The Hatherleigh Guide

to

Ethics in Therapy

The Hatherleigh Guides series

1. Psychiatric Disorders
2. Psychotherapy
3. Managing Depression
4. Issues in Modern Therapy
5. Child and Adolescent Therapy
6. Marriage and Family Therapy
7. Treating Substance Abuse, Part I
8. Treating Substance Abuse, Part II
9. Vocational and Career Counseling
10. Ethics in Therapy

The Hatherleigh Guide

to

Ethics in Therapy

Hatherleigh Press • New York

The Hatherleigh Guide to Ethics in Therapy

Project Editor: Joya Lonsdale
Indexer: Angela Washington-Blair, PhD
Cover Designer: Gary Szczecina
Cover photo: Christopher Flach, PhD

© 1997 Hatherleigh Press
A Division of The Hatherleigh Company, Ltd.
1114 First Avenue, Suite 500, New York, NY 10021-8325

Compiled under the auspices of the editorial boards of *Directions in Mental Health Counseling, Directions in Clinical Psychology,* and *Directions in Rehabilitation Counseling.*

Library of Congress Cataloging-in-Publication Data

The Hatherleigh guide to ethics in therapy — 1st ed.
       p. cm. — (The Hatherleigh guides series; 10)
    Includes bibliographical references and indexes.
    ISBN 1-886330-51-4 (alk. paper)
    1. Psychotherapy — moral and ethical aspects. 2. Counseling — moral and
      ethical aspects. I. Hatherleigh Press. II. Series.
    RC456.H38 1996 vol.10
    [RC455.2.E8]
    174'.2 — dc21   96-50305
                                                CIP

First Edition: March 1997

10 9 8 7 6 5 4 3 2 1

About the photograph and the photographer

Versailles, France, 1995
A long, peaceful walk by the river, surrounded by silhouettes of trees blowing in the wind.

Christopher Flach, PhD, is a psychologist in private practice in San Francisco, California. An avid photographer for more than 20 years, his favorite subjects include people and nature. He has studied photography with Ansel Adams, and his work has been on display in public galleries and in private collections.

Compiled under the auspices of the editorial boards of *Directions in Mental Health Counseling, Directions in Clinical and Counseling Psychology,* and *Directions in Rehabilitation Counseling*:

Table of Contents

List of Illustrations ix

Introduction xi
Barbara Herlihy, PhD, NCC, LPC, and Gerald Corey, EdD,
ABPP, NCC

1. Current Ethical Issues in the Practice of Psychology 1
    Sharon E. Robinson Kurpius, PhD

2. Ethical Considerations in the Development of
    Counseling Goals 17
    Kerry Brace, PsyD

3. Codes of Ethics as Catalysts for Improving Practice 37
    Barbara Herlihy, PhD, NCC, LPC, and Gerald Corey, EdD,
    ABPP, NCC

4. Preparing Rehabilitation Counselors to Deal with Ethical
    Dilemmas 57
    Carolyn Rollins, PhD

5. Ethics in Supervision: Managing Supervisee Rights and
    Supervisor Responsibilities 75
    J. Michael Tyler, PhD, and Catherine L. Tyler, MBA

6. Expert Witness Testimony: Ethical, Practical, and Legal
   Issues 97
   Robert L. Sadoff, MD

7. Lawsuit Prevention Techniques.. 109
   Barbara E. Calfee, JD, LSW

8. The "Duty to Protect" Others from Violence 127
   Michael L. Perlin, Esq

9. Ethics, Insanity Pleas, and Forensic Psychology 147
   Michael W. Millard, PhD, BCFE

10. The Multifaceted Ethical Dimension of Treating the
    Mentally Ill 161
    Mary Ann Carroll, PhD

11. Dual/Multiple Relationships: Toward a Consensus of
    Thinking 183
    *Gerald Corey, EdD, ABPP, NCC, and Barbara Herlihy, PhD,
    NCC, LPC*

12. Sexual Boundary Violations 195
    Silvia W. Olarte, MD

13. Ethical Standards in Counseling Sexually Active Clients
    with HIV 211
    Elliot D. Cohen, PhD

14. Ethics and Multiculturalism: The Challenge of
    Diversity 235
    Courtland C. Lee, PhD, and Virginia Kurilla, MEd

Name Index 249

Subject Index.. 253

About the Contributors 261

Illustrations

Appendix 2.1 For Further Reading on Ethical
Considerations in the Development of Counseling
Goals 35

Table 4.1 Title and Purpose of Each Instructional Unit
of The Ethical Case Management Practices Training
Program (in-service) 66

Table 4.2 Titles and Content of the Instructional
Modules of the Ethical Practices in Rehabilitation
Training Modules (pre-service) 68

Table 5.1 A "Bill of Rights" for Supervisees 88

Appendix 10A Ethical Considerations in Treating the
Mentally Ill: Two Case Studies 180

Table 13.1 Ethical Guidelines (EGs) 220

Table 13.2 Ethical Rules (ERs) 228

Introduction

In today's complex and changing world of practice, therapists and counselors are confronted with a range of ethical issues for which there are no easy answers. At a minimum, they are expected to be aware of the codes of ethics of their professional organizations and to be able to use good judgment in applying these codes to specific situations that arise in their practice. Ethically conscientious practitioners, however, require more of themselves. Rather than simply following the letter of their ethical codes, they practice aspirational ethics and strive to meet the spirit that underlies the standards. Their decisions are motivated by a sincere desire to provide their clients with the most effective services possible. Although they want to avoid charges of unethical or unprofessional conduct, they are more concerned about examining their own practices, looking for subtle ways in which they might not be acting in the highest ethical manner, and keeping current with the profession's expectations for best practice.

Codes of ethics offer us guidance, yet in the final analysis, each of us is responsible for our own actions. The challenge is for us, as professionals, to be willing to examine the subtle ways that we might not be functioning at the highest ethical level and to wrestle with the ambiguities that we encounter. We need to be open to struggling with questions that do not have obvious answers and to engage in self-reflection that will enable us to decide how to act in ways that will further the best interests of our clients.

Keeping up to date with professional ethical standards is an ongoing task. Our knowledge base must constantly expand to keep current with the developments in our environments; today, the environments in which psychotherapy is practiced are undergoing some profound changes. New ethical issues, some of which were not even anticipated at the time when many seasoned practitioners were originally trained, now present themselves. Some examples are a possible duty to warn partners of sexually active clients who are HIV positive; client rights and informed consent in a managed care environment; ethical implications of new technologies used to support psychotherapy services; and issues of therapist competence to counsel with an ethnically, racially, and culturally diverse client population. One way that busy practitioners can stay abreast of developments is by reading, reflecting on, and applying to their own work the information contained in books such as *The Hatherleigh Guide to Ethics in Therapy.*

Becoming an ethical and effective practitioner is a process rather than a state at which we arrive. Many ethical issues need to be reexamined periodically throughout our professional lives, and skills and strategies for dealing with new issues need to be developed and refined. The process of developing an ethically responsible psychotherapy practice is never really finished.

The Hatherleigh Guide to Ethics in Therapy explores a range of ethical and legal issues that will be extremely useful to practitioners as they examine and work to improve their practices. The chapters, written by some of the leading thinkers in the area of professional ethics, provide mental health professionals with current information on a number of issues that are particularly troubling and complex. This book will assist therapists and counselors as they grapple with ideas pertaining to a wide variety of topics that are an integral part of ethical practice, including setting goals, the role of codes of ethics in practice, supervision, legal issues related to ethics, strategies for preventing malpractice suits, boundary issues in therapy, confidentiality in working with sexually active clients with HIV/AIDS, and meeting the needs of diverse client populations.

The opening chapter by Sharon Robinson Kurpius emphasizes ethical dilemmas pertaining to confidentiality. Kurpius identifies situations that require counselors to breach confidentiality, such as those in which clients are a danger to themselves, or children or incapacitated adults are being abused. She also offers guidelines for dealing with confidentiality limits when working with clients who have HIV/AIDS. A number of helpful suggestions are given regarding record keeping, which is an issue closely related to confidentiality. Ideas for dealing with dual or conflictual relationships are also offered.

In Chapter 2, Kerry Brace addresses ethical dimensions in formulating goals for counseling. Brace reminds practitioners of the special ethical responsibilities we assume because of our power position in therapeutic relationships; in counseling or therapy, clients may make decisions that change the course of their lives. Models of ethical reasoning and the principles of respect for the client's welfare and self-determination are explored. Practitioners will find particularly useful, as they work to translate these principles into action, a proposed set of rules to guide goal development in therapy.

Our chapter on the role of ethical codes as catalysts for improving practice describes the purposes that codes of ethics serve, their underlying principles, and some of their limitations. We highlight some issues that are addressed in new ways in *The Code of Ethics and Standards of Practice of the American Counseling Association* (ACA, 1995), including diversity and multicultural issues; reporting of contagious, fatal diseases; dual relationships; *pro bono* service; and sexual intimacies with clients. We conclude by offering suggestions for individual practitioners to make the best use of their ethics codes.

Chapter 4 addresses rehabilitation counselors' increased interest in raising their level of preparation to resolve ethical issues they encounter in practice. Carolyn Rollins articulates the need for rehabilitation counselors to have ethical reasoning skills as they deal with increasing job complexity and conflicting demands. She discusses approaches and resources for ethics education that can foster the development of these skills.

In Chapter 5, which addresses ethical aspects of supervision, J. Michael Tyler and Catherine Tyler explore a range of issues including competence, role conflicts, dual relationships, transference and countertransference, diversity, confidentiality, and personal values in supervision. The authors draw important distinctions, and point to similarities, between supervision and counseling, as well as between supervision and consulting. The "bill of rights" for supervisees they propose is especially useful; it will help supervisors, supervisees, and institutions resolve critical ethical concerns appropriately.

A comprehensive book on ethics in therapy must address related legal dimensions of professional practice. Four chapters in this guide provide information that psychotherapists will find extremely helpful when their work takes them into the legal arena.

Chapter 6 by Robert Sadoff on expert witness testimony is "must reading" for therapists who may be contemplating their first venture as an expert witness, and is an excellent refresher for those who are experienced. Sadoff offers practical, sound advice on preparing for trial, coping with the demands of direct examination, and dealing with hypothetical questions, as well as specific strategies for ensuring one's effectiveness as a witness.

Chapter 7, which presents lawsuit prevention techniques, opens with both good and bad news for mental health professionals: lawsuits against psychotherapists are few, but their number is on the rise. The author, Barbara Calfee, an attorney and social worker, provides useful guidelines for preventing malpractice actions. She defines the grounds for professional negligence and focuses on specific types of negligence, including abandoning the client, employing unorthodox therapy methods, failing to obtain informed consent, mishandling transference and countertransference, practicing beyond one's scope of competence, engaging in sexual intimacies with clients, treating clients inappropriately because of inaccurate diagnosis, and failing to control dangerous clients.

Michael Perlin, also an attorney, focuses and expands on

one of the issues raised by Calfee : the "duty to protect" others from violence. Chapter 8 discusses the controversial benchmark *Tarasoff v. Regents of the University of California* case, the critical response that followed in its wake, and subsequent court decisions that have variously adopted, extended, limited, or declined to follow the ruling in the case. Under *Tarasoff*, therapists are responsible for their ability to predict the potential for violence committed by clients.

Forensic psychology is the subject of Chapter 9 by Michael Millard, which explores ethical and legal issues pertaining to insanity pleas. This chapter includes an interesting case study that illuminates how ethical issues—particularly issues regarding the psychologist's competency—can arise throughout the sanity evaluation process. Millard also points out that forensic psychologists are given a great deal of power and they must recognize their own personal values and beliefs and know how these might interfere with their work.

The remaining chapters in the book deal with special ethical issues. Chapter 10, by Mary Ann Carroll, focuses on the multifaceted ethical aspects of working with the mentally ill. Carroll suggests criteria for distinguishing between treatments that are appropriate for mentally healthy clients versus those that are appropriate for working with those who are mentally ill. She describes ways in which many issues—including obtaining valid consent, confidentiality, and the right to treatment and to refuse treatment—take on a different meaning when applied to mentally ill clients. Practitioners who work with mentally ill clients need to guard against the potential for coercion and to be able to deal with the moral dilemmas that are inherent in their practice.

In Chapter 11, we discuss the controversy that has surrounded dual and multiple relationships and review the diverse perspectives on this ethical issue. We look at the positions recently taken by the major professional associations toward sexual and nonsexual dual or multiple relationships, and suggest that some consensus is emerging. We draw distinctions between avoidable and unavoidable dual relationships and offer guidelines to minimize the risk of exploitation or harm to clients.

Chapter 12 by Silvia Olarte deals with one kind of unethical dual relationship: sexual intimacies with clients. Olarte describes the harmful effects of sexual boundary violations and explores in some detail the dynamics of the sexually abusive therapist and the effects of sex-role socialization. She maintains that it is the profession's responsibility to evaluate and, when possible, treat and rehabilitate offenders to avoid a repeat of their unethical behavior and protect clients from harm.

There are both ethical and legal considerations in treating sexually active clients who are HIV positive. In Chapter 13, Elliot Cohen demonstrates that the answers tend to be complex, especially when issues of confidentiality and harm to third parties are examined. Although confidentiality is crucial in any counseling relationship, there are certain restrictions to confidentiality exist when clients who are HIV positive may be putting others at risk. Cohen provides some guidelines to assist practitioners in determining when they have a moral and ethical obligation to disclose.

Courtland Lee and Virginia Kurilla contribute the final chapter, which deals with the ethics of multicultural counseling. These authors see continuing education as a pathway to achieving competence in working ethically and effectively across cultures. Ethical practice demands that practitioners who have not received adequate training in counseling individuals from diverse backgrounds participate in ongoing professional development to become culturally effective counselors. Practitioners who cannot open-mindedly and effectively treat clients from different cultures or with different worldviews are ethically obligated to seek consultation or refer these clients.

All the chapters in this book, although addressing diverse topics, are unified by the premise that ethical practice involves careful consideration of moral principles that undergird our work in the helping professions. These principles — respect for autonomy (self-determination), beneficence (promoting good for others), nonmaleficence (avoiding harm), justice (being fair and providing equal treatment), and fidelity (honoring commitments) — emerge throughout the book.

Conscientious professionals must struggle to determine the best course of action when, as often happens, these moral principles compete with one another in a given situation. There are no easy answers, but the material in this book provides mental health professionals with new insights into difficult ethical issues that arise in today's rapidly changing mental health care environment. It increases their repertoire of strategies for resolving the ethical dilemmas they encounter in their work. Equipped with these insights and strategies, professionals will be better prepared to provide services in a manner that meets the helping professions' expectations for the highest ethical practice.

Barbara Herlihy, PhD, NCC, LPC
New Orleans, Louisiana

Gerald Corey, EdD, ABPP, NCC
Fullerton, California

Dr. Herlihy is Associate Professor of Counseling, Loyola University, New Orleans, LA. Dr. Corey is Professor of Human Services and Counseling, California State University, Fullerton, CA. Drs. Herlihy and Corey have coauthored three books: Dual Relationships in Counseling *(1992), the* ACA Ethical Standards Casebook *(5th ed.) (1996), and* Boundary issues in counseling: Multiple roles and relationships *(in press), all of which are published by the American Counseling Association.*

1

Current Ethical Issues in the Practice of Psychology

Sharon E. Robinson Kurpius, PhD

Dr. Robinson Kurpius is Professor of Counseling Psychology, Division of Psychology in Education, Arizona State University, Tempe, AZ.

KEY POINTS

- One of the most important developments in contemporary psychology is the attempt to establish ethical guidelines.

- Three ethical issues are discussed in this chapter: confidentiality, dual relationships, and record keeping.

- Situations in which a possible breach of confidence is universally required include cases of child abuse, adult abuse, and danger to clients or others.

- The American Psychological Association (APA) guidelines for breaching versus maintaining the confidentiality of clients with HIV/AIDS provide that, unless there is an identifiable victim and the client refuses to behave in a manner that protects this person, the covenant of confidentiality should not be broken.

- Dual relationships occur when professionals assume two or more roles simultaneously or sequentially with a person seeking counseling. Many psychologists find themselves in a conflicting relationship with clients, which puts the therapeutic relationship at risk. The APA guidelines for dual relationships are outlined.

- Conscientious record keeping and the security or control of access to records is an important responsibility of mental health professionals. The author discusses issues related to record keeping. These include what is minimal storage, laws affecting the retention of records, the release of records to other mental health professionals, and the destruction of old records.

INTRODUCTION

When one looks at the evolution of professional psychology, the changes encountered since the founding of the American Psychological Association (APA) in 1892 have been monumental. Foremost among these changes have been attempts to provide workable ethical guidelines for psychologists. Since the first code of ethics was published in 1953, the concerns of society and individual clients have become more complex, and potential areas of ethical conflict have expanded considerably beyond the initial issues "of plagiarism and of academic freedom" (Rich, 1952, p. 440). To meet the evolving needs of society and clients, the 1992 APA *Ethical Principles for Psychologists* attempts to deal with the many diverse ethical challenges facing psychologists practicing in a society where litigation is rampant and allegations of unethical behavior are readily made.

In 1992, Pope and Vetter published the results of their national survey on the ethical dilemmas encountered by the members of the APA. They found that among the 679 respondents, the primary concern was confidentiality. Although only 2% of all cases reported to the APA Ethics Committee involved confidentiality, 18% of the 703 ethically troubling incidents described by survey respondents involved questions of confidentiality. Closely following confidentiality was the issue of blurred, dual, or conflicted relationships, which was identified as a critical ethical dilemma 17% of the time. Although farther down the list of critical issues, record keeping and appropriate release of information are closely linked to the issue of confidentiality.

These three issues — confidentiality, dual relationships, and record keeping — form the core of the discussion to follow. Pressing societal concerns, however, such as child and adult abuse, violence and dangerousness, and clients with acquired immunodeficiency syndrome (AIDS) must be considered within the parameters of confidentiality.

DEFINING CONFIDENTIALITY

The Fourth Amendment in the Bill of Rights grants that "The right of the people to be secure in their persons, houses, papers, and effects, against unreasonable searches and sei- zures, shall not be violated, and no Warrants shall issue, but upon probable cause, supported by Oath or affirmation, and particularly describing the place to be searched, and the per- sons or things to be seized." It is evident from this amendment that the writers of the Constitution of the United States of America valued privacy. Privacy is the cornerstone of per- sonal rights; the courts have interpreted privacy as "the free- dom of individuals to choose for themselves the time and the circumstances under which and the extent to which their beliefs, behaviors, and opinions are to be shared or withheld from others" (Siegel, 1979, p. 251). A person has the right to control whether others have access to his or her thoughts, words, and behaviors. These rights have been deemed per- sonal and private by persons entrusted with interpreting the Constitution.

The concept of privacy is the foundation for the legal right of privileged communication and the professional concept of confidentiality. Although psychologists tell clients that they will hold confidential what is said in therapy, what they are actually referring to is privileged communication. *Confidenti- ality* is a professional term used by therapists for telling clients that they will protect from disclosure any information shared in therapy. *Privileged communication* is a legal term that pro- tects clients from having their communications disclosed in a court of law. The privilege is granted legally to clients of all certified or licensed mental health professionals.

For communication to be privileged, it must meet four criteria: (a) the communication must originate in confidence that it will not be disclosed, (b) the confidentiality of informa- tion must be essential to the full and satisfactory maintenance of the relationship, (c) the relationship must be one that should

be sedulously fostered in the opinion of the community, and
(d) injury to the relationship by disclosure of the communication must be greater than the benefit gained by the correct
disposal of litigation regarding the information (Schwitzgebel
& Schwitzgebel, 1980).

The psychologist-client relationship traditionally has been
valued by society, and clients have had the benefit of privileged communication. To breach clients' confidentiality without just cause is legally viewed as an invasion of their consti-
tutional right of privacy (Everstine et al., 1980). Despite this
view, in a national study, 62% of psychologists reported that
they had unintentionally violated their clients' confidentiality
and 21% reported intentionally violating it (Pope, Tabachnick,
& Keith-Spiegel, 1987). These statistics reveal that psychologists are at risk for violating this core legal and ethical component of the psychologist-client relationship. Psychologists
should be aware of their state's laws governing the parameters
of confidentiality between psychologists and clients and whether confidentiality also extends to secretaries who make client
appointments, gather initial intake information, and type case
notes. In most states, secretaries are considered extensions of
psychologists.

WHEN TO BREACH CONFIDENTIALITY

Certain issues (just causes) require psychologists to breach
client confidentiality. In such cases, courts of law and professional associations such as the APA have determined that the
benefit to society of such disclosure is greater than the potential harm to the individual client. Global issues requiring
breach of confidentiality include cases of child abuse, adult
abuse, and danger to clients or others.

Because laws or the APA (1992) require psychologists to
breach confidentiality under selected circumstances, it is vital
that clients be informed regarding such disclosures before
beginning therapy, if at all possible. Once adequately in-

formed of the information that cannot remain confidential, clients can make an informed choice regarding discussion of these issues in therapy.

The APA (1992) stated that informed consent implies "the person has the capacity to consent, has been informed of significant information concerning the procedures, has freely and without undue influence expressed consent, and consent has been appropriately documented." Not only does the client consent to accepting responsibility for what is discussed in therapy, but also he or she is informed regarding what information must be released to courts, insurance companies (if a third party is paying the bill), and courts of laws.

Information released to insurance companies typically includes the client's name, services provided, and a DSM-IV (APA, 1994) diagnosis. Clients should be aware that this diagnosis is a label that will remain in their permanent insurance records and that psychologists have no control over who has access to these records within the insurance company. Often, clients do not fully comprehend the possible ramifications of using a third-party payer; psychologists should discuss this with them.

Psychologists also have a responsibility to tell clients that their records can be subpoenaed. Many psychologists do not realize that the only subpoena to which they must respond is the one issued by a court of law and handed directly to them. The psychologist has no legal obligation to respond to a subpoena issued by an attorney. If the subpoena is a subpoena *duces tecum*, psychologists must appear in court and bring the client's records with them. If the subpoena is a "plain" subpoena, they should not bring records to court. Regardless of the type of subpoena, psychologists initially should claim the privilege for the clients that forces the court to order the psychologists to breach confidentiality or allows the court to honor the clients' right of privileged communication.

A recent court case in California ruled that even a client's personal journals and diary may not be private (Pope & Vasquez, 1991). In this case, a rape victim kept a diary as part of her therapeutic homework; however, because the issues being discussed were related to the court case, the diary was not considered private.

In some instances, a client automatically waives privilege by the nature of his or her actions. According to Corey and colleagues (1988), clients automatically waive the privilege by filing a lawsuit or ethical grievance against their therapist, by introducing their mental condition as grounds for a legal claim or defense, by revealing an intention to harm themselves, or by indicating that they intend to harm an identifiable person. If a client is being seen in a court-ordered capacity, confidentiality is limited, particularly if the psychologist's responsibility is to evaluate the client for the court. Finally, if the best professional judgment of the psychologist dictates that the client needs hospitalization, he or she can breach confidentiality to the extent necessary to obtain the professional help needed for the client.

As mentioned previously, there are universal instances that require psychologists to breach confidentiality or at least to consider seriously the ramifications of not breaching confidentiality. These instances include child abuse, adult abuse, and danger to clients or others.

Child Abuse:

Every state has laws requiring mental health professionals to report child abuse to the appropriate government agency. The duty of psychologists is to protect minors from the "future harm of continued abuse or neglect and to protect children who are insufficiently autonomous to act on their own behalf" (Sattler, 1990, p. 105). In most states, a *minor* is defined as someone younger than the age of 18; however, some states recognize a 16-year-old person as an *emancipated minor*. It would behoove psychologists to become familiar with the laws in their individual states regarding the reporting of child abuse. In Arizona, for example, the law requires mental health professionals to observe evidence of injury, sexual molestation, death, abuse, or physical neglect that appears to have been inflicted on a child by other than accidental means. A parent's confession of child abuse is not enough to require reporting the abuse to state officials. Psychologists must actually see the child and the signs of abuse.

Adult Abuse:

In addition to child abuse, in many states, mental health professionals are responsible for reporting cases of abuse, neglect, or exploitation of incapacitated adults. If an adult is not incapacitated, the responsibility for seeking help rests with him or her. In Arizona, *incapacitated* is defined as "an impairment by reason of mental illness, mental deficiency, mental disorder, physical illness or disability, advanced age, chronic use of drugs, chronic intoxication, or other cause to the extent that the person lacks sufficient understanding or capacity to make or communicate responsible decisions" (American Psychological Association [APA] Board of Professional Affairs, 1992). A legal finding of incapacity is not necessary for psychologists to be required to report incidents of adult abuse. With the increasing incidents of physical and sexual abuse as well as financial exploitation of the elderly, psychologists must be sensitive to their role in preventing such abuse if they are aware of it.

Danger to Clients or Others:

It is unlikely that any psychologist is unfamiliar with the *Tarasoff* case (*Tarasoff v. Regents of the University of California,* 1974, 1976), in which the psychologist employed at the University of California was charged with being liable for not protecting Tatiana Tarasoff from harm by warning her that an exboyfriend intended to kill her. This case laid the foundation for the concept of duty to warn and made mental health professionals responsible for assessing the dangerousness of their clients and acting on their judgments to breach confidentiality and warn potential victims.

The APA (1992) made two statements regarding this issue: (a) "Psychologists take reasonable steps to avoid harming the patients or clients, research participants, students, and others with whom they work and to minimize harm where it is foreseeable and unavoidable"; and (b) "Psychologists disclose confidential information without the consent of the individual only as mandated by law, or where permitted by law for a valid purpose, such as. . . to protect the patient or client or others from harm." In both guidelines, psychologists must protect clients from harm and break confidentiality, if necessary, to accomplish this end.

Other court cases holding mental health professionals responsible for protecting third parties (i.e., those who are not clients) have built on the *Tarasoff* case. For example, in *McIntosh v. Milano* (1979), the court found Dr. Milano liable because his client had specified a victim, his ex-girlfriend. Because there was an identifiable victim, there was a duty to warn. In *Lipari v. Sears, Roebuck & Co.* (1980), the court ruled against the therapist for failing to detain a potentially violent client who had purchased a gun, although no identifiable victim was named. A similar ruling was made in *Peterson v. State* [of Washington] (1983); a therapist was held responsible for releasing a potentially dangerous client who had drug-related mental problems. On release, while under the influence of drugs, this client was in a car accident that injured another person. The court ruled that the therapist should have foreseen the potential for dangerousness. In each of these cases, the courts have held mental health professionals liable for the violence of their clients. In reaction to these rulings, some states (e.g., California, Colorado, and Kentucky) have passed legislation protecting mental health professionals from civil liability for invasion of privacy if they issue warnings and make predictions of dangerousness in an attempt to protect someone from potential harm (Herlihy & Sheeley, 1988).

Regardless of these court rulings and laws, no psychologist or therapist should practice without liability insurance. "Going bare" — practicing without professional insurance — in this age of litigation is too risky, especially when psychologists are increasingly being expected to diagnose potential dangerousness and to take steps to ensure that intended victims are not harmed (Gross & Robinson, 1987).

GUIDELINES FOR CLIENTS WITH AIDS

A discussion of breaching confidentiality would be incomplete without evaluating the current ethical concerns engendered when working with clients with AIDS. The professional debate is growing regarding the need to protect others from becoming infected with the human immunodeficiency virus (HIV) versus the need to maintain the confidentiality of a client who is HIV positive. As Erickson (1993) pointed out, traditional approaches to maintaining client confidentiality are greatly challenged by the advent and rapid spread of AIDS.

The APA has taken a leadership role in this area, and at its August 1991 convention, the Council of Representatives passed several resolutions regarding clients who are HIV positive. The first, addressing the APA's position on confidentiality and the prevention of HIV transmission, stated that:

- A legal duty to protect third parties from HIV infection should not be imposed.

- If, however, specific legislation is considered, then it should permit disclosure only when the provider knows of an identifiable third party who the provider has a compelling reason to believe is at significant risk for infection; the provider has a reasonable belief that the third party has no reason to suspect that he or she is at risk; and the client/ patient has been urged to inform the third party and has either refused or is considered unreliable in his/her willingness to notify the third party.

• If such legislation is adopted, it should include immunity from civil and criminal liability for providers who, in good faith, make decisions to disclose or not to disclose information about HIV infection to third parties. (APA, 1991)

This resolution provides concrete guidelines for breaching versus maintaining the confidentiality of clients with AIDS. Unless there is an identifiable victim and the client refuses to behave in a manner that protects this person, the covenant of confidentiality should not be broken.

Few decisions regarding confidentiality are truly clear-cut, except for those protecting clients from committing suicide and those warning a clearly identifiable victim about potential harm. Aside from these two areas, many gray areas call for psychologists' best professional judgment. For guidance in making these types of ethical judgments, psychologists should consult respected colleagues and ethics committees.

DUAL RELATIONSHIPS

A discussion of current ethical issues would be remiss if dual relationships were not addressed. Dual relationships occur when professionals assume two or more roles simultaneously or sequentially with a person seeking counseling (see Chapter 11). These situations include professional and secondary relationships such as a friendship, intimate relationship, social or business relationship, or financial relationship.

The APA (1992) specifically stated that "a psychologist refrains from entering into or promising another personal, scientific, professional, financial, or other relationship to their clients." Despite this warning, many psychologists find themselves in a conflicting relationship with clients, which puts the therapeutic relationship at risk.

Although certain dual relationships, such as bartering for services with a client who cannot afford to pay for therapy or attending a social affair given by a client, may not always be harmful, they most often result in hampering the psychologist's ability to remain totally objective and be completely honest in therapy. As Corey and Herlihy note in Chapter 11, the potential for harm always exists and the potential for exploiting the client is always a danger. One should remember that a power differential exists between therapists and clients and a differential exists between expectations and responsibilities. Moreover, the natural boundaries of the fiduciary relationship are voided when a secondary relationship occurs. In each of these instances, clients are the ones who are in danger of harm.

Clients are particularly vulnerable when a psychologist engages them in an intimate relationship, as are students when an academic psychologist becomes intimate with them. When sexual contact becomes part of a therapeutic relationship, the expectation of trust that is fundamental to the process of therapy is violated (Thoreson, Shaughnessy, Heppner, & Cook, 1993). Although attraction may occur between therapists and clients, acting on this attraction results in serious ethical violations.

The shortest and most explicit of all the APA's (1992) ethical principles involved intimate relationships: "Psychologists do not engage in sexual intimacies with current patients or clients." The APA also clearly specified the inappropriateness of seeing a client with whom one has been intimate and of becoming intimate with a former client. According to the APA, psychologists should not become sexually involved with a client for at least 2 years after termination of therapy – and then only under unusual circumstances.

Keith-Spiegel and Koocher (1985) pointed out that the profile of therapists who become sexually involved with clients closely resembles that of impaired helpers. They cite research indicating that these therapists usually have severe personal problems and are attempting to meet their own needs — particularly their need to be loved — through their clients. Regardless of the reason for becoming involved intimately with clients, it is unethical and, in many states, illegal. Psychologists who find themselves attracted to clients should be wary of beginning the cycle of nonerotic touching, "innocent" kissing, or erotic thoughts that easily lead to greater intimacy. Perhaps the best step for psychologists who find themselves in this position is for them to ask themselves whether they must hide what they are doing with a client. If the answer is yes, they need to seek consultation or supervision immediately and put an end to such behaviors.

RECORD KEEPING

An issue closely related to confidentiality is appropriate record keeping. Conscientious record keeping not only benefits clients through accurate documentation of service, but it also benefits psychologists by guiding plans for therapy, allowing a review of the therapeutic endeavor as a whole, and fostering self-monitoring (APA Board of Professional Affairs, 1992). *Record-Keeping Guidelines* provides suggestions for content, control, retention, and disclosure of records. "Records for psychological services minimally include identifying data; dates of services; types of services; fees; any assessment, plan for intervention, consultation, and/or summary reports as may be appropriate; and any release of information obtained" (p. 6). Snider (1987) suggested that if an error is made in a record, a single line should be drawn through the written text, which is initialed and dated by the psychologist. Text should never be erased or whited out; courts of law frown on altered records.

The security or control of access to records is the ultimate responsibility of psychologists (APA, 1992). Snider (1987) stressed that a locked file cabinet is absolutely minimal storage. To be even safer, psychologists should consider "minimal storage" to be a locked file cabinet in a locked office.

According to the APA Board of Professional Affairs (1992), psychologists should initially be aware of any laws affecting the retention of records. In the absence of such laws, psychologists should keep full client records for 3 years after the termination of therapy. At this time, psychologists can choose to summarize the records or maintain the entire record for an additional 12 years before record disposal. If the client is a minor, the records should be kept for 3 years after the client reaches the age of majority.

If a client asks for his or her records, psychologists must decide whether the client would obtain therapeutic value from reading this information. At the 1993 convention for the Arizona State Psychological Association, one expert, an attorney and psychologist, indicated that records do not have to be given to clients simply because they ask for them. If psychologists decide that sharing the records is not in the client's best interest, they can refuse to give the records to the client. However, psychologists must notify the client in writing of the reasons for this decision and inform the client that this decision can be appealed to the State Board of Examiners. It might be important for psychologists to determine whether their states have passed similar legislation related to the release of client records.

According to the APA (1992), a psychologist cannot prevent clients from viewing their records just because the fee has not been paid. This can be viewed as holding a client's records hostage. It is acceptable, however, to charge a client a reasonable amount for reproduction and release of records.

Related to the release of records to a client is the release of records to other mental health professionals. It is imperative for psychologists to have written informed consent from the client to release personal information. The client should be informed as to what information is being released, to whom, for what purpose, and the time period for which the signed consent for release is valid.

When records become outdated or psychologists have kept them for the suggested time period, records should be properly destroyed. If records are just thrown away, it is possible someone will find them and read them. To protect client confidentiality, records must be completely destroyed by such means as shredding or burning.

A final note on record keeping is necessary. It is the responsibility of psychologists to keep their records in such order that the transition of a client to a new therapist is easily facilitated in the case of their death, incapacity, or withdrawal from practice (APA, 1992). Regardless of the aspect of record keeping being discussed, psychologists are responsible for maintaining accurate, thorough, timely records that reflect the services provided to their clients.

REFERENCES

American Psychological Association. (1953). *Ethical principles of psychologists*. Washington, DC: Author.

American Psychological Association. (1991). APA Council of Representatives adopts new AIDS policies. *Psychology and AIDS Exchange, 7,* 1.

American Psychological Association. (1992). *Ethical principles of psychologists*. Washington, DC: Author.

American Psychological Association. (1994). *Diagnostic and statistical manual of mental disorders* (4th ed.). Washington, DC: Author.

American Psychological Association Board of Professional Affairs. (1992). *Record-keeping guidelines* (Draft 5.2). Arizona Revised Statute 46-451.

Corey, G., Corey, M. S., & Callanan, P. (1988). *Issues and ethics in the helping professions*. Pacific Grove, CA: Brooks/Cole.

Erickson, S. H. (1993). Ethics and confidentiality in AIDS counseling: A professional dilemma. *Journal of Mental Health Counseling, 15,* 118–131.

Everstine, L., Everstine, D. S., Haymann, G. M., True, R. H., Frey, D. H., Johnson, H. G., & Seiden, R. H. (1980). Privacy and confidentiality in psychotherapy. *American Psychologist, 35*, 828-840.

Gross, D. R., & Robinson, S. E. (1987). Ethics and violence: Hear no evil, see no evil, speak no evil. *Journal of Counseling and Development, 65*, 334-344.

Herlihy, B., & Sheeley, V. L. (1988). Counselor liability and the duty to warn: Selected cases, statutory trends, and implications for practice. *Counselor Education and Supervision, 27*, 203-215.

Keith-Spiegel, P., & Koocher, G. P. (1985). *Ethics in psychology: Professional standards and cases.* New York: McGraw-Hill.

Lipari v. Sears, Roebuck, & Co, 497 F. Supp. 195D (Neb. 1980).

McIntosh v. Milano, 403 A.2d.500 (1979).

Peterson v. State, 671 P2d. 230 (Wash. 1983).

Pope, K. S., Tabachnick, B. G., & Keith-Spiegel, P. (1987). Good and poor practices in psychotherapy: National survey of beliefs of psychologists. *Professional Psychology: Research and Practice, 19*, 547–552.

Pope, K. S., & Vasquez, M. J. T. (1991). *Ethics in psychotherapy and counseling: A practical guide for psychologists.* San Francisco: Jossey-Bass.

Pope, K. S., & Vetter, V. A. (1992). Ethical dilemmas encountered by members of the American Psychological Association: A national survey. *American Psychologist, 47*, 397–411.

Rich, G. L. (1952). A new code of ethics is needed. *American Psychologist, 7*, 440–441.

Sattler, H. A. (1990). Confidentiality. In B. Herlihy & L. Golden (Eds.), *ACD ethical standards casebook* (4th ed., pp. 102-110). Alexandria, VA: American Association for Counseling and Development.

Schwitzgebel, R. L., & Schwitzgebel, R. K. (1980). *Law and psychological practice.* New York: John Wiley & Sons.

Siegel, M. (1979). Privacy, ethics, and confidentiality. *Professional Psychology, 10*, 249-258.

Snider, P. D. (1987). Client records: Inexpensive liability protection for mental health counselors. *Journal of Mental Health Counseling, 9*, 134–141.

Tarasoff v. Regents of the University of California, 118 Cal., Rptr. 129.529 P.2d 533 (1974).

Tarasoff v. Regents of the University of California, 113 Cal., Rptr. 14.551 P.2d 334 (1976).

Thoreson, R. W., Shaughnessy, P., Heppner, P. P., & Cook, S. W. (1993). Sexual contact during and after the professional relationship: Attitudes and practices of male counselors. *Journal of Counseling and Development, 71*, 429–434.

2

Ethical Considerations in the Development of Counseling Goals

Kerry Brace, PsyD

Dr. Brace is a psychotherapist with Allegheny East MHMR Center, Pittsburgh, PA.

KEY POINTS

- This chapter shows how counselors can apply ethical principles to the development of end goals and instrumental goals with clients.

- Two universally applicable principles are discussed: respect for the client's best interest or welfare and respect for the client's self-determination. Rules for applying these principles are provided with case examples.

- The principle of respect for the client's welfare is the central ethical consideration in counseling. This guiding principal is essential because the fundamental purpose of counseling is to enhance the client's welfare.

- Although subordinate to the principle of respect for the client's welfare, the principle of respect for client self-determination is important. This principle should be observed in counseling goal development; the client should set his or her own counseling goals.

- Research suggests that clients tend to adopt mental health professionals' personal values during the course of treatment. Counselors, to avoid imposing their personal values on clients, must make their own values explicit and make it clear to clients that clients can choose the degree to which they want to adopt these values.

- The tenants of moral philosophy can provide counselors with a rational basis for goal development that is not limited by personal values and beliefs.

INTRODUCTION

Each counseling session presents mental health and rehabilitation professionals with choices that affect the client's life. The impact of these decisions can be dramatic. During counseling, clients often arrive at decisions that significantly change their outlook, behavior, and, indeed, the course of their lives. Thus, the counselor is placed in a position of power, and, consequently, holds ethical responsibilities unequaled in other professions.

To guide moment-to-moment choices as to what to say or not to say to a client, the counselor may rely on some theory or theories about how change occurs in counseling and about what changes are desirable. However, theories are numerous and diverse. Most counselors are probably drawn to one particular approach by virtue of personal liking or value preferences (Lowe, 1976). For instance, the person who feels most competent and comfortable functioning in the realm of thought and reason most likely subscribes to cognitive-behavioral theory, whereas one who relishes the riches of emotional life might take an experiential approach. In short, counselors' personal values influence the means or "instrumental goals" they use to help clients achieve end goals.

Furthermore, counselors' values influence the choice of end goals themselves. Evidence indicates that, during the course of psychotherapy, clients tend to adopt the beliefs and values of their therapists (Beutler, 1983; Murray, 1956; Strong, 1978; Truax, 1966), and the same is likely to be applicable to counseling. Because goals are usually based on values and beliefs, a client is likely to adopt goals that the counselor holds as beneficial for the client.

A counselor reflecting on this situation may well experience a sense of what might be called "moral discomfort": Is it acceptable to exert a potentially major influence on a client based on one's own personal values or beliefs? For counselors who do not feel comfortable with this question—who would like to have something more as a basis for the choices they make in developing instrumental and end goals with their clients—help may be found in the field of moral philosophy, which is directed toward elucidating "how we ought to live," to quote Socrates (Rachels, 1986, p. 1). Moral philosophy asks what can be considered good and bad, and what can be considered acceptable or unacceptable means to ends.

In the context of counseling, moral reasoning particularly applies to choices of end goals and instrumental goals. *End goal development* is the clarification of what the client wants to accomplish through counseling, and *instrumental goal development* involves choosing and activating particular means to accomplish end goals. The purpose of this chapter is to illustrate how counselors can apply ethical principles to their development of end and instrumental goals with clients, and, in doing so, provide themselves with a rational basis for goal development that is not limited by their particular personal values and beliefs.

LEVELS OF ETHICAL CONSIDERATIONS IN COUNSELING

An understanding of the model of levels of ethical considerations presented by Kitchener (1984) is useful in applying ethical thinking to goal development. Drawing from the work of Hare (1981), Kitchener distinguished between intuitive and critical-evaluative approaches to ethical issues. *Intuitive understanding* involves a person's "immediate, prereflective response to most ethical situations based on the sum of their prior ethical knowledge and experience" (Kitchener, 1984, p. 44). The idea that it might not be right to influence clients solely on the basis of one's personal views is an example of thinking on this level.

The *critical-evaluative level* involves the use of explicit reasoning and evaluative processes in addressing ethical issues. On the basis of work by Drane (1982), Kitchener shows that this level can be divided into three sublevels: (a) *ethical rules,* "directives which prescribe or proscribe certain acts" (Drane, 1982, p. 26); (b) *principles*, "ethical values in verbal or propositional form which either have or presume to have universal applicability" and on which the particular rules are based (Drane, 1982, p. 31); and (c) *ethical theory*, the philosophical or religious thinking that supports or explains the ethical principles.

The following discussion centers on two principles that can be viewed as universally applicable in the development of counseling goals: respect for the client's best interest or welfare and respect for the client's self-determination.

THE CLIENT'S WELFARE

The principle of respect for the client's welfare can be seen as the basic or central ethical consideration in counseling. It means that what the counselor does or says in the counseling context should be for the purpose of benefiting the client, and that the counselor should be careful to avoid causing harm to the client. At the micro level, this means each statement or question during the counseling process should be intended to benefit the client and that the counselor should have reasonable grounds for believing that a particular statement or question could benefit the client. For example, in asking a client whether time with his or her family or advancement in the workplace is more important to him or her, the counselor may believe that reflecting on this could lead the client to more self-fulfilling time management. Of course, it may not be possible to maintain constant awareness of this obligation to foster the client's welfare. But by maintaining constant awareness as much as possible, counselors are likely to enhance their effectiveness.

Respect for the client's welfare is logically indispensable in counseling because the purpose of counseling is to enhance the client's welfare. The counselor makes an implicit or explicit promise to benefit the client, and the continued existence of the profession depends of the fulfillment of this promise. One might argue that counselors of different theoretical or value orientations will differ on what will benefit a client, and that the counselor may think something beneficial that the client does not. However, the fact that people differ as to what they consider beneficial (in the present context, as to what goals are worthy of adoption), does not belie the fact that counseling must be directed to the attainment of some benefit for the client.

CLIENT SELF-DETERMINATION

Self-determination may be defined as a person's sense of acting according to his or her own wishes or intentions when these are consciously and willingly determined by that person. The principle of respect for the client's self-determination can be viewed as subordinate to the principle of respect for the client's welfare.

Self-determination is closely related to the concept of freedom: To determine one's own actions, one must be free from having them determined by someone else. The contemporary moral philosopher Bernard Gert (1988) considers "do not deprive of freedom" to be a *universal* moral rule; that is, no rational person would advocate that it is acceptable to deprive someone of freedom unless there is a justification for doing so that would be accepted by any impartial, rational person. In the context of counseling, this would imply that the client should not be deprived of self-determination.

Another consideration that supports the importance of respect for self-determination is based on the "golden rule" that is central in various traditional views of morality. Because counselors as rational persons would not want their own self-determination to be curtailed (unless they believed this to be in their best interest), counselors should not deprive clients of their self-determination unless it is justified by some particular circumstance.

Self-determination in counseling means that *the client* should determine what "being benefited" means; that is, what his or her goals are to be. The client may alter his or her initial goals during the course of counseling on the basis of knowledge or values contributed by the counselor. Still, the purpose of counseling remains the achievement of end goals willingly chosen by the client. These considerations support the importance of respect for the client's self-determination as a principle to be observed in counseling goal development.

COUNSELORS' VALUES AND CLIENTS' SELF-DETERMINATION

Research findings (Beutler, 1983; Murray, 1956; Strong, 1978; Truax, 1966) suggest that the personal values held by psychotherapists or counselors — for example, positive valuation of independence or intimacy — tend to be adopted by clients during the course of treatment. This can happen with or without the counselor's conscious intent. The inequality inherent in the counseling relationship, with the assumption that the helper has more knowledge about the issues under consideration, may promote this process (Owen, 1986).

It is generally accepted that it is impossible for therapists or counselors to remain value free in what they say to their clients (Bergin, 1980, 1985; Owen, 1986). This can create a problematic situation with regard to clients' self-determination. Clients generally do not enter a counseling relationship intending to change their personal values to accord with the counselor's personal values; rather, their goal is to remedy some problem or achieve some positive end. If the client does change values in this way, without being aware of what he or she is doing, this constitutes a deprivation of self-determination.

Because no one can speak in a way that is completely free of personal values, counselors, to avoid imposing their personal values on clients, must make their own values explicit, and must make it clear to clients that they can choose the degree to which they want to adopt these values (Bergin, 1985; Oliver & Rogers, 1986). Of course, not all of the counselor's values will be relevant to any particular client, and only when they are relevant do they need to be discussed.

A counselor is seeing Ms. A, who wants to improve her intimate relationships. The counselor may place a high value on "openness" (the ability to tell one's intimate partner both positive and negative thoughts and feelings, and to hear the same from the partner). To avoid unwittingly imposing this value on Ms. A, the counselor can label it as a value, explain the reasons for holding it, and mention the possible validity of alternative values. The counselor might, for example, mention that others may think it better to avoid hurting a partner's feelings except when this has to be done to preserve one's own self-esteem or other alternative views of the issue of openness.

FROM PRINCIPLES TO RULES FOR GOAL DEVELOPMENT

Even at the abstract level of ethical principles, ethical consideration implies action. The implication intended in the above discussion is that counselors should observe the principles of respect for client's best interest and respect for the client's self-determination in what they say to the client. This makes it necessary to move from the level of ethical principles to the level of rules for applying them. The question of what I would have to do to observe the principles in my own practice led me to propose a set of rules that could guide goal development in psychotherapy or counseling (Brace, 1992). These rules are intended to exclude cultural or personal value preferences so as to be applicable regardless of the counselor's values or theoretical orientation. Following is a list of the rules with a brief discussion of each.

Rules Based on Respect for Clients' Best Interest:

1. *The goals stated should be examined before adoption to be as sure as possible that they are in the client's best interest.* To do this, it is usually necessary to inquire into the client's reasons for having a particular goal, possible pressures from other people that may be influencing goal selection, and alternative goals that might not have occurred to the client.

   A naïve client, Mr. B, enamored with someone who has repeatedly delayed a decision about whether to enter into a committed relationship with him, might come to counseling with a goal of developing the patience to keep waiting for his lover's decision. Discussion of the situation and other options could lead the client to determine that a different goal might actually be in his better interest.

2. *The goals should be mutually consistent.* Sometimes clients seek out counseling with a combination of goals such that one of the goals would interfere with, or preclude accomplishment of, another of the goals – but the client has not recognized the incompatibility or acknowledged it. In this situation, the counselor needs to identify the incompatibility so that the client can choose goals that can be achieved. Goal incompatibility can occur when one of the client's goals is for someone else to change, or to learn what to do to get someone to change. A goal of reducing conflict with the other person may accompany this goal. However, the nature of the relationship may be such that attempts to get the other to change escalate the conflict. If the counselor helps the client realize the incompatibility in such a context, the client will have the opportunity to formulate a workable goal. If not, the counselor is setting the client up for failure.

3. *There should be adequate reasons for pursuing a chosen end goal rather than not pursuing it, or for pursuing other end goals.* A client may seek counseling to make a lifestyle change. But given the opportunity to examine and express reasons for doing so, the client might discover that the change is unnecessary.

Ms. C feels apprehensive before going to social functions and thinks she should not feel this way. The counselor investigates and learns that this does not keep her from going out when she wants to go, and that she generally forgets about the apprehension once engaged in socializing. The counselor could get her to question whether there is really a need for her to be free of the apprehension, rather than agreeing immediately to help her with this goal.

4. *The choice of particular instrumental goals should be based on adequate reasons; if the ones chosen are found to be ineffective, they should be replaced with others that are effective.* These points should be obvious to practicing professionals, but we do well to remind ourselves repeatedly of them. Adequate reasons could be found in research evidence for the effectiveness of certain procedures for certain conditions (e.g., systematic desensitization) or certain ways of relating with clients. One's own clinical experience or the advice of consultants or supervisors can also provide such bases for action. Specific occasions for monitoring progress toward the stated end goals should be regularly scheduled to verify that the chosen instrumental goals are indeed working.

5. *All causal and contributory factors that may pertain to the goal should be assessed as much as possible.* The attainment of a particular goal may require changes

at any or all of the various systemic levels of human functioning, including biologic, intrapsychic, interpersonal, family, and social settings. The counselor needs to be aware that some problems or concerns presented by clients require attention at levels other than the level of the client's own thoughts and behavior. For example, some emotional or cognitive problems may be caused by organic disorders. When this is a possibility, the counselor must ensure that the client is examined adequately by a medical specialist (i.e., an endocrinologist or a psychiatrist) to rule out organic etiology before working on counseling goals. The counselor's failure to do so can be fatal to the client. Similarly, some family or work situations are so stressful that it would be futile for the client to pursue a goal related to increased emotional well-being without a change in environment.

6. *The counselor should avoid or correct errors in clinical judgment that could adversely affect goal attainment.* A number of authors and researchers (Arkes, 1981; Dawes, 1986; Jordan, Harvey, & Weary, 1988; Snyder & Thomsen, 1988) have expounded certain types of errors in judgment to which clinicians are prone. By being aware of these errors, counselors can better avoid acting against the client's best interest. A good example of such erroneous thinking is the biasing effect of preconceived notions (Arkes, 1981). There is a tendency to selectively attend to, or selectively elicit, aspects of the client's presentation that confirm one's initial impression or a preconception about the client. This can easily lead to misjudgment of the client's nature or situation.

It is common experience that after attending a workshop or reading a book about some disorder or problematic behavior, counselors find many more clients of that particular type in their caseloads. This shows a preconception exerting an effect on judgment. Just being interested in a particular disorder (e.g., dissociative identity disorder [DID]), may lead a counselor to attend to selectively, elicit, and interpret a client's discourse so as to become mistakenly convinced the client has the disorder. Also, the counselor's actions may elicit behavior from the client that would appear to confirm the counselor's belief, perhaps by inadvertently reinforcing DID-like statements. (The references cited at the beginning of this section explain other types of errors in clinical judgment.)

7. *The treatment should not harm the client; if some harm is necessary for the treatment, it should be outweighed by the treatment's potential benefit and should have the client's informed consent.* Harm in the context of counseling can be understood as infliction of emotional suffering or as influencing clients in such a way as to lead them into conditions less desirable to themselves. Harm in the latter sense is avoided by regular assessment of the client's progress toward end goals, with shifting of instrumental goals or referral to different treatment when necessary.

In the former sense, harm is probably typical (though not necessarily inevitable) in counseling or psychotherapy because the process often involves confrontation of difficult feelings and disturbing thoughts and change in habitual behavior patterns. The counselor must have reasonable grounds for believing that the benefits will outweigh the suffering entailed in the counseling process.

8. *The counselor should keep any implicit or explicit promises made to the client.* In the counseling context, an implicit promise is to serve the client's best

interest, which can be fulfilled by observing the other rules discussed here. A treatment contract specifying end goals and instrumental goals is essentially a set of explicit promises; thus, it should not be taken lightly or forgotten as counseling proceeds. It often happens that new issues not covered in the initial treatment contract emerge as counseling proceeds. When this happens, the counselor needs to discuss any revisions in goals with the client to make it clear that what is promised is being revised. This also helps foster efficacious goal achievement by helping the client maintain a clear focus on goals.

9. *When counseling involves more than one person, equal importance should be given to the welfare of each of them as far as possible.* In couples or family therapy, the counselor often finds one or more of the clients more likeable or more compatible in views or values. The counselor must avoid influencing the situation unfairly in favor of the better-liked client. Sometimes, one of the clients believes something to be in his or her own interest that would be harmful to the welfare of another client. The controlling or abusive spouse and the overprotective parent are prime examples. In such cases, the counselor must protect more vulnerable clients from harm and encourage the harming clients to see that harm to a spouse or child is not in their own best interest.

10. *The counselor should consider possible effects of the client's instrumental and end goals on others so as to minimize harm.* This rule goes beyond respect for the client's best interest to include respect for the interest of those in the client's environment. Of course, the counselor does not have the same kind of contractual responsibility to these others as he or she does to the

client. But he or she may want to assume the general human moral responsibility of avoiding unnecessary harm to others (Gert, 1988). This involves finding out enough about those in the client's environment to gauge how the client's changes might affect them. If there appears to be a potential for harm, it may be necessary to invite the other person(s) to participate in counseling or to recommend separate treatment for the other person(s).

Rules Based on Respect for Clients' Self-determination:

1. *Counselors should make explicit to the client any of their values that could affect goal development.* To do this, counselors need to be aware of their own personal values and to reflect on their own words to notice those words that are laden with values. When they find themselves saying something to a client that derives from these values, they can explicitly label the statement as based on their personal values. For example, "Life becomes more meaningful if one allows oneself to think about death's inevitability. This is something I have found to be of value in my own life."

   This rule implies recognition that certain views and values contrary to one's own views and values may be just as valid. It may take special attention to remember this in the counseling situation, where the power differential between counselor and client may lead the former to assume his or her values to be superior and worthy of adoption.

2. *If clients change their values or goals during the course of counseling to ones espoused by the counselor, this should happen with clients' conscious volition.* This rule is to help counselors be aware of and avoid

intentional or unintentional imposition of their personal values (and goals based on them) on their clients. The counselor who wants to respect clients' self-determination may point out when clients express a value or goal that appears to have been adopted from the counselor. Counselors should let clients know that they have the choice to adopt such a value, and ask them to consider whether it is really something they now want. The counselor could take these steps, for example, if a client who initially preferred an isolated lifestyle would set a goal of increased social activity as a result of the counselor's commending the benefits of socializing.

3. *Any paternalistic actions by the therapist should be justifiable.* In this context, *paternalism* refers to an action by a professional intended to benefit a client but done without that person's consent. Involuntary hospitalization is an obvious example. Culver and Gert (1982) provided a relatively straightforward rule for determining when paternalism is justifiable. The rule they propose is as follows: If the harm prevented for the client by the action clearly is greater than the harm caused to the client, and if the harm prevented by always taking this type of action in similar situations would be greater than the harm caused, the action is justifiable.

Paternalism is usually not difficult to avoid: Just obtain the client's informed consent for whatever treatments or interventions are used.

A counselor may believe that recall and expression of some traumatic event is needed for Mr. D to be relieved of symptoms of anxiety or depression. If the counselor explains to Mr. D the reasons for eliciting the memories, gives warning about the potential pain involved, and finds out that he wants to proceed, he or she avoids paternalistic action. If the counselor evokes Mr. D's traumatic memories without these preliminary explanations, this may constitute an unjustified abrogation of the client's self-determination. If it is not certain that the harm prevented by the recall and expression outweighs the harm caused, then the action would not be justified.

Questions relating to paternalism have given rise to extensive discussion in the field of medical ethics. For further information, the reader is referred to Culver and Gert's book (1982) or an article by Brace and VandeCreek (1991) on paternalistic actions in psychotherapy.

4. *The counselor should avoid deceiving the client in the development of end and instrumental goals.* The application of Culver and Gert's method (1982) for determining the justifiability of paternalistic actions rules out most use of deceptive interventions in counseling, because deception involves acting without the client's informed consent. There might be a particular situation in which less harm would come to a client if the counselor misleads him or her about something (e.g., about the motives of the person who is jilting him or her). If, however, counselors were to mislead clients routinely (even to spare their feelings), the profession would lose all credibility. Thus, the harm prevented by always acting in this way would not be greater than the harm caused by doing so. The issue of justifiability of deception is discussed in detail by Brace and VandeCreek (1991).

5. *The counselor should reach an explicit agreement with the client that the end goals and instrumental goals are in the client's best interest and are to be pursued.* This rule is to ensure that clients participate in the

development of their goals and give their informed consent to them. Counselors, in their enthusiasm to be helpful, may often risk losing sight of the fact that what seems obviously good or desirable to them may not be what their clients want. Repeatedly asking for the client's agreement on goals not only respects their self-determination, but it also increases the chances of successful outcome; clients are more likely to work with means of treatment and toward goals they really want. This repeated inquiry into the client's views of the means and goals of counseling gives an implicit message that the client and his or her views are important. This should contribute to the enhancement of positive self-valuation, which is so important for many clients.

CONCLUSION

Consider the complexity of any client's life, the multitude of theoretical models for understanding people, their relationships, and the problems to which they are subject, as well as the various approaches to counseling. Is it any wonder that counselors often feel uncertain about how best to help their clients, and that they question whether what they think is good is indeed good for their clients? The purpose of this chapter has been to offer practical guidelines for reducing uncertainty—by describing the primary principles of respect for the client's best interest and respect for the client's self-determination, and by suggesting rules for the application of these principles in goal development. Being aware of these principles and rules should increase the effectiveness of practice because doing so fosters a practical focus on what is best for the client. Also, observance of the suggested rules would provide for achievement of specific goals and use of justifiable means to goal attainment. This stands counselors in good stead when it becomes necessary to account for their work.

REFERENCES

Arkes, H. R. (1981). Impediments to accurate clinical judgment and possible ways to minimize their impact. *Journal of Consulting and Clinical Psychology, 49,* 323–330.

Bergin, A. E. (1980). Psychotherapy and religious values. *Journal of Consulting and Clinical Psychology, 48,* 95–105.

Bergin, A. E. (1985). Proposed values for guiding and evaluating counseling and psychotherapy. *Counseling and Values, 29,* 99–116.

Beutler, L. F. (1983). *Eclectic psychotherapy.* New York: Pergammon Press.

Brace, K. (1992). Nonrelativist ethical standards for goal setting in psychotherapy. *Ethics and Behavior, 2,* 15–38.

Brace, K., & VandeCreek, L. (1991). The justification of paternalistic actions in psychotherapy. *Ethics and Behavior, 1,* 87–103.

Culver, C. M., & Gert, B. (1982). *Philosophy in medicine: Conceptual and ethical issues in medicine and psychiatry.* New York: Oxford University Press.

Dawes, R. M. (1986). Representative thinking in clinical judgment. *Clinical Psychology Review, 6,* 425–441.

Drane, J. F. (1982). Ethics and psychotherapy: A philosophical perspective. In M. Rosenbaum (Ed.), *Ethics and values in psychotherapy: A guidebook* (pp. 15–50). New York: Free Press.

Gert, B. (1988). *Morality.* New York: Oxford University Press.

Hare, R. (1981). The philosophical basis of psychiatric ethics. In S. Block & P. Chodoff (Eds.), *Psychiatric ethics.* Oxford, England: Oxford University.

Jordan, J. S., Harvey, J. H., & Weary, G. (1988). Attributional biases in clinical decision making. In D. C. Turk & P. Salovey (Eds.), *Reasoning, inference, and judgment in clinical psychology* (pp. 90–106). New York: Free Press.

Keith-Spiegel, P., & Koocher, G. P. (1985). *Ethics in psychology: Professional standards and cases.* New York: Random House.

Kitchener, K. S. (1984). Intuition, critical evaluation, and ethical principles: The foundation for ethical decisions in counseling psychology. *The Counseling Psychologist, 12*(3), 43–55.

Lowe, C. M. (1976). *Value orientations in counseling and psychotherapy: The meanings of mental health* (2nd ed.). Cranston, RI: Carroll.

Murray, E. J. (1956). A content-analysis method for studying psychotherapy. *Psychological Monographs, 70* (13, Whole No. 420).

Oliver, P., & Rogers, S. J. (1986). The virtue of explicit values in the social sciences. *Australian Psychologist, 21,* 195–210.

Owen, G. (1986). Ethics of intervention for change. *Australian Psychologist, 21,* 211–218.

Rachels, J. (1986). *The elements of moral philosophy.* Philadelphia: Temple University Press.

Snyder, M., & Thomsen, C. J. (1988). Interactions between therapists and clients: Hypothesis testing and behavioral confirmation. In D. C. Turk & P. Salovey (Eds.), *Reasoning, inference, and judgment in clinical psychology* (pp. 124–152). New York: Free Press.

Strong, S. R. (1978). Social psychological approach to psychotherapy research. In S. L. Garfield & A. E. Bergin (Eds.), *Handbook of psychotherapy and behavior change* (pp. 101–135). New York: John Wiley & Sons.

Truax, C. B. (1966). Reinforcement and nonreinforcement by Rogerian psychotherapy. *Journal of Abnormal Psychology, 71,* 1–9.

Appendix 2.1
FOR FURTHER READING ON ETHICAL CONSIDERATIONS IN THE DEVELOPMENT OF COUNSELING GOALS

Aside from the sources recommended in the chapter for additional information on errors in clinical judgment and on paternalism, the following sources will be useful to those who want to know more about issues raised in this chapter. Full bibliographic information is provided in the list of references.

- *The Elements of Moral Philosophy* by Rachels is an interesting, readable, and wonderfully concise introduction to the field. In my opinion, exposure to this work is likely to enhance any counselor's ethical awareness and practice.

- Kitchener's 1984 article "Intuition, critical evaluation, and ethical principles: The foundation for ethical decisions in counseling psychology" is helpful for explaining the meaning of important ethical principles and clarifying their place in counseling.

- My 1992 article "Nonrelativist ethical standards for goal setting in psychotherapy" provides a more detailed discussion of some of the issues covered in this chapter.

- *Ethics in Psychology: Professional Standards and Cases* by Keith-Spiegel and Koocher provides an excellent discussion of a wide range of ethical matters of concern to counselors.

3

Codes of Ethics as Catalysts for Improving Practice

Barbara Herlihy, PhD, NCC, LPC, and Gerald Corey, EdD, ABPP, NCC

Dr. Herlihy is Associate Professor of Counselor Education at Loyola University of New Orleans. Dr. Corey is Professor of Human Services and Counseling at California State University at Fullerton.

KEY POINTS

- Professional codes of ethics inform counseling professionals and the general public about their responsibilities, provide a mechanism for professional accountability, and protect clients from unethical practices.

- One basic function of a code of ethics is to provide professionals with a means to improve their own practice.

- Five fundamental moral principles are reflected in all ethics codes: autonomy, beneficence, nonmaleficence, justice, and fidelity. These principles are illustrated with examples from the American Counseling Association code of ethics.

- The authors discuss four major problems with ethics codes: they can be lengthy and have inherent inconsistencies; the proliferation of codes makes it a daunting task for professionals to be sufficiently familiar with every code; opinions vary widely in how much latitude should be taken in interpreting the codes; and they are difficult to enforce.

- Codes of ethics are living documents, some of which may change over time. They can only reflect the current state of knowledge.

- Recent changes in the ethical codes are presented. These include diversity and multicultural issues; reporting of contagious, fatal diseases; dual relationships; *pro bono* service; and sexual relationships.

PURPOSES OF ETHICS CODES

Professional codes of ethics serve a number of purposes. They educate counseling professionals and the general public about our responsibilities. They provide a mechanism for professional accountability, and, through their enforcement, protect clients from unethical practices. For practicing counselors, the codes can serve as a basis for self-monitoring and improving practice.

Education:

In our opinion, the most basic function of codes of ethics is to further the education of counselors. Future members of our profession need to learn about the ethical responsibilities that will be expected of them. As counselor educators, we certainly do much more in our counselor training programs than distribute codes of ethics and ask students to learn them. Hopefully, students are provided with opportunities at every stage of their training to apply the ethical standards to issues and dilemmas they encounter. Students often say that they had not thought about certain ethical questions until they were posed in an ethics class or until they carefully read through the ethical codes. The codes can educate by helping to expand awareness of the range of ethical concerns and can develop ethical sensitivity.

Ethical issues also need to be addressed routinely in the education of practitioners. Continuing education programs, such as this ethics guide, help to further this purpose. When we pause to read and reflect, codes can challenge us to explore our thinking and to clarify our values. They can assist us in raising significant questions, many of which may not have simple or definitive answers.

It is equally important that we inform clients about our ethical responsibilities. One means for accomplishing this goal is through our professional disclosure statements, by including information about our ethical obligations and what recourse clients have if they are dissatisfied with our services. Beyond informing our own clients, we would hope that counselors take a proactive role in educating the general public about the ethical standards of our profession.

Accountability:

In addition to education, ethical standards provide a mechanism for professional accountability. Professional associations and certification boards (such as the National Board for Certified Counselors and the Commission on Rehabilitation Counselor Certification), through their ethics committees, hold their members accountable to the principles they set forth in their codes. State counselor licensure boards serve the same purpose through the mechanisms they have established for processing complaints about licensees. The ultimate end of ethics code enforcement is to protect the public.

Codes can have an impact in legal proceedings as well. One of the best ways to protect ourselves if we are sued for malpractice is to practice in accordance with the ethics codes of our profession. If we have violated an ethical standard and we are involved in a lawsuit, we are certainly more vulnerable to malpractice allegations. We are likely to be asked why we felt justified in not following a given standard.

Improving Practice:

Finally, codes of ethics can serve as a catalyst for improving practice. Codes of ethics typically address a broad range of issues and behaviors. They describe minimal standards of behaviors and identify and prohibit behaviors that are unethical, such as sexual intimacies with clients.

Mandatory ethics is a term that has been used to describe a level of ethical functioning at which counselors simply act in compliance with these minimal standards.

Codes also attempt to foster *aspirational ethics* by describing the highest standards of conduct to which members can aspire

(Austin, Moline, & Williams, 1990; Corey, Corey, & Callanan, 1993). We would hope that counselors use the codes to further these aspirational ethics. We can do this by asking ourselves questions like, "How can I best monitor my own behavior?" "How can I develop increased honesty with myself?" and "How can I ensure that I am thinking about what is best for my clients?"

For practitioners, codes can provide a structure and raise topics for consideration that we might overlook. Moreover, they can foster personal reflection. When we seriously study our codes, apply relevant standards to situations we encounter, and periodically review them with an eye to how we can improve our own performance, ethics documents can be a vehicle to enhance and strengthen our profession.

UNDERLYING PRINCIPLES OF ETHICS CODES

Mandatory ethics require knowledge of the codes, with an intent to comply with "the letter of the law." Aspirational ethics require that we do more — that we understand the spirit behind the codes and the principles on which they rest. Kitchener (1984) has described four fundamental moral principles: (a) autonomy, (b) beneficence, (c) nonmaleficence, and (d) justice. A fifth principle, fidelity, can be identified as well. Although codes of ethics are living documents that change over time (a point discussed later), these moral principles are constant and are reflected in all professional codes. We define each of these principles below and provide examples from various sections of the *Code of Ethics and Standards of Practice* of the American Counseling Association (ACA, 1995) to illustrate some ways these principles are reflected in the code.

Autonomy:

Autonomy signifies self-determination. It undergirds our belief that clients are free to choose their own direction and that we have an ethical obligation to decrease client dependency and foster independent decision making. One statement in Section B, "Counseling Relationships," reads, "The member must recognize the need for client freedom of choice."

Standard A.1.b. states, "Counselors encourage client growth and development in ways that foster the client's interest and welfare; counselors avoid fostering dependent counseling relationships."

Beneficence:

Beneficence means to promote good for others; in the counseling relationship, it refers to promoting mental health and wellness. Standard A.1.a. reads, "The primary responsibility of counselors is to respect the integrity and promote the welfare of the client." And, according to Standard E.3.b., "The examinee's welfare, explicit understanding, and prior agreement determine the recipients of the test results."

Nonmaleficence:

Nonmaleficence means to do no harm. As counseling professionals, we must take care that our actions do not risk hurting clients, even inadvertently. Counselors recognize how their personal needs and values influence their work. According to Standard A.5.a., "In the counseling relationship, counselors are aware of the intimacy and responsibilities inherent in the counseling relationship, maintain respect for clients, and avoid actions that seek to meet their personal needs at the expense of clients." Standard A.5.b. adds, "Counselors are aware of their own values, attitudes, beliefs, and behaviors and how these apply in a diverse society, and avoid imposing their values on clients."

Standard G.1.c. reads, "Counselors who conduct research with human subjects are responsible for the subjects' welfare throughout the experiment and take reasonable precautions to avoid causing injurious psychological, physical, or social effects to their subjects."

Justice:

We have a commitment to providing equal, *fair* treatment to all clients. We believe that all persons are entitled to equal access to counseling services.

Consider Standard A.10.c.: "In establishing fees for professional counseling services, counselors consider the financial status of clients and locality. In the event that the established fee structure is inappropriate for a client, assistance is provided in attempting to find comparable services of acceptable cost."

Standard A.12.c. reads, "Counselors provide for equal access to computer applications in counseling services."

So that an increased number of client populations have equal access to professional services, counselors are encouraged to offer *pro bono* services. Standard A.10.d. reads, "Counselors contribute to society by devoting a portion of their professional activity to services for which there is little or no financial return (pro bono)."

Fidelity:

Counselors should make honest promises and be faithful to these promises by honoring commitments to their clients.

According to Standard A.3.a., "When counseling in initiated, and throughout the counseling process as necessary, counselors inform clients of the purposes, goals, techniques, procedures, limitations, potential risks, and benefits of services to be performed, and other pertinent information."

INTERPERSONAL DYNAMICS AND PRINCIPLES OF ETHICS CODES

These moral principles underlie certain interpersonal dynamics in the counseling relationship. Pope and Vasquez (1991) have identified three dynamics – trust, power, and caring—that seem fundamental to us. These authors remind us that both individual clients and our society invest a sacred trust in counselors and the counseling profession. This trust is a source of power that we must use to benefit, and never to harm or exploit, those who seek our help. Finally, caring for and about our clients represents the foundation of our work. Caring assumes that our ethics are aspirational, that our attitude of caring "is incompatible with a goal of meeting the lowest possible standards, doing as little as possible to get by, or using explicit regulations to resist, obscure, and evade professional responsibilities" (Pope & Vasquez, 1991, p. 41).

We believe that two other dynamics should be added: respect and hope. Respect for the fundamental human dignity of our clients and respect for diversity seem basic to us. Hope is another dynamic that underlies our work with clients— hope that change is possible and that counseling can help.

As professionals who help others, we share a commitment to these moral principles and interpersonal dynamics. When we attempt to codify and apply these principles, however, we discover that codes of ethics have certain limitations.

LIMITATIONS OF ETHICS CODES

We can identify four problems with codes of ethics as they presently exist. First, because the codes attempt to serve so many purposes simultaneously, they tend to evolve into lengthy documents with inherent inconsistencies—both prescribing what is desired and proscribing what is prohibited, setting forth both mandatory or minimal expectations and aspirational or desired conduct, and mixing principles and behaviors in both general and specific terms. This can be confusing to professionals who are trying to make optimal use of the codes.

Second, there has been a proliferation of ethics codes. Many counselors find themselves bound to abide by the codes of more than one professional association of which they are a member, the divisional standards of several different ACA divisions, one or more national certification boards, and the ethics code contained in the licensure law of the state in which they practice. Although these various codes may not contradict each other in significant ways, it is a daunting task for any conscientious professionals to become sufficiently familiar with every applicable code to know that they can honor its provisions.

Third, opinions vary widely regarding just how much latitude for interpretation professionals should assume in reading the codes. As we have noted in another work (Herlihy & Corey, in press), we do not always agree with each other on this point. Corey emphasizes that ethics codes should be viewed as guidelines rather than as rigid prescriptions and that professional judgment and flexibility play crucial roles in applying the standards. He reminds us that codes of ethics are creations of human beings, not divine decrees that deliver universal truths. Herlihy sees a danger that questionable behaviors could be too easily justified "as differences in interpretation," and emphasizes the importance of consultation when uncertain as to how to apply the standards. We do agree, however, that no code of ethics could possibly delineate what would be the appropriate or best course of action in every conceivable situation that one might encounter, and that codes are no substitute for sound professional judgment.

Finally, codes of ethics are difficult to enforce. The common perception is that sanctions imposed by professional associations "have no teeth." It is true that a professional association can impose no sanction more serious than loss of membership, which is voluntary to begin with, accompanied by an embarrassing public announcement. However, the ACA notifies state licensing boards when members have been found guilty of serious infractions of its *Code of Ethics*. This in turn can trigger investigations that may result in the offender's loss of licensure.

Another argument that has been made regarding the difficulty of enforcing ethical standards is that the majority of unethical behavior is difficult to detect (Corey et al., 1993). We agree that this may in fact be the case. Some of the more subtle manipulations and careless or slipshod practices undoubtedly do continue undetected – much to the detriment of clients who have placed their trust in our profession and to the ultimate detriment of the profession itself. Some examples are:

- Prolonging the number of sessions because a counselor needs the client more than the client needs the counselor (perhaps the counselor is experiencing financial difficulties)

- Using techniques that are inappropriate for certain clients because of their cultural background (such as using highly emotive techniques with clients before trust is established, when their culture prizes keeping emotions to oneself)

- Using techniques as a gimmick to "get things moving," instead of paying attention to cues given by clients

- Being unaware of our own countertransference, or failing to deal with it in a therapeutic manner when we are aware

- Being so anxious about getting approval from clients that we avoid confrontation and resort to giving advice

ETHICS CODES AS LIVING DOCUMENTS

Codes of ethics are living documents that change over time. They can do no more than reflect our state of knowledge and general consensus on ethical issues at the time they are written. The ACA, for instance, first adopted a code of ethics in 1961. The *Ethical Standards* were revised in 1974 and have been revised every 7 years since then. In 1995, the *Code of Ethics and Standards of Practice* were adopted, which represented a major restructuring of the prior standards (Herlihy & Corey, 1996). To give an example of how ethics codes reflect changes in our thinking, consider that the 1981 code did not contain a specific standard prohibiting sexual intimacies with current clients, nor did the 1988 code make specific reference to sexual intimacies with former clients. It was a measure of our growing concern about the harm done to clients by such relationships that new standards were included in the ACA's (1995) *Code of Ethics*. Standard A.7.a. reads, "Counselors do not have any type of sexual intimacies with clients and do not counsel persons with whom they have had a sexual relationship." Regarding former clients, Standard A.7.b. states, "Counselors do not engage in sexual intimacies with former clients within a minimum of 2 years after terminating the counseling relationship." This does not imply that such relationships are necessarily ethical even after a 2-year period, for the burden of proof is on the counselor to demonstrate that such relations were not exploitative in nature and did not harm the client.

In developing the 1995 *Code of Ethics and Standards of Practice*, it was the goal of the ACA Ethics Committee to offer a comprehensive set of codes and standards that would be acceptable to all groups of professional counselors that currently have their own sets of standards. The 1995 *ACA Code of Ethics and Standards of Practice* together address both mandatory and aspirational ethics. The *Standards of Practice* were developed in response to the needs of nonmembers of ACA to understand our minimal expectations for ethical behavior and to enforce these expectations in legal arenas. Increasingly, courts of law and state licensure boards are demanding that the counseling profession define its minimal standards to which all counselors may be held accountable. The *Standards of Practice* are comparatively brief and specify minimal behaviors required of professional counselors (mandatory ethics) that can be understood and evaluated by individuals outside the counseling profession. The *Code of Ethics* is lengthier, gives more detailed guidance regarding the standards of practice, and includes statements describing the best practice that represents the ideals of the profession (aspirational ethics) (Herlihy & Corey, 1996). Although the changes in the 1995 ethical codes are far too numerous to mention in this article, we have selected five issues to focus on: (a) diversity and multicultural issues; (b) reporting of contagious, fatal diseases; (c) dual relationships; (d) *pro bono* service; and (e) sexual relationships.

Diversity and Multicultural Issues:

The Preamble to the ACA's *Code of Ethics* acknowledges the importance of recognizing diversity in our society and embracing a cross-cultural approach to the theory and practice of counseling. Multiculturalism occupies a central place in the 1995 version of the ACA's *Code of Ethics*. Respecting diversity implies a commitment to acquiring the knowledge, skills, and personal awareness that are essential to working effectively with diverse client populations. Becoming a culturally effective counselor begins with self-understanding, especially with the counselor's recognition of how his or her values, prejudices, and biases are likely to affect the counseling process. Counselors who do not possess the knowledge and skills required to work with people from diverse backgrounds are aware that ethical practice demands that they find ways to acquire multicultural competence. They recognize that the reality of working in a pluralistic society entails learning a variety of perspectives to meet the unique needs of clients.

ACA's (1995) *Code of Ethics* emphasizes the role of respecting diversity as a basic part of the counseling relationship. Section A.2.a. provides guidance on nondiscrimination: "Counselors do not condone or engage in discrimination based on age, color, culture, disability, ethnic group, gender, race, religion, sexual orientation, marital status, or socioeconomic status." The importance of respecting differences is found in Standard A.2.b., which reads, "Counselors will actively attempt to understand the diverse cultural backgrounds of the clients with whom they work. This includes, but is not limited to, learning how the counselor's own cultural/racial identity impacts her or his values and beliefs about the counseling process."

The current *Code of Ethics* specifically addresses diversity perspectives as they apply to diagnosis of mental disorders, testing, research, and training programs.

- Standard E.5.b. states: "Counselors recognize that culture affects the manner in which clients' problems are defined. Clients' socioeconomic and cultural experience is considered when diagnosing mental disorders."

- Standard E.6.b. states: "Counselors are cautious when selecting tests for culturally diverse populations to avoid inappropriateness of testing that may be outside of socialized behavioral or cognitive patterns."

- Standard E.8 states: "Counselors are cautious in using assessment techniques, making evaluations, and interpreting the performance of populations not represented in the norm group on which an instrument was standardized. They recognize the effects of age, color, culture, disability, ethnic group, gender, race, religion, sexual orientation, and socioeconomic status on test administration and interpretation and place test results in proper perspective with other relevant factors."

- Standard G.1.f. states: "Counselors are sensitive to diversity and research issues with special populations. They seek consultation when appropriate."

In the education and training of counselors, the faculty of counselor education programs must make a concerted effort to infuse diversity perspectives as a basic part of the curriculum. This involves integrating material related to cultural, ethnic, racial, gender, socioeconomic status, and sexual orientation in various courses. Furthermore, ethical practice demands that counselor educators explore with students the cultural limitations and biases associated with traditional theories and techniques for counseling. The issue of diversity in training programs is found in Standard F.2.i., which reads, "Counselors are responsive to their institution's and program's recruitment and retention needs for training program administrators, faculty, and students with diverse backgrounds and special needs."

How would you assess your own competency in the area of working with diverse client populations? What do you consider to be the pressing issues in multicultural counseling? What steps can you take to practice from a multicultural perspective?

Reporting on Contagious, Fatal Diseases:

In recent years, counselors have been faced with taking a position on their ethical duty to warn and to protect a third party when a client is HIV positive or has AIDS and may be putting others at risk. Until this 1995 version of the *Code of Ethics*, ACA has been silent on this topic. However, a new guideline addresses this issue. When a counselor has confirmed information "that a client has a disease commonly known to be both communicable and fatal," the counselor is justified in disclosing information to an identifiable third party who is at a high risk of contracting the disease. However, counselors do not take this action except as a final measure and only after they have ascertained that the client has not already informed the third party and does not intend to do so in the immediate future. This issue is an example of how ethical and legal duties might conflict. Although the ethical course of action might be to warn the partner of a client who refuses to disclose his or her HIV status to a third party, legal opinions are conflicting. Indeed, a counselor could be sued for breaching confidentiality, especially if the counselor's state does not have a statute allowing this kind of disclosure.

What are your thoughts on the matter of warning partners of clients who have a contagious, fatal disease—if they refuse to disclose their status? Why would you warn or not warn? How much time might you wait?

Dual Relationships:

With respect to the spirit of the 1995 version of the code dealing with dual relationships, the message is that it is best to avoid them when possible. Standard A.6.a. states, "Counselors are aware of their influential positions with respect to clients, and they avoid exploiting the trust and dependency of clients. Counselors make every effort to avoid dual relationships with clients that could impair professional judgment or increase the risk of harm to clients. (Examples of such relationships include, but are not limited to, familial, social, financial, business, or close personal relationships with clients.) When a dual relationship cannot be avoided, counselors take appropriate professional precautions such as informed consent, consultation, supervision, and documentation to ensure that judgment is not impaired and no exploitation occurs."

Although the code pertaining to dual relationships states that counselors are not to exploit clients, not all dual relationships can be avoided. There are some appropriate precautions to take in assessing the risks of entering into dual relationships. (For more information on dual relationships, see Chapter 11.)

What is your own stance toward dual relationships? It is clear that managing dual relationships is a complex issue and is not solved by simplistic solutions. What guidance does the above code provide to you in deciding a course of action in dual relationship situations?

Pro Bono Service:

Earlier editions of the *Ethical Standards* did not specifically suggest that counselors should devote some of their professional time to individuals and the community without regard to financial renumeration. The 1995 codes state: "Counselors contribute to society by devoting a portion of their professional activity to services for which there is little or no financial return (pro bono)."

It seems to us that this new code challenges counselors to practice aspirational ethics. Both of us teach ethics courses at our universities, and we tell our students that being ethical involves more than merely following the codes and abiding by mandatory standards. We suggest that it means giving away some of our time and talents to further our professional responsibility to improve the world (or a segment of it). However, we also realize that teaching about an ideal is different from putting it into practice.

As a mental health professional, what are your thoughts about this standard? How might it influence your practice? For instance, would you fulfill your obligation to *pro bono* service by offering free or reduced-fee counseling to clients who can no longer afford to pay? There is disagreement over this question (Kimmerling, 1993). Would you offer *pro bono* services in a context separate from your practice (such as at a crisis hotline or a United Way agency)? Would you consider yourself unethical if you did not provide *pro bono* service?

Sexual Relationships:

Sexual relationships between therapists and clients have come to public attention and have been the source of serious concern. At least fifteen states have now made it a felony for a therapist to engage in a sexual relationship with a client. Professionals have become increasingly concerned about the issue of sexual relationships with former clients. Some professional codes of ethics and state licensure boards have established waiting periods (typically 1 or 2 years) that must elapse between the termination of a counseling relationship and the establishment of a sexual one, whereas others have created a prohibition with no time limit.

Standard A.7.b. reads, "Counselors do not engage in sexual intimacies with former clients within a minimum of 2 years after terminating the counseling relationship."

Although a consensus exists among counselors that it is inappropriate to enter into a sexual relationship with a former client soon after a counseling relationship has ended, their opinions vary regarding the waiting period. Some of our colleagues have argued, quite convincingly, that time periods are artificial. It does seem absurd, for instance, that what we considered unethical for 365 days could become acceptable on the 366th day. Also, it is a point well taken that clients often return to their counselor, even several years after termination, and that the door to reestablishing the counseling relationship can be kept open only when no intervening relationship has developed.

On the other hand, equally persuasive arguments have been made that it is absurd to prohibit sexual relationships forever. For example, a practicum student (student member of ACA) working at a university counseling center might see a fellow student for a limited number of sessions. They could both graduate and go on to lead separate lives, then meet again almost as strangers many years later and feel a mutual attraction. It could be argued that the proposed standard is too stringent in forbidding an intimate relationship between them at this time.

What are your thoughts about the 2-year waiting period? Some maintain that "once a client, always a client." Some argue that because sexual intimacies are frequently harmful to former clients and that because these intimacies undermine public confidence in the counseling profession, they should be prohibited regardless of the amount of time elapsed since termination. What do you think?

MAKING YOUR CODES OF ETHICS WORK FOR YOU

To conclude this chapter, we highlight some ways that individual practitioners can make the best use of their codes of ethics.

When necessary, do your part to foster professional accountability. Although each of us has an ethical duty to take action when we suspect that a fellow professional is behaving unethically, counselors have been extremely reluctant to report a colleague. As one of us (Herlihy) has learned from her experience as a member of the ACA Ethics Committee, the role of "policeperson" can be extremely uncomfortable. The role seems antithetical to the very core of who we are as counselors, with our commitments to helping rather than punishing and accepting rather than judging. Nonetheless, it is clear that unless we police our own profession, the courts will do it for us. More important, public confidence in a profession is based in large measure on the extent to which the public believes that the profession holds its members accountable to acceptable standards of behavior. A public perception that members of a profession "protect their own," and close ranks to protect an unethical or incompetent practitioner, diminishes the profession. Counseling is a relatively young profession; this presents us with a unique opportunity to deal with unethical behaviors in a way that enhances the trust that our clients and society have invested in us.

On an ongoing basis, we believe the most important use to which any professional can put a code of ethics is to improve one's own practice. When confronted with a question or an ethical dilemma, put the codes of ethics to work for you in helping to resolve it, at the same time recognizing that reliance on the codes will not be sufficient. Several writers have offered models for ethical decision making (Austin et al., 1990; Corey et al., 1993; Kitchener, 1984; Paradise & Siegelwaks, 1982; Stadler, 1986).

Forester-Miller and Davis (1995) describe a seven-step approach to thinking through ethical dilemmas:

1. Identify the problem.

2. Apply the ACA *Code of Ethics.*

3. Determine the nature and dimensions of the dilemma.

4. Generate potential courses of action.

5. Consider the potential consequences of all options. Choose a course of action.

6. Evaluate the selected course of action.

7. Implement the course of action.

You will need to find a model that works best for you. What is important to note here is that, in reasoning through any ethical issue, various practitioners will arrive at different decisions (Lanning, 1997). There is rarely a singular, ideal course of action.

Although codes of ethics do help to guide us, in the final analysis each of us is responsible for our own actions. Codes do not make decisions for us. We must be willing to struggle, to raise questions, to discuss ethical concerns with others, and to continually clarify our values and examine our motives.

We believe that the field of ethics is best seen from a developmental perspective. We have looked at issues as students, and then later as professionals; with time and experience, our views are likely to have taken on a collective new form. Ethical reasoning takes on new meaning as we encounter a variety of ethical dilemmas. Professional maturity implies that we are open to questioning, and are willing to discuss our quandaries with colleagues and engage in continual self-monitoring.

REFERENCES

American Counseling Association. (1995). *Code of ethics and standards of practice*. Alexandria, VA: Author.

Austin, K. M., Moline, M. E., & Williams, G. T. (1990). *Confronting malpractice: Legal and ethical dilemmas in psychotherapy*. Newbury Park, CA: Sage.

Corey, G., Corey, M. S., & Callanan, P. (1993). *Issues and ethics in the helping professions* (4th ed.). Pacific Grove, CA: Brooks/Cole.

Forester-Miller, H., & Davis, T. E. (1995). *A practitioner's guide to ethical decision making*. Alexandria, VA: American Counseling Association.

Herlihy, B., & Corey, G. (1996). *ACA ethical standards casebook* (5th ed.). American Counseling Association: Alexandria, VA.

Herlihy, B., & Corey, G. (in press). *Boundary issues in counseling: Multiple roles and relationships*. Alexandria, VA: American Counseling Association.

Kimmerling, G. F. (1993). The business side of a helping profession. *American Counselor, 2*(4), 5-6.

Kitchener, K. S. (1984). Intuition, critical evaluation and ethical principles: The foundation for ethical decisions in counseling psychology. *The Counseling Psychologist, 12*(3), 43-55.

Lanning, W. (1997). Ethical codes and responsible decision making (pp. 111-113). In J. A. Kottler (Ed.), *Finding your way as a counselor*. Alexandria, VA: American Counseling Association.

Paradise, L. V., Siegelwaks, S. (1982). Ethical training for group leaders. *Journal for Specialists in Group Work, 7*(3), 162-166.

Pope, K. S., & Vasquez, M. J. T. (1991). *Ethics in psychotherapy and counseling*. San Francisco: Jossey-Bass.

Stadler, H. A. (1986). *Confidentiality: The professional's dilemma – Participant manual*. Alexandria, VA: American Association for Counseling and Development.

4

Preparing Rehabilitation Counselors to Deal with Ethical Dilemmas

Carolyn Rollins, PhD

Dr. Rollins is Assistant Professor in the Department of Rehabilitation, Social Work, and Addictions in Denton, TX.

KEY POINTS

- In recent years, the rehabilitation community has expressed an increased interest in the need to prepare rehabilitation counselors for resolving the ethical issues that arise in their practice.

- Rehabilitation counselors are encountering ethical dilemmas more frequently. They fulfill their professional roles in an environment that is undergoing constant change and in which societal expectations and attitudes often conflict; this has rendered their tasks increasingly complex.

- In some situations, rehabilitation counselors may have to choose between adhering to professional standards of practice (supporting fidelity) and meeting clients' immediate needs (supporting nonmaleficence).

- Society's expectations of rehabilitation counselors have increased. At the same time, they have new responsibilities resulting from the passage of the Americans with Disabilities Act and limited opportunities. These factors present a substantial challenge. To meet this challenge, rehabilitation counselors must possess ethical decision-making skills and a broad range of technical competencies.

- Ethical decision making is a skill that can be learned. A course in ethics should be included in rehabilitation counselors' training. Various resources on ethical decision making are offered.

INTRODUCTION

In recent years, the rehabilitation community has expressed an increased interest in the need to prepare rehabilitation counselors for resolving ethical issues in the course of practice (Patterson, 1988, 1989a, 1989b; Rubin, Garcia, Millard, & Wong, 1988; Wilson, Rubin, & Millard, 1988). This interest has been stimulated by an elevated awareness of unethical behavior by rehabilitation counselors (Pape & Klein, 1986) and enhanced by a realization that many rehabilitation counselors experience difficulty recognizing and dealing with ethical dilemmas. For example, it has been noted that rehabilitation professionals have attempted to resolve ethical issues by using an *intuitive* process rather than an *ethical reasoning* process (Emener, Wright, Klein, Lavender, & Smith, 1987). Recent work has indicated that reliance on intuition is not an effective approach for resolving the complicated ethical situations counselors encounter when providing rehabilitation services to persons with disabilities (Wong, Rubin, & Millard, 1991).

An ethical dilemma occurs when the counselor must choose between actions that seem to adhere to one ethical principle while simultaneously compromising another. Rehabilitation professionals have a responsibility to act in a manner consistent with the following ethical principles: (a) beneficence (promoting client growth), (b) autonomy (respecting the client's choices and decisions), (c) nonmaleficence (avoiding or preventing harm to the client), (d) justice (treating clients fairly), and (e) fidelity (keeping one's promises and commitments, both stated and implied) (Wilson et al., 1991). These principles shape rehabilitation counselors' beliefs about how they should practice (Patterson, Buckley, & Smull, 1989; Rubin & Millard, 1991; Tarvydas, 1987; Welfel, 1987; Wilson et al., 1991).

THE NEED FOR ETHICAL REASONING SKILLS

Rehabilitation counselors fulfill their roles in an environment that is undergoing constant change and in which societal expectations and attitudes often conflict; this has rendered their tasks increasingly complex. Therefore, it is not surprising that rehabilitation counselors are encountering ethical dilemmas more frequently. Such encounters have occurred, for example, in situations regarding surrogacy, goal setting, and familial obligations in head trauma rehabilitation (Wong & Millard, 1992); quality assurance, differing professional perspectives of the obligation to and autonomy of the client, and role delineation in rehabilitation teams (Lucignano & Lee, 1991; Purtillo, 1983). Furthermore, the growth of insurance rehabilitation, the emergence of acquired immunodeficiency syndrome (AIDS) as a disabling condition, the increasing numbers of employee assistance programs, and the increasing numbers of rehabilitation clients who are chemically dependent all have complicated the ethical conflicts involved in rehabilitation and have made issues of confidentiality and accessibility more problematic for rehabilitation counselors (Backer, 1988; Cohen, 1990; de Miranda & Cherry, 1989).

The examples that follow illustrate the potential for ethical conflict as rehabilitation counselors attempt to address two issues that can arise simultaneously when providing quality rehabilitation services.

> Two years ago, Nancy, a 22-year-old woman who has mild retardation, was placed in a sheltered workshop, where she had performed well. She is legally competent, acting as her own guardian. The workshop director contacted you—the rehabilitation counselor—indicating that Nancy might do well in competitive employment and that he would like to reopen her case. However, Nancy has told him that she wants to keep working at the workshop because all of her friends are there. She has also told the workshop director that she does not want to see a rehabilitation counselor again at this time.

> Although the workshop director thinks that Nancy's needs would be better served in competitive employment, he is not sure if he should respect her wish to remain at the workshop or

refer her to you for job placement services. The director asks
your opinion as Nancy's rehabilitation counselor; he will likely
be strongly influenced by your response (Rubin, Wilson, Fischer,
& Vaughn, 1991, p. 97).

The workshop director and the client may differ in their
view of which actions represent the client's best interests.
Whose view should be given precedence — the client's (principle of autonomy) or the workshop director's (principle of
beneficence)?

Even the decision to engage in training to develop expertise
or refine existing skills is not always clear-cut. Rehabilitation
counselors sometimes may find themselves having to choose
between adhering to professional standards of practice (supporting fidelity) and meeting clients' immediate needs (supporting nonmaleficence).

> Your case load of clients whose disability resulted from head
> injury has steadily increased. You request approval to attend a
> 2-day continuing education workshop for counselors working
> with clients with head injures. The request was approved, and
> the course begins the following Tuesday. To attend the work
> shop, you must postpone scheduled home visits with several
> active clients who are having problems and need guidance and
> counseling services. You must decide whether to attend the
> workshop or make the scheduled home visits (Rubin, Wilson,
> et al., 1991).

Some guidance in such situations can be found in laws,
regulations, and organizational policy. Peer consultation and
professional codes of ethics also are useful. However, in many
situations, issues can emerge for which these resources offer
little or no guidance. As rehabilitation counselors provide
more services in a wider range of settings to persons with a
broader range of disabling conditions and with more severe
disabilities, the ethical issues that arise in these situations
become more complex (Patterson, 1989b). These factors,

coupled with the limited guidance and resources available for resolving ethical dilemmas, necessitate the continuing review and practice of ethical reasoning skills by all rehabilitation professionals.

INCREASING JOB COMPLEXITY FOR REHABILITATION COUNSELORS

The early emphasis of public vocational rehabilitation counseling in the United States was restricted to persons with physical disabilities acquired through military service or agricultural or industrial employment. In the 1940s and 1950s, the client pool expanded to include persons with mental retardation and mental illness. Since the 1960s, activism by consumer disability organizations has led to several distinct changes: (a) more disability categories are eligible for services (e.g., learning disabilities), (b) the order in which clients are served has been prioritized (e.g., the most severely disabled first), and (c) the field has emphasized environmental accessibility and the integration of persons with disabilities into mainstream society (Rubin & Roessler, 1987).

As a result of this activism, society's expectations of the rehabilitation counselor have increased; simultaneously, legislation has mandated that gains be achieved with clients who have very severe disabilities and limited vocational potential (Rubin & Roessler, 1987). This means that rehabilitation counselors are working in an environment with persons who require more time and resources and for whom there is less potential for successful vocational outcome.

Societal expectations have been boosted further by legislation of the 1990s, which attempts to ensure equal status and protect the rights of disabled persons. At the same time, societal attitudes continue to be influenced by prejudices and biases that perpetuate differential treatment and unequal opportunity. The Americans with Disabilities Act (ADA) seeks to ensure accessibility, accommodation, and equal opportunities for persons with disabilities, in both public and private employment (Doyon, 1990).

One role of rehabilitation counselors in ensuring the implementation of the ADA is that of a "broker": that is, a provider of services designed to forge a stronger relationship between the business community and the community of persons with disabilities (Douglas, 1992). Employers are concerned with how to provide accommodation for different jobs, cost-effective job restructuring, and the ADA's impact on workers' compensation claims (Gilbride, Stensrud, & Connolly, 1992). As brokers, rehabilitation counselors will be in a position to provide training and technical assistance for employers and promote collaboration with consumer advocacy groups to create opportunities for trust and understanding.

Rehabilitation counselors simultaneously will have to move from the current service-based focus to a client-based focus (Douglas, 1992; Patterson & Marks, 1992). In other words, counselors will not be able to serve as brokers in promoting the spirit of the ADA without an adjustment of their "service delivery" mindset; they must move from the current "good cause" way of thinking to a "service marketing" manner of thought and behavior. Such behavior will demonstrate an understanding of employers' needs and suggest the capacity to provide appropriate consultation and disability management services (Douglas, 1992; Gilbride et al., 1992). The atmosphere stimulated by the ADA requires that rehabilitation counselors provide training and education and possess skills in consumer advocacy, professional collaboration, and client consultation (Benshoff & Souheaver, 1991; Schmidt, 1991).

In this environment of heightened societal expectations, limited opportunity, and mandated change, rehabilitation counselors must balance the need for successful closures against the need to achieve maximal client rehabilitation gains. Such a balance cannot be achieved without confronting ethical issues. To meet these demands, rehabilitation counselors must possess ethical decision-making skills as well as a broad range of technical competencies.

APPROACHES FOR TEACHING DECISION MAKING IN ETHICS

Formal ethics training is one way to prepare rehabilitation counselors to make effective decisions in ethically laden situations. For this reason, it is important to view ethical decision making as a skill that can be learned and that should be included in rehabilitation counselors' educational training (Cottone, 1987; Handelsman, 1986). However, until recently, opportunities for formal instruction in ethics were limited. For example, among the rehabilitation educators surveyed by Rollins and Rubin (1993), less than half indicated having taken a course that focused on ethics.

Although more attention is being given to ethics in rehabilitation education, the number of courses focusing on ethics that are available to future counselors is unlikely to increase significantly. When offered, ethics more likely will be integrated into existing courses (Patterson, 1989; Rollins & Rubin, 1993).

The ability of professional rehabilitation counselors to be more analytical when confronting ethical issues can be enhanced through in-service training (Hastings Center, 1990), which has been provided in many regions throughout the United States. Rehabilitation professionals who have participated in ethical decision-making training generally believe that the training has a positive effect on their professional skills by enhancing their ability to recognize and develop resolutions for ethical dilemmas; consequently, the training is beneficial for their clients.

Educators who teach ethics for rehabilitation counselors should consider the fact that there is no consensus on the best approach for ethics education. However, the instructor should have some experience in teaching ethics in rehabilitation and be familiar with the language, concepts, and analytic methods of ethics, as well as be able to critique participants' responses (Fisher, Rollins, Rubin, & McGinn, 1993). Instructional strategies for ethics education can include presentations of ethical theory; the use of case studies, role playing, and debates; and the use of video presentations.

Teaching methods vary, depending on the skills, resources, and background of both educators and students (Hastings Center, 1990). Training in ethical reasoning should include values, principles, and theories; codes of ethics; case situations containing ethical dilemmas; and ethical decision-making models (Cottone, 1987; Patterson, 1989a; Rubin et al., 1988; Rubin & Millard, 1991; Wilson et al., 1991).

• Instruction should promote an understanding of the ethical principles of beneficence, autonomy, nonmaleficence, fidelity, and justice. Howie, Gatens-Robinson, and Rubin (1992) have conducted especially helpful research on this topic.

• Instruction in rehabilitation should promote familiarity with and an understanding of the *Code of Professional Ethics for Rehabilitation Counselors* as a guide for decision making.

• Instruction should provide practice in identifying and analyzing the types of ethical dilemmas encountered in the rehabilitation service-delivery process.

• An ethical decision-making model for resolving ethical dilemmas that are likely to occur in rehabilitation practice should be taught.

The choice of a decision-making model is a critical decision. Diverse models of decision making in ethics have ranged from a process of professional self-exploration (Corey, Corey, &

Callahan, 1984), to the development of moral reasoning (Kitchener, 1984), to moral development (Van Hoose & Kottler, 1984), to a process of ethical reasoning (Wilson et al., 1991), to a hierarchical model of ethical practice (Tarvydas & Cottone, 1991). Some of these decision-making models are cognitively based, requiring that the user assess the value systems present in the situation, gather and analyze the relevant situational and technical information, identify the options and the consequences associated with each option, and make a logically justifiable choice. One of the models is based on an integrative approach, which applies greater consideration to the social and organizational-contextual variables that may influence ethical practice (Tarvydas & Cottone, 1991).

The inclusion of ethics in rehabilitation education may have been influenced by the limited resources available for teaching ethics (Rubin et al., 1988). Areas of professional responsibility for which rehabilitation educators have identified a need for instructional materials include: confidentiality of information, assessment and client evaluation, professional relationships with referral sources including insurance and third-party payers, consumer advocacy, relationships with colleagues and other professionals, multicultural relationships, fees and financial practices, and counselor advertising of services (Rollins & Rubin, 1993).

Two resources for teaching ethical decision making, *The Ethical Case Management Practices Training Program* (Rubin, Millard, Wong, & Wilson, 1991) and *The Ethical Practices in Rehabilitation Training Modules* (Rubin, Wilson, et al., 1991), can be obtained from the National Clearing House of Rehabilitation Materials at Oklahoma State University. *The Ethical Case Management Practices Training Program* is an in-service training curriculum designed to provide rehabilitation counselors with: (a) an understanding of the five ethical principles mentioned above, (b) an increased understanding of the *Code of Professional Ethics for Rehabilitation Counselors* as a guide for case-management decision making, (c) practice in identifying and analyzing ethical dilemmas encountered in the rehabilitation case-management process, and (d) an ethical decision-making model for rationally resolving ethical dilemmas likely to occur in the rehabilitation case-management process. Table 4.1 describes the instructional units (Rubin, Millard, et al., 1991).

Table 4.1
TITLE AND PURPOSE OF EACH INSTRUCTIONAL UNIT OF
THE ETHICAL CASE MANAGEMENT PRACTICES TRAINING
PROGRAM
(IN-SERVICE)

Unit 1:   *Conflicting valued actions in case management*
(1h)   Trainees are provided with an opportunity to identify their many valued case-management actions and to associate these actions with five ethical principles. Unit 1 is designed to increase their awareness of ethical conflicts present in such choices and the frequency with which these conflicts occur.

Unit 2:   *Identifying and analyzing ethical dilemmas*
(1h)   Trainers are provided with practice in identifying ethical dilemmas in rehabilitation case-management situations. Through the exercises contained in Unit 2, trainees should gain a greater understanding of the characteristics of ethical dilemmas encountered in the rehabilitation case-management process.

Unit 3:   *The* Code of Professional Ethics for
(4 h)   Rehabilitation Counselors
           Trainees are introduced to the *Code of Professional Ethics for Rehabilitation Counselors* as a source of guidance for their service-delivery behavior. They are also introduced to the relationships between ethical principles and the content of the *Code.* Via exercises, trainees learn to use the *Code* as a guide for resolving ethical dilemmas, as well as other ethically laden case-management situations.

Unit 4:   *An ethical decision-making model for rehabilita-*
(4 h)   *tion*
Trainees are introduced to a six-step ethical decision-making model. Through practice exercises
that apply the model to case-management situations, trainees learn how to use the model for
resolving ethical dilemmas.

Unit 5:   *Further application of the ethical decision-mak-*
(4 h)   *ing model*
Trainees are provided with further practice in
resolving ethical dilemmas as well as with opportunities to discuss ethical dilemmas they have
encountered personally.

Adapted from *The Ethical Case Management Practices Training Program,* the *Ethical Practices in Rehabilitation Training Modules* are designed for use in pre-service education to increase
the following skills of future rehabilitation counselors:

- Ability to identify and analyze ethical dilemmas
  encountered in the rehabilitation service-delivery
  process

- Understanding of the strengths and limitations of
  the *Code of Professional Ethics for Rehabilitation
  Counselors* as a guide for rehabilitation decision
  making

- Ability to develop rationally defensible resolutions
  to ethical dilemmas encountered in the rehabilitation
  service-delivery process

The instructional materials outlined in Table 4.2 are
organized in a modular fashion. The instructor of a compre-

Table 4.2
TITLES AND CONTENT OF THE INSTRUCTIONAL MODULES OF THE
ETHICAL PRACTICES IN REHABILITATION TRAINING MODULES
(PRE-SERVICE)

Module 1 — An easy-to-understand introduction to ethical principles for rehabilitation practitioners
This module introduces students to the five ethical principles that form the foundation for ethical behavior in rehabilitation and the human service professions. It provides an opportunity for students to clarify the values that influenced their choice of a career in rehabilitation and some of the ways that ethical principles influence their personal values and many everyday decisions. Desirable actions are identified and associated with five ethical principles.

Module 2 — Value conflicts in the rehabilitation-service delivery process
This module promotes an awareness of ethical choices faced by rehabilitation practitioners.

Module 3 — Introduction to the Code of Professional Ethics for Rehabilitation Counselors
This module introduces the canons and rules of the *Code* and the relationship between ethical principles and the content of the *Code*.

Module 4 — Teachings of the Code
Students process the content of the *Code* to increase their understanding of what the *Code* teaches.

Module 5 — Consulting the Code for resolutions for ethical dilemmas
This module provides an opportunity to seek guidance from the *Code* for dealing with situations containing ethical dilemmas. In addition, an increased awareness of the limitations of the *Code* as a guide for resolving ethical dilemmas is facilitated.

Module 6 — An ethical decision-making model for rehabilitation practitioners
A six-step ethical decision-making model is introduced. Exercises provide practice use of the model for resolving ethical dilemmas that arise in rehabilitation situations.

Module 7 — Further application of the ethical decision-making model
This module provides additional practice using the ethical decision-making model and a discussion of students' experiences involving ethical dilemmas.

hensive ethics course such as "Legal and Ethical Aspects of Rehabilitation" can use all of the modules, whereas the instructor of a more general course such as "Introduction to Rehabilitation" or "Rehabilitation Case Management" can use individual modules to address specific instructional topics. Both sets of materials use several instructional methods, including lecture, visual aids, individual activities, group discussion, and debate. Also included are opportunities to deal with case situations that involve ethical issues, some of which are ethical dilemmas. Instructors of ethics in rehabilitation must, for the most part, develop their own approaches; they must discover what works best for them and alter their approach to meet varying class needs, objectives, and abilities (Hastings Center, 1990). These resources provide a starting point.

CONCLUSION

Persons who enter the rehabilitation counseling profession already may have a strong orientation to helping others but do not yet understand the complexities of the helping relationship. The study of ethics often helps these professionals clarify their own values and better perceive the interrelationships between such values as treating all people fairly (justice) and respecting client choices (autonomy). By analyzing these relationships more clearly, rehabilitation counselors may be better able to develop their philosophy of helping. Conscious ethical decision-making processes should aid rehabilitation counselors in making policy and service-delivery decisions that are appropriate and equitable (National Institute on Disability and Rehabilitation Research, 1989).

REFERENCES

Backer, T. (1988). The future of rehabilitation in the workplace: Drug abuse, AIDS, and disability management. *Journal of Rehabilitation, 19,* 38–40.

Benshoff, J. J., & Souheaver, H. G. (1991). Private-sector rehabilitation and the Americans with Disabilities Act. *Journal of Applied Rehabilitation Counseling, 22,* 27–31.

Cohen, E. (1990). Confidentiality, counseling, and clients who have AIDS: Ethical foundations of a model rule. *Journal of Counseling and Development, 68,* 282–286.

Corey, G., Corey, M., & Callanan, P. (1984). *Professional and ethical issues in counseling and psychotherapy.* Monterey, CA: Brookes/Cole.

Cottone, R. (1987). From the book of Genesis to the Ten Commandments: Ethical and moral renewal in rehabilitation counseling. *Journal of Applied Rehabilitation Counseling, 18,* 53–54.

de Miranda, J., & Cherry, L. (1989). California responds: Changing treatment systems through advocacy for the disabled. *Alcohol Health Research World, 13,* 154–157.

Douglas, R. (1992). The Americans with Disabilities Act (ADA) — What it's really about for rehabilitation professionals. *Journal of Rehabilitation Administration, 16,* 38–39.

Doyon, M. (1990). The practical impact of the Americans with Disabilities Act. In *Rehabilitation USA.* Reston, VA: National Rehabilitation Association.

Emener, W., Wright, T., Klein, L., Lavender, L., & Smith, D. (1987). Rules of ethical conduct and rehabilitation counseling: Results of a national survey. *Journal of Applied Rehabilitation Counseling, 18,* 3–15.

Fisher, J., Rollins, C., Rubin, S., & McGinn, F. (1993). The ethical case management practices training program: An evaluation. *Rehabilitation Education, 7,* 7–16.

Gilbride, D., Stensrud, R., & Connolly, M. (1992). Employers' concerns about the ADA: Implications and opportunities for rehabilitation counselors. *Journal of Applied Rehabilitation Counseling, 23,* 45–46.

Handelsman, M. M. (1986). Problems with ethics training by "osmosis." *Professional Psychology: Research and Practice, 17,* 371–372.

Hastings Center. (1990). *The teaching of ethics in higher education.* Hastings-on-Hudson, NY: Author.

Howie, J., Gatens-Robinson, E., & Rubin, S. E. (1992). Applying ethical principles in the rehabilitation context. *Rehabilitation Education, 6,* 41–55.

Kitchener, K. S. (1984). Intuition, critical evaluation, and ethical principles: The foundation for ethical decisions in counseling psychology. *The Counseling Psychologist, 12,* 43–55.

Lucignano, G., & Lee, S. (1991). Ethical issues involved in the role of psychologists in medical settings. *Journal of Rehabilitation, 57,* 55–57.

National Institute on Disability and Rehabilitation Research. (1989). Ethics and disability services. *Rehabilitation Brief, 12,* 1–4.

Pape, D. A., & Klein, M. (1986). Ethical issues in rehabilitation counseling: A survey of rehabilitation practitioners. *Journal of Applied Rehabilitation Counseling, 17,* 8–13.

Patterson, J. B. (1988). Ethics education: A literature review. *Rehabilitation Education, 2,* 121-128.

Patterson, J. B. (1989a). Ethics and rehabilitation supervision. *Journal of Rehabilitation, 55,* 44-49

Patterson, J. B. (1989b). Ethics training in rehabilitation counseling programs: A national survey. *Rehabilitation Education, 3,* 155-161.

Patterson, J. B., Buckley, J., & Smull, M. (1989). Ethics in supported employment. *Journal of Applied Rehabilitation Counseling, 20,* 12-20.

Patterson, J. B., & Marks, C. (1992). The client as customer: Achieving service quality and customer satisfaction in rehabilitation. *Journal of Rehabilitation, 58,* 16-21.

Purtillo, R. (1983). Ethics in allied health education: State of the art. *Journal of Allied Health, 12,* 210-221.

Rollins, C., & Rubin, S. (1993). The need for ethics instructional materials: A national survey. *Rehabilitation Education, 7,* 27-34.

Romano, M. D. (1989). Ethical issues and families of brain-injured persons. *Journal of Head Trauma Rehabilitation, 94,* 33-41.

Rubin, S. E., Garcia, J., Millard, R., & Wong, H. (1988). Preparing rehabilitation counselors to deal with ethical dilemmas: A major challenge for rehabilitation education. In S. Rubin & N. Rubin (Eds.), *Contemporary challenges to the rehabilitation counseling profession* (pp. 303-315). Baltimore, MD: Paul H. Brookes.

Rubin, S. E., & Millard, R. (1991). Ethical principles and American public policy on disability. *Journal of Rehabilitation, 57,* 13-16.

Rubin, S. E., Millard, R. M., Wong, H., & Wilson, C. (1991). *Ethical case management practices: A training package for dealing with ethical dilemmas encountered by rehabilitation counselors in their case management process* (2nd ed.). Carbondale, IL: Rehabilitation Institute, Southern Illinois University.

Rubin, S. E., & Roessler, R. (1987). *Foundations of the vocational rehabilitation process* (3rd ed.). Austin, TX: ProEd.

Rubin, S., Wilson, C., Fischer, J., & Vaughn, B. (1991). *Ethical case management practices: A preservice training package for dealing with ethical dilemmas encountered by rehabilitation counselors.* Carbondale, IL: Rehabilitation Institute, Southern Illinois University.

Schmidt, M. J. (1991). The role, function, and responsibilities of rehabilitation consumers and professionals in disability policy and law. *Journal of Applied Rehabilitation Counseling, 22,* 32–35.

Tarvydas, V. (1987). Decision-making models in ethics: Models for increased clarity and wisdom. *Journal of Applied Rehabilitation Counseling, 18,* 50–52.

Tarvydas, V., & Cottone, R. (1991). Ethical responses to legislative, organizational, and economic dynamics: A four level model of ethical practice. *Journal of Applied Rehabilitation Counseling, 22,* 26–33.

Van Hoose, W. H., & Kottler, J. A. (1984). *Ethical and legal issues in counseling and psychotherapy* (2nd ed.). San Francisco: Jossey-Bass.

Welfel, E. (1987). A new code of ethics for rehabilitation counselors: An achievement or a constraint? *Journal of Applied Rehabilitation Counseling, 18,* 9–11.

Wilson, C., Rubin, S., & Millard, R. (1991). Preparing rehabilitation counselors to deal with ethical dilemmas. *Journal of Applied Rehabilitation Counseling, 22,* 30–33.

Wong, H., & Millard, R. (1992). Ethical dilemmas encountered by independent living service providers. *Journal of Rehabilitation, 58,* 10–15.

Wong, H., Rubin, S., & Millard, R. (1991). Ethical dilemmas encountered by rehabilitation counselors. *Rehabilitation Education, 5,* 19–27.

5

Ethics in Supervision: Managing Supervisee Rights and Supervisor Responsibilities

J. Michael Tyler, PhD, and Catherine L. Tyler, MBA

Dr. J. Michael Tyler is Assistant Professor in the Department of Counseling, University of South Florida, Fort Myers, FL. Catherine L. Tyler is a former supervisor with the State of Indiana, Division of Family and Children.

KEY POINTS

- Drawing from ethics theory as it has been applied to counseling, consulting, and supervising, this chapter develops a framework within which supervisors and supervisees can better understand the ethical concerns in the supervisory process.

- Because supervisors bear a disproportionate level of power in the relationship, they also shoulder a large share of the responsibility for maintaining ethical interactions.

- Supervisees enter into the supervisory process in an inherently weak position. This chapter, unlike much of the literature, which focuses on the supervisor's responsibilities, discusses the supervisee's rights.

- The authors propose a "bill of rights" for supervisees. The rights are divided into three areas that affect different aspects of the supervisory relationship: defining the parameters, creating an equitable and mutual relationship, and ensuring quality and appropriateness.

- It is unethical for supervisors to provide therapy for supervisees.

- To ensure that clients receive the best possible services, a system of training and credentialing of clinical supervisors is necessary.

INTRODUCTION

In the fields of counseling and psychology, issues in ethics have gained increasing attention over the past 10 years (Sherry, Teschendorf, Anderson, & Guzman, 1991). The focus changed from the 1970s to the early 1990s. Writings from the early 1970s tended to address demographic correlates in relation to therapists' abilities to make ethical judgments or identify ethical behaviors. In the 1980s, the focus shifted slightly to models of ethical decision making and theory testing. So far in the 1990s, more emphasis has been placed on teaching ethics in graduate programs.

Little has been written on the issues of ethics in supervision throughout this period. The *Ethical Standards Casebook* (Callis, Pope, & DePauw, 1982) does not even directly discuss ethical issues in supervision in relation to counseling. Although *Ethical Principles of Psychologists and Code of Conduct* (American Psychological Association, 1992) addressed the issues of dual relationships and sexual exploitation, little direction was provided to supervisors.

The literature includes only brief discussions of potential ethical concerns that may arise in supervisory relationships. It is no surprise that these articles, written almost entirely by academicians, focus on the supervision of counseling trainees in graduate programs. Issues that may be important to practicing therapists or supervisors outside universities and practicums have received virtually no attention.

Many authors have noted that the supervisor-supervisee relationship is similar in many respects to the therapist-client relationship (Brodsky, 1980; Upchurch, 1985). As such, the tendency has been to apply ethical concepts relevant to the counseling process to the supervisory process as well (Kurpius, Gibson, Lewis, & Corbet, 1991). Although this transfer of theory seems applicable in many instances, we feel that such an incorporation is inadequate to address the special needs of the supervisory process.

Additional sources of material that may shed light on the

issues of ethics in supervision include writings in consultation. Because supervision is triadic in nature, it often mimics the consultative relationship and process. As with the counselor-client metaphor, the consultation metaphor is beneficial but not comprehensive.

Drawing from ethics theory as it has been applied to counseling, consulting, and supervising, this chapter develops a framework within which supervisors and supervisees can better understand the ethical concerns in the supervisory process.

IDENTIFYING ETHICAL CONCERNS

Competence:

Wolberg (1954, p. 642) defined *supervision* as "essentially a teaching procedure in which an experienced psychotherapist helps a less experienced individual acquire a body of knowledge aimed at a more dexterous handling of the therapeutic situation." A premise seen throughout the literature is the notion that it is unethical to practice beyond one's level of competence. Given that the role of supervisors is to increase competence, they bear a high level of responsibility to ensure that their supervisees are working within their own area of competence. Similarly, supervisors have an ethical responsibility to supervise only those therapist-client relationships wherein they possess a level of competence.

This focus on competence is one area in which supervision deviates from counseling or consultation. As the persons responsible for assisting supervisees in their professional development, supervisors must assist therapists in understanding the limitations or extent of their abilities.

Role Conflicts:

A potential problem area identified by Sherry (1991) is the

presence of role conflicts. Because both supervisors and supervisees may have multiple roles in the training process, a clear delineation may be difficult. Beginning professionals often may be working as supervisors to one group while still being supervised themselves. These multiple roles may lead to some confusion as supervisees struggle to determine the amount and type of involvement that may be appropriate with students or other staff members.

Accountability:

Supervisors generally have a number of parties to whom they must be accountable. Although a primary responsibility of supervisors is to protect clients and to ensure adequate services, there are other potentially conflicting demands. Supervisors must help supervisees develop and grow professionally. To the general public, supervisors owe some assurance that supervisees will have the capacity to provide quality services. Finally, the institution has expectations of both supervisors and supervisees. In an ideal world, these roles would work to support each other. In practice, however, these varying roles often result in competitive, rather than complementary, expectations.

SUPERVISORY ISSUES SIMILAR TO THOSE IN COUNSELING RELATIONSHIPS

Supervisors find themselves confronted with many of the same concerns that confront therapists. Among these issues are transference and countertransference, dual relationships, diversity, and personal values and beliefs (Kurpius et al., 1991).

Transference and Countertransference:

Issues of transference and countertransference are commonly addressed by therapists, almost all of whom are aware of the potential problems surrounding dependency and power (Sherry, 1991). However, these issues may be less commonly addressed in the supervisory relationship.

The supervisory relationship may develop into a close and supportive environment where supervisees can feel the safety required to undertake significant self-exploration. To the extent that this exploration focuses on issues of professional performance, it is appropriate and within the realm of supervision. However, this limited focus does not prohibit the development of transference in the relationship any more than a goal-focused orientation prohibits its development in counseling.

Dual Relationships:

Another area of concern that is often overlooked is the issue of dual relationships. By the very structure of many organizations that employ therapists, supervisors perform many tasks that affect counselors in a variety of ways. A clear and increasingly difficult example involves the supervisor who is responsible to the organization for maintaining a profit while overseeing the clinical care of individual clients through supervision. In this situation, it may be difficult for a supervisor to meet the sometimes conflicting demands imposed by superiors and clients.

A more direct and potentially dangerous type of dual relationship is established when a supervisor agrees to counsel a supervisee. Roberts, Murrell, Thomas, and Claxton (1982) found that 56% of surveyed counselor educators believed it was ethical to engage in ongoing counseling with a student. Many others, however, disagree with the appropriateness of supervisors' having a therapeutic relationship with supervisees (Burns & Holloway, 1989; Sherry, 1991; Whiston & Emerson, 1989; Wise, Lowery, & Silverglade, 1989).

Two reasons for this objection are the power differential and the issue of informed consent. Sherry (1991) argued that because of the inherent power difference in the supervisor-supervisee relationship and the aspects of performance evaluation involved, supervisees cannot give true informed consent to any type of therapeutic relationship. The expressed consent always will be unduly influenced by the superior power of the supervisors. Even when consent is given, therapy will likely be compromised because of the supervisees' concerns that what they reveal about themselves may negatively affect their evaluation and future academic and professional career. These dual relationships in graduate training programs model dangerous, inappropriate behavior for students who later may expect similar services from clinical supervisors or who may offer services when they become supervisors themselves.

More commonly identified as unethical are sexual relationships between supervisors and supervisees. One report (Pope, Tabachnik, & Keith-Spiegel, 1987) indicated that although there is widespread agreement on this issue, it is not universal or at least does not translate into universal actions. Sexual relationships between supervisors and supervisees are always inappropriate. When such relationships exist before the initiation of supervision, every effort must be made to provide alternative supervision to the supervisees. (For a more detailed discussion of dual relationships, see Chapter 11.)

Diversity:

As American society continues to become increasingly diverse, mental health professionals in all settings find their case loads diversifying as well. In response, many graduate training programs are addressing issues of diversity as a core component of training. However, students in counseling and counseling psychology generally express dissatisfaction with the level of training received in this area (Guth, Tyler, McDonnell, & Mendoza, 1993). It may be expected that supervisors are no better prepared to handle diversity than university faculty. Without the assistance of knowledgeable supervisors, therapists can hardly be expected to recognize and confront their own biased behaviors. Furthermore, if supervisors are not adequately prepared in diversity issues, they may inadvertently reinforce their supervisees' biased behaviors. It should be acknowledged that issues of gender and ethnicity are increasingly being addressed, and university students tend to rate their training in these areas as relatively good. However, issues centered around sexual preferences as well as religious diversity are not well covered and will require special consideration by most supervisors.

Personal Values and Beliefs:

Attention should be drawn to the potential for supervisors to impose their own values, belief systems, or styles on their supervisees. Therapists receive specific instruction in methods designed to allow clients to remain autonomous in their decision making. Recognizing that a completely value-free stance is not possible, many training programs address the impact of individual values on the counseling process. This recognition also is noted in texts and other writings. The process of supervision may actually be an area in which it is even more difficult to withhold one's values.

SUPERVISORY ISSUES SIMILAR TO THOSE IN CONSULTING RELATIONSHIPS

Kurpius and associates (1991, p. 49) proposed that ". . .the supervisory relationship is triadic, rather than dyadic." Upchurch (1985) outlined several separate relationships emphasizing the triadic nature of supervision: supervisor-trainee, counselor-client, and supervisor-client relationships. The unique ethical problems presented by this triadic relationship are similar to those experienced in consultation. Upchurch (1985) stated that both supervisees and clients are consumers of the supervisors' expertise. As such, supervisors must address the rights and needs of both parties.

Client Identification:

Given the triadic nature of supervision, ethical questions may be raised concerning the identification of clients. Because supervisory clients may be defined as supervisees or supervisees' clients, supervisors may have difficulty in focusing on their most salient obligation. Lowman (1985) suggested that in some consultative relationships, there may also be a "hidden class" of clients. In supervision, other clients being seen by supervisees as well as other individuals with whom clients interact may be included. It is conceivable that supervisors may identify clients' family members as the level of intervention, thereby bringing them indirectly into the supervisory process.

Goal Identification:

Another potential problem area concerns conflicts among the goals of supervisors, supervisees, and clients. Although clients often enter therapy with some specific goals, therapists may determine a secondary agenda toward which to work. These differing goals can be most readily seen in inpatient and other restrictive settings. In such cases, the supervisor and the supervisee may not agree on goals, or both may agree with each other while disagreeing with the client. Our own understanding of client rights suggests that it is the client's responsibility and right to choose treatment goals. We believe that conflicts between supervisors and supervisees can be resolved by allowing the clients to direct the course of treatment and by focusing on the process of interaction between supervisors and supervisees.

Credentials and Presentation:

The APA's (1992) *Ethical Principles of Psychologists and Code of Conduct,* as well as the professional codes of other organizations, address the issue of self-presentation. Professionals have an obligation to present their credentials in a responsible manner. To allow clients to make informed choices, it is suggested that credentials be presented to them at the start of any relationship; this allows clients to determine whether the person has the level of expertise and knowledge they believe is necessary. Although not covered by any ethical codes, it seems appropriate that clients should also be presented with the credentials of anyone supervising their case. Clients may never meet supervisors or fully understand the role they play, but informed consent suggests that they are entitled to as much information about supervisors as they possess about counselors.

Confidentiality:

Another area of ethical importance is confidentiality (Sherry, 1991). Most disclosures concerning confidentiality are limited to issues of harm to self and others and abuse. However, counselors regularly discuss clients with supervisors and outside consultants without the clients' knowledge. In addition, clients may be discussed in group formats, where a number of counselors gather to receive supervision. Therapists may be reluctant to disclose such supervisory procedures to clients because of concerns that clients will become resistant. However, to withhold such information is to deprive clients of their own right to autonomy. We believe that therapists should provide full disclosure and address any concerns clients may have regarding supervisory issues during therapy.

MANAGING ETHICAL CONCERNS

Upchurch (1985) noted that supervisors are responsible for defining supervision, the supervisory process, and supervisory expectations and outcomes. Because supervisors bear a disproportionate level of power in the relationship (Upchurch, 1985), we believe they also shoulder a large share of the responsibility for maintaining ethical interactions. To facilitate this relationship at its highest level, a special process of certification should be implemented to ensure supervisory competence (Borders & Leddick, 1987; Kurpius et al., 1991; Newman, 1981; Upchurch, 1985).

Separating Therapy From Supervision:

One method of decreasing potential problems is to separate clinical supervision from administrative supervision. This effectively removes some of the administrative voice from supervisors, thereby allowing counselors to interact more freely regarding clinical issues.

Although supervision is not counseling, there are circumstances under which some interaction similar to that in the counseling process may prove to be beneficial to both clients and supervisees. Supervisors must ensure that trainees' rights of due process are addressed before recommending counseling services. One step is to inform students or supervisees in advance of the possibility that therapy may be required or recommended (Kurpius et al., 1991). The possibility of supervisees requiring therapeutic intervention is real. We maintain that it is unethical (as well as potentially ineffective and harmful) for supervisors to provide therapy for supervisees. If supervisees are having difficulty working with a particular client, it is appropriate for supervisors to explore this issue with them.

Whiston and Emerson (1989) used Egan's (1986) three-stage model as a practical method of defining the appropriate boundaries of the therapeutic relationship in the supervisory process. They proposed that the initial stage of exploring and clarifying the problem situation is appropriate for this relationship. Supervisees must be given the responsibility for resolving the issue in another therapeutic venue outside the supervisory relationship.

Additional methods have been proposed to determine whether a supervisory relationship is crossing the boundary into a therapeutic one (Whiston & Emerson, 1989). The first way is to examine the goals of the relationship. The goal of supervision is the professional development of trainees, whereas the goal of therapy is to increase clients' well-being. A second distinction is supervisors' response to trainees' statements about thoughts and feelings. Whiston and Emerson (1989, p. 322) proposed that when "a supervisor shifts from what the trainee thought or felt to why or what caused these personal dynamics to occur, then the focus shifts from supervising to counseling." In some instances, however, this shift may be appropriate for trainees to understand what is interfering in their work with clients. The burden remains with supervisors to demonstrate the appropriateness of this level of interaction.

Because supervisors embrace particular theoretical orientations consistent with their individual values and cannot be adept at all orientations, it is unrealistic to expect supervision to remain unbiased regarding styles of intervention, values in counseling, or even client goals. Therefore, we recommend that supervisors be as direct as possible about their own biases. Whenever possible, counselors should freely choose from several supervisors, allowing for a "goodness of fit." If this is not possible, supervisors should remain as flexible as possible in their approach and work to create an egalitarian relationship that empowers supervisees.

Agencies may find it beneficial to cooperate with other organizations, providing clinical supervision across organizational boundaries. This type of arrangement not only increases counselors' choice of supervisors, but also may decrease the potential impact of dual relationships.

Upchurch (1985) stated that the following issues should be provided by supervisors: setting fees for supervision; issuing behavioral objectives to supervisees; providing notification of a grievance procedure for failing to meet training objectives; and making timely, relevant, useful, and objective evaluations. They should be explicitly clarified in advance and should be provided to supervisees in a written statement before the start of supervision.

In the counseling relationship, therapists should be respon-

sible for understanding and managing transference and countertransference. This responsibility rests with therapists because of their role and training and by virtue of the power
differential implied in the relationship. Similarly, we believe
that supervisors are responsible for identifying any transference or countertransference that exists in supervision and
addressing the issue professionally.

Kurpius and colleagues (1991) suggested that supervisors
receive regular feedback and consultation concerning their
supervisory styles and interactions. They also recommended
that supervisors engage continually in self-exploration to uncover inconsistencies and biases in their own interactions.
Furthermore, ongoing self-assessment of counseling styles
and staying current with counseling outcome literature to
provide supervisees with the latest information are worth-
while.

Patrick (1989) addressed the unique ethical concerns of
training sites where therapists also participate as clients in a
counselor training laboratory. She stated that informed consent is especially important in these situations and that
supervisees must be told that information revealed in counseling will be used to evaluate their ability to be effective counselors.

Finally, established policies should be implemented by
supervisors to protect supervisees in the case of a grievance or
dispute. Such a policy should carefully outline the procedure
for mediation. There may be a tendency in the design of such
procedures to focus on protection of the institution or agency
involved. However, because supervisees are in an inherently
weaker position, policies should be designed to protect their
rights.

ADDRESSING THE RIGHTS OF SUPERVISEES

Authors often adopt ethical statements concerning the therapist-client relationship and apply the concepts to the supervisor-supervisee relationship. Because of the power differential

inherent in both relationships, the potential for abuse, and the focus on growth, similar ethical concerns occur in both settings. We believe it is beneficial to discuss the rights of supervisees in much the same way as others have addressed the rights of clients.

Supervisees enter into the supervisory process in an inherently weak position. Supervision, by its nature, contains some evaluative component and implies a differentiation in power between those persons involved. Typically, authors in this area have focused on the supervisor's responsibilities. We believe it is beneficial to focus on the supervisee's rights. When focusing on the supervisor, the power differential is increased because the control and responsibility for the relationship remain with the supervisor. When focusing instead on the supervisee's rights, the supervisee is empowered to express expectations, make decisions, and be a more active participant in the supervisory process.

Building on the ideas of Weinrach and Morgan (1975), we propose a "bill of rights" for supervisees (Table 5.1). Three separate areas address a different aspect of the supervisory relationship. Because supervisory relationships are found in a variety of settings for a variety of reasons, this list is not designed to be inclusive — nor is it universally applicable. In some contexts, supervisees find they have no choice about who acts as their supervisor. Although this is not ideal, it represents reality. It is certainly unrealistic to expect that all institutions or agencies can provide an unlimited number of supervisors with different orientations from which to choose. Therefore, we propose these rights as ideals toward which to strive rather than mandates to be imposed.

We recognize that not all supervisees are at the same developmental level. Theories of justice, such as that of Kitchener (1984), require that supervisees receive equal treatment unless individual differences mandate differential treatment to achieve equal outcomes. Therefore, although all mental health professionals have rights regarding the supervisory process, the supervisor's behavioral response to these rights may vary from individual to individual based on develop-

---

Table 5.1
A "BILL OF RIGHTS" FOR SUPERVISEES

Group 1 — Defining the Parameters

Supervisees have the right to:

- Choose among potential supervisors
- Choose to terminate supervision with any given supervisor
- Freely determine the amount of personal disclosure made in supervision
- Be assured of a supervisor's competence based on thorough disclosure of his or her training, experience, and orientation

Group 2 — Creating an Equitable and Mutual Relationship

Supervisees have the right to:

- A supervisory period free from interruptions and distraction provided by supervisors who are interested in their professional growth
- Be fully informed of supervisors' approaches to supervision and the use of any experimental techniques
- Set goals for themselves in the manner in which they choose to proceed in their professional work and development
- Choose or decline to participate in group supervision
- Choose or decline to participate in being taped for use with other supervisees, trainees, or research endeavors
- Continual access to any records maintained through the supervisory relationship
- Expect the maintenance of complete confidentiality with regard to their own disclosure as well as that of clients, except as mandated by law

Group 3 — Ensuring Quality and Appropriateness

Supervisees have the right to:

- Provide feedback to supervisors concerning the efficacy of supervision
- Seek consultation from other professionals as necessary

mental and training needs. We do not believe that an entry-level therapist should have the right to refuse supervision or to refuse to respond to a supervisor's directives. However, we do believe that a more accomplished and experienced counselor has the right to make therapeutic interventions in a manner consistent with his or her style, even when they conflict with those of a particular supervisor, provided the therapist can explain his or her rationale for the intervention.

Group 1 — Defining the Parameters:

The rights proposed in this area focus on the general parameters of the supervisory process. Supervision, like counseling, is not a singularly applicable model that meets everyone's needs. Different supervisees will require different models of supervision, sometimes throughout their professional development. Although it is assumed that supervisors have the most knowledge about these models and their potential impact, supervisees have a right to assist in defining the parameters within which supervision will occur.

The first right a supervisee has in this area is the right to choose among potential supervisors. A supervisory relationship is a personal one that is potentially important professionally. Just as clients have a right to choose their own counselor, supervisees should choose their own supervisor.

It is not always possible for an agency or institution to offer a number of supervisors from which to choose. In these instances, exercising this right may not be realistic. However, if more than one supervisor is available, supervisees should have the right to choose among those available. Such a choice allows supervisees control over their own development and is likely to promote a healthier interaction between supervisors and supervisees.

Once a supervisor has been chosen, the supervisee may find that the choice is not beneficial. If the supervisory process is not meeting the needs of the persons involved, and cannot be restructured to meet these needs, then supervision should be terminated. Institutions should create policies to handle such terminations and the reassignment of the supervisee to a new supervisor.

Supervision is *not* therapy; however, many models of supervision acknowledge a great deal of similarity between the two. It is realistic for supervisors to expect full disclosure of interactions between clients and counselors. Occasionally, supervisors will identify a personal concern of supervisees that is interfering with the therapeutic process. At this point in supervision, supervisees should decide what level of personal disclosure they choose to make to a given supervisor. Although supervisors can legitimately expect that personal concerns are addressed appropriately, supervisees may choose to do so in a venue outside supervision. Because of professional standards against dual relationships, we believe it is incumbent on institutions of all sizes to maintain policies that support the personal growth of their staff outside the institution. In many cases, this may be accomplished through creative contracting with other agencies, in training settings and universities, or with private practitioners. In every case, such outside assistance must include a provision for complete confidentiality.

Finally, supervisees have a right to be assured of a supervisor's competence. Before entering supervision, potential supervisors should make full disclosure to supervisees of their training, background, and qualifications. This information allows supervisees to make an informed choice, thereby protecting their own autonomy. To assist in this process, institutions should require that all supervising counselors be appropriately trained, provide both basic and renewal training, and arrange for consultants to supervisors on an as-needed basis.

Group 2—Creating an Equitable and Mutual Relationship:

This section focuses on ongoing issues in the relationship. Recognizing the power differential inherent in the supervisory relationship, we believe that supervisees have a basic right to expect that steps will be taken to minimize this differential, and we propose the following rights as specific steps in this process.

First, supervisees have the right to a supervisory period that is focused on them and their needs. Supervisors are likely to be busy with other roles and duties. There also may be a tendency to allow other responsibilities to intrude on supervisory time. We maintain that such a practice projects a lack of concern for supervisees and expresses the sentiment that supervision is not as important as other duties.

Second, supervisees should be fully informed of the supervisors' approach to supervision, including specific techniques. Only through full disclosure can supervisees be truly autonomous and make fully informed decisions. Supervisees must also be allowed to set goals for themselves in supervision. All supervisees develop at a different pace and choose to focus energy into specific channels at various points in their development. We respect supervisors' rights to focus on specific skill deficits and to provide whatever interventions are necessary to protect the welfare of clients. However, this focus should not be considered as providing supervisors with complete authority. Supervisees must remain free in directing the course of their own professional development whenever possible.

Within a given setting, certain policies may exist concerning the use of group versus individual supervision. Because supervision requires some level of personal disclosure, group supervision occasionally is not appropriate for a particular supervisee or situation. The decision to participate in group supervision ultimately must remain an individual one. If a decision is made to avoid all group supervision, and the decision appears to be without merit or substance, it becomes an issue to be addressed in supervision.

Supervisors or institutions may find it expedient to videotape or audiotape supervision for training purposes. Because such an act may violate the confidentiality of supervisees (as well as that of the client[s] being discussed), such taping can only be permitted after full disclosure of the purposes of the taping and its uses, as well as with the written consent of the supervisees. Supervisees may be reluctant to decline to allow such taping because of the implications of this decision. Therefore, we believe that actual taping of supervisory sessions should be made with great care and that great pains should be taken to ensure that supervisees can decline to participate without penalty, the threat of penalty, or the perception of penalty. Written records maintained by supervisors should be considered in the same category as other professional records. Specifically, supervisees should be allowed complete access to any of these written records.

Finally, supervisees should be assured of complete confidentiality regarding their own disclosures or those of clients. Supervision is entered into as a private relationship, with the goal of assisting in professional development. Occasionally, personal information may be shared or implied. Supervisors and institutions should take appropriate precautions to protect the fidelity of these relationships.

Group 3 — Ensuring Quality and Appropriateness:

This final area focuses on the right of supervisees to seek the highest quality of supervision possible. Because of the "trainee" status of supervisees, there is often an unexpressed philosophy that what *they* believe is less important simply because their knowledge base is not as wide as that of their supervisor. Such an approach disempowers them and spuriously increases the power of the supervisor.

Supervisees have a right to provide feedback to supervisors and to be listened to with respect and concern. If supervisees are to be allowed to control their own development, they must be granted equal status. Through the process of listening to feedback, supervisors can demonstrate the equality of the relationship as well as their respect for the supervisees' knowledge.

Furthermore, supervisees have a right to seek consultation from other professionals as necessary. At times, supervisees will find that their individual needs are not being met by supervision. In these circumstances, seeking the assistance of an outside consultant is an appropriate professional step to help ensure the quality of services to clients, as well as to aid in professional development.

SUMMARY

Ethics in supervision is an important and complex issue receiving increased attention in the literature. Some of the ethical concerns we have identified are similar to concerns in counseling and consultation, whereas others are unique to the supervisory process. Awareness of and attention to managing these critical concerns will lead to an improved relationship for both supervisors and supervisees. In turn, this will lead to greater professional development and better services to clients.

To ensure that clients receive the best possible services, a system of training and credentialing of clinical supervisors is necessary. The American Association of Marriage and Family Therapy is a leader in this area, providing guidelines concerning the qualifications for supervisors. Other professional associations can assist their members as well as consumers of mental health services by following this lead. Any system of supervisory credentialing must include a demonstrated knowledge of relevant research, supervised experience in clinical supervision, and a knowledge of the specific ethical and legal concerns in supervision.

Implicit in our proposed bill of rights for supervisees are corresponding responsibilities that have implications for training and practice. These responsibilities have not been clearly defined; further development of these ideas will benefit supervisees and supervisors at all levels. Clearly delineated rights and responsibilities will help supervisors, therapists, and institutions resolve ethical concerns appropriately. When these issues are addressed in advance, some ethical dilemmas may be avoided entirely, and a healthier climate will be created for all mental health practitioners and consumers.

Psychology has been slow to address ethics in supervision. Therefore, guidelines in this area are less developed than those in the counseling process or research. We hope this chapter stimulates discussion and contributes to the development of a more mature understanding of ethics in supervision.

REFERENCES

American Psychological Association. (1992). Ethical principles of psychologists and code of conduct. *American Psychologist, 47,* 1597–1628.

Borders, L. D., & Leddick, G. R. (1987). *Handbook of counselor supervision.* Alexandria, VA: Association for Counselor Education and Supervision.

Brodsky, A. (1980). Sex role issues in the supervision of therapy. In A. K. Hess (Ed.), *Psychotherapy supervision: Theory, research, and practice* (pp. 509–522). New York: John Wiley & Sons.

Burns, C. I., & Holloway, E. L. (1989). Therapy in supervision: An unresolved issue. *The Clinical Supervisor, 7*(4), 47–60.

Callis, R., Pope, S. K., & DePauw, M. E. (1982). *Ethical standards casebook.* Falls Church, VA: American Personnel and Guidance Association.

Egan, G. (1986). *The skilled helper: Models, skills, and methods for effective helping* (3rd ed.). Monterey, CA: Brooks/Cole.

Guth, L., Tyler, J. M., McDonnell, K., & Mendoza, D. (1993). *Assessment of graduate students' attitudes toward training in diversity issues.* Paper presented at the meeting of the American Psychological Association, Toronto.

Kitchener, K. (1984). Intuition, critical evaluation, and ethical principles: The foundation for ethical decisions in counseling psychology. *The Counseling Psychologist, 12*(3), 43–55.

Kurpius, D., Gibson, G., Lewis, J., & Corbet, M. (1991). Ethical issues in supervising counseling practitioners. *Counselor Education and Supervision, 31,* 48–57.

Lowman, R. L. (1985). Ethical practice of psychological consultation: Not an impossible dream. *The Consulting Psychologist, 13*(3), 466–472.

Newman, A. S. (1981). Ethical issues in the supervision of psycho- therapy. *Professional Psychology, 12,* 690–695.

Patrick, K. D. (1989). Unique ethical dilemmas in counselor training. *Counselor Education and Supervision, 28,* 337–341.

Pope, K. S., Tabachnik, B. G., & Keith-Spiegel, P. (1987). Ethics of practice: The beliefs and behaviors of psychologists as therapists. *American Psychologist, 42,* 993–1006.

Roberts, G. T., Murrell, P. H., Thomas, R. E., & Claxton, S. (1982). Ethical concerns for counselor educators. *Counselor Education and Supervision, 22,* 8–14.

Sherry, P. (1991). Ethical issues in the conduct of supervision. *The Counseling Psychologist, 19*(4), 566–584.

Sherry, P., Teschendorf, R., Anderson, S., & Guzman, F. (1991). Ethical beliefs and behaviors of college counseling center professionals. *Journal of College Student Development, 32,* 350–358.

Upchurch, D. W. (1985). Ethical standards and the supervisory process. *Counselor Education and Supervision, 25,* 90–98.

Weinrach, S. G., & Morgan, L. B. (1975). A bill of client rights and responsibilities. *Personnel and Guidance Journal, 53*(8), 557–562.

Whiston, S. C., & Emerson, S. (1989). Ethical implications for supervisors in counseling of trainees. *Counselor Education and Supervision, 28,* 318– 325.

Wise, P. S., Lowery, S., & Silverglade, L. (1989). Personal counseling for counselors in training: Guidelines for supervisors. *Counselor Education and Supervision, 28,* 326–336.

Wolberg, L. P. (1954). *The technique of psychotherapy.* New York: Grune & Stratton.

6

Expert Witness Testimony: Ethical, Practical, and Legal Issues

Robert L. Sadoff, MD

Dr. Sadoff is Clinical Professor of Psychiatry and Director of the Center for Studies in Social-Legal Psychiatry, University of Pennsylvania, Philadelphia, PA.

KEY POINTS

- This chapter provides mental health professionals who have been subpoenaed by attorneys to appear in court as expert witnesses with practical suggestions for each stage of the legal process, including preparation for trial, direct examination, and cross-examination.

- Expert witnesses, unlike standard witnesses, are expected to present their opinion as evidence to the extent that it is relevant to the issues being tried in court. Counselors in court essentially act as teachers; they clarify, explain, and help the judge and jury understand certain complex issues involved in the case.

- Counselors are always free to remove themselves from a case, but they cannot subsequently consult with the opposing attorney.

- Expert witnesses must be ready to corroborate their opinion or deal with neutralizing material that may negatively influence their evaluation.

- It is critical to distinguish between the counselor-defendant relationship and the counselor-client relationship.

- Counselors should get full fee for time in court (not for testimony) before testifying in criminal cases when for the defendant and in civil cases when for the plaintiff.

INTRODUCTION

When counselors are called on to testify in court, it is because they have special information, training, and experience in a particular area that bears on the case being heard. They are not witnesses to fact, such as someone who has been an eyewitness to a crime or accident. However, *standard witnesses* are not permitted to present their judgments or impressions; they must stick to the pertinent facts about which they may be asked, usually concerning events that they have actually seen or heard. By contrast, *expert witnesses* are expected and allowed to present their opinion as evidence to the extent that it is relevant to the issues being tried in court. Therefore, the rules of evidence are modified to permit them to perform their task.

Of course, the counselor is only one type of expert witness. Engineers, accountants, nurses, and physicians are among the many kinds of expert witnesses who may be called on for opinion. It is their experience and expertise that is being tapped. Because this is the context in which they are being asked to appear, counselors in court should regard themselves more or less as teachers — clarifying, explaining, and helping the judge and jury understand certain complex issues involved in a particular case. Ideally, expert witnesses are not regarded as adversaries; rather, they should be viewed as credible and honest persons whose testimony derives from their experience and is relatively unbiased.

Counselors should feel free to consult with attorneys for either side (but not both!) on various issues, such as for the defense in a criminal case or for the plaintiff in a civil case (and vice versa). Whatever the setting, they should remain objective throughout in assessing the materials provided with respect to each case.

Counselors should feel comfortable informing the attorney who has engaged their services that their opinion may go contrary to the intent of that attorney in court; they then remain free to dissociate themselves from the case. Of course, if they make such a choice, they should not subsequently accept the responsibility for consulting with the attorney for the other side. After all, the adversary system of justice does pit one side against the other in a battle to determine the truth in court—or, at least, to win the point in dispute. It would be unethical for counselors to review the information presented to them by the first attorney, reject the case, and then consult with the attorney for the opposition.

If, on the other hand, they feel that they are able to give a sound opinion in the matter—one that will be of help to the attorney who has first called on them—they should carefully plan a comprehensive evaluation of the issues to prepare for their appearance in court. Their opinion should be neutral and unbiased.

A number of outstanding professionals (e.g., Diamond, 1968) have taken the position that no mental health professional can be totally impartial. They note what they believe to be an inherent bias built into the system and ultimately expressed by counselors' presence in court. It is, they feel, inhuman for counselors not to have a point of view. This is true to some extent, but at the very beginning of involvement in any case, the counselor should try to be open minded and without prejudice as he or she approaches an assessment of the issues. A truly credible counselor will be available to properly consult with attorneys for either side of various cases and maintain neutrality while doing so. He or she should definitely not behave in such a way that will result in being labeled by attorneys as "prosecution-oriented" or "defense-oriented," because the testimony offered will be expected to mirror the counselor's preference, and this will soon become known in the legal community. His or her testimony would then lose credibility; it would become routine, weak, and easily discredited. It is far better to be able to demonstrate that one has testified on different occasions as an expert for the defense and as an expert for the prosecution, and that no bias is held other than what emerges in the study of the material connected to each case. When the counselor has carefully assessed the particulars of a case and eventually develops an opinion helpful to one side, he or she is often considered to be an advocate for that opinion and will tend to be called on by other attorneys who feel that such opinion can be of help.

Once called on by an attorney to help prepare a case, the counselor owes allegiance to that attorney during the course of the trial. The opinion may not be discussed with the attorney for the opposing side or with others who may neutralize or minimize the effectiveness of the attorney's case. Any contact with the opposing attorney must be made with the permission of the attorney with whom the counselor is working.

One of the counselor's tasks may be to help the attorney prepare cross-examination of the mental health professional serving as the witness for the other side. As for the counselor's testimony, he or she must prepare the attorney to ask questions in the most effective language so that, as the expert witness, he or she can fully benefit from the questions and answers and express ideas effectively. The counselor must also consider any weaknesses in his or her opinion and intended testimony, finding alternative ways to view the situation to deal with anticipated attacks by the opposing attorney. This planning will strengthen the presentation and lend a more believable quality to the testimony in the eyes of the judge and the jury.

There will usually be cross-examination, which often can be incisive and well thought out. During this experience, the counselor should remain composed and try to avoid becoming angry or defensive. If the cross-examination presents material damaging to the counselor's opinion, he or she must acknowledge certain points and hope that the attorney who called him or her will stand ready to neutralize the damage during what is called redirect examination. The expert witness should neither argue with the cross-examining attorney nor permit himself or herself to be manipulated during this procedure. If provocative remarks are made, the expert witness should feel confident that either the lawyer who has brought him or her into the case or the judge will properly attend to the matter.

PREPARATION FOR TRIAL

Preparation begins with the first moment of consultation. One of the most important considerations is that expert witnesses must be ready to corroborate their opinion or deal with neutralizing material that may negatively influence their evaluation. For example, a battery of psychological tests may be helpful in delineating and clarifying subsurface issues, such as character trends or underlying pathology. Expert witnesses must spend enough time with the attorney to orient their testimony along the lines of the particular trial and issues and to help the attorney understand the therapeutic content in the case. Experts may want the consultation benefit of other specialists (e.g., a psychiatrist, a neurologist), or special tests (e.g., an electroencephalogram, computed tomography scan, skull radiographs, blood studies), depending on the points they wish to establish. When examining a defendant, experts should determine the consistency, reliability, and validity of the client's statements to determine the extent to which the person may be distorting the facts to advance his or her own best interests. The counselor-*defendant* relationship is not the same as the counselor-*client* relationship; the nature of the contract is different. The former is asking for helpful evidence; the latter is seeking help for problems. This is a critical distinction, considering the need of the expert witness to retain as much freedom from bias as possible.

After reading all relevant materials and carefully examining the client, the counselor is ready to consult with the attorney to develop the case. The attorney will want to know in detail the counselor's credentials so that they can be presented in court in the most effective way possible. Counselors should alert attorneys to the complex issues involved and the best way to approach them during direct examination so that they can be effectively brought out in a manner acceptable to the court. They should also make clear the weaknesses in the presentation—problem areas could be the target for a good cross-examination — and together they should try to fill in the gaps and adequately prepare to deal with them. Attorneys will usually advise speaking in understandable language, particularly when a jury is present, and to avoid using technical language whenever possible or, at least, to explain in clear terms the concepts and information intended.

It is the attorney's role to instruct the expert witness in courtroom behavior. For example, counselors should not argue with the attorney from the other side. When explaining matters, they should face the judge and jury and make allowance for the fact that the members of the jury, while they may be intelligent and educated men and women, may not be sophisticated in mental health matters. Moreover, jury members may possess biases about counselors and their testimony before they even appear before the court. If expert witnesses cannot cut through their misconceptions by clarity of expression, what they have to say may not be heard, have little weight, and essentially be wasted.

What demeanor should expert witnesses use? They should dress in a conservative manner consistent with the professional image they must convey. They should carry their notes with them for easy reference during examination or cross-examination. And, of course, they must be serious. The judge and the jury will appraise their demeanor and assess the credibility of their presentation on the basis of factors they may not consider the least bit relevant — gait, for example, or manner of speech, the tone in which they communicate, the subtleties of their bearing. The degree to which they represent authority may often mean more than the content of their testimony.

DIRECT EXAMINATION

During direct examination, the attorney who has subpoenaed or called the counselor as a consultant will question him or her on the stand. First, the counselor will be asked to discuss his or her credentials—institution attended, degrees earned, and specialty training or area of expertise within the mental health field. For example, in child-custody cases, it is important for expert witnesses to have a background in the field of child behavior and to clarify for the court the extent of their experience in this area and how it may be relevant to the case at hand. This kind of carefully established pertinence can carry considerable weight if counselors who are called on to testify for the other side have less relevant credentials. Any additional qualifications that make counselors particularly suitable and authoritative witnesses to the issues under consideration may influence their testimony.

When speaking of previous work and experience, counselors should be frank and specific and should under no circumstances either underplay or overplay their authority. Arrogance or boastfulness can hurt their cause as much as understatement. If they have published articles or books in a given area or have academic and hospital appointments, these should be spelled out, including the matter of board certification. It is helpful if they can say honestly that they have testified for attorneys representing the other side of similar issues in the past; this can increase faith in their objectivity.

After the counselor's qualifications have been explored, the opposing attorney has the right to cross-examine the witness if he or she believes that the case so warrants; for instance, efforts may be made to diminish the relevance of a counselor's credentials to the case, or perhaps to contrast the expert witness with a consultant of the opposing attorney who is thought to represent a stronger authority in the matter. For example, if alcoholism is an issue, the opposing attorney may wish to explore the possibility that the counselor has no special qualifications in the treatment or understanding of alcoholics. The attorney may even try to have the witness disqualified. This rarely happens, even if the attorney requests it, because judges usually allow the counselor to testify if the discrepancy between the issues and the witness's experience is not patently great. Expert witnesses should not interpret such a move, if it occurs, as a personal affront to their training and professional position; it is often a ploy or strategy of an opposing attorney, intended to shake their confidence before proceeding with the serious matter of presentation. Counselors should keep in mind that the trial is by nature an adversarial situation and that if the matters in question could have been solved in more peaceful and thoughtful ways, they would probably not be in court at all.

The counselor who testifies will hear objections from the opposition at various points. Sometimes they are justified; often they are not. They may be raised to interrupt the tone and rhythm of the testimony if the opposition feels that they are working against them, thereby diminishing this influence on the jury. Once an objection is raised, the expert witness should halt the testimony and wait before answering until the judge rules on the objection and allows him or her to proceed. If the objection is sustained, the counselor will not be allowed to answer the attorney's question during the direct examination.

During direct examination, counselors usually have few problems because they have had the opportunity to be well prepared and rehearsed. Here they have the freedom to expand on their opinion when asked open-ended questions permitted in direct examination. Of course, the rules of evidence forbid the attorney's directing the questions to be leading or asking queries that are simply rhetorical. Attorneys must ask questions so that the witness can fill in the answers.

A word of caution: Counselors should not go beyond the scope of any particular question in an adversarial way; sometimes, when developing their testimony, expert witnesses are tempted to expand beyond the question they have been answering to impress the jury. They can hurt their testimony should they do so because they may give the opposing attorney the opportunity to object to the extra information indicative of bias on the part of the counselor. Always remember that it is not the expert witness's trial to win or lose but, rather, that of the attorney and, of course, the client represented. Witnesses are free to respond as clarifiers, but they should avoid thinking they can become a coercive or convincing influence on the judge or the jury.

THE HYPOTHETICAL QUESTION

The attorney who calls the counselor may ask what are referred to as hypothetical questions. This is done because the witness has not been present in court to hear the prior testimony. Of course, the expert witness is knowledgeable of this testimony, and he or she is asked to assume that such information is true and is expected to base an opinion on those data. Upon direct examination he or she will have already been prepared for such questions, having rehearsed them long before appearing in court.

However, during cross-examination, the hypothetical questions may be different; opposing attorneys generally emphasize another set of facts. Counselors must base responses on those facts alone; they may not introduce other facts about which they have not been asked. If a question is allowed by the judge and is limited, the witness's response can sometimes go against the side that has called them.

This is an intentional move to make witnesses appear less credible, and it is accentuated if witnesses maintain a stubborn position in the face of uncontroverted opposition. Expert witnesses must be flexible enough to adapt their testimony to the specific questions asked during cross-examination, knowing that the opposing attorney is fully entitled to his or her viewpoints even if they are made at the expense of counselors' testimony.

In order to test the credibility of the witnesses during cross-examination, the opposing attorney will often ask them relatively simple questions, the answers to which are obvious to the jury. Should witnesses be caught in the trap of denying the obvious, the jury will discount their previous testimony. Thus, it is always important for witnesses to give as truthful and accurate answers as they can, even if they then seem to risk hurting the side of the case for whom they have been called. They will always have the chance to clarify or strengthen a position later, if the attorney with whom they work chooses redirect examination.

SPECIAL GUIDELINES

Counselors who are called on to testify for the defense in a criminal case (nonpublic defender) or for the plaintiff in a personal injury or other civil suit should obtain their fee, or a substantial portion of it, before they actually appear in court. This way, they can usually testify more comfortably, without worrying about honest statements that may hurt the side that hired them and that might anger their attorney's client so much that they might not be paid. Of course, in criminal cases, the defendant may end up in jail; and, if not paid in advance, the counselor may never be compensated. Attorneys routinely demand retainers, and counselors should use the same method, basing their fee on the value of the time (usually at least half a day) they must subtract from practice or other professional activities to be available; there will always be time wasted while waiting to be called into the courtroom. Lawyers and judges tend to make every reasonable effort to put mental health professionals on the stand as soon as possible, but various circumstances often will interfere with such expediency and efficiency. Should counselors be called on behalf of an insurance company or a prosecutor from the district attorney's office, they can usually feel secure about being paid.

Courtroom demeanor and behavior are important. When witnesses are communicating ideas to the judge or the jury, they should talk directly to them, turning in the seat, facing them, and speaking in normal conversational tones without appearing to be giving a speech. This does not mean that counselors should not speak with authority, particularly if dealing with such issues as the accepted definitions of mental disorders about which they are obviously expert. If they need them, they should feel free to use slides, charts, or diagrams. The important thing is clarity of expression; they should use concepts and language that will make understandable complex concepts they themselves may have spent years to grasp.

There is no reason for witnesses to feel defensive and worried about challenges to their credibility, reputation, or opinion, even at the most heated moments. After all, they are not on trial. As should be expected, some counselors simply are not comfortable in such adversarial situations and will prefer to avoid being witnesses unless absolutely required.

Rarely is psychological testimony so clear-cut that it cannot be appropriately attacked by the opposing attorney in a good cross-examination. The side he or she represents is seldom entirely correct; the opposition is rarely entirely wrong. Particularly during cross-examination, counselors should answer questions graciously and even acknowledge, if appropriate, intelligent but differing points raised by the other side's attorney. The attorney who has called them will have the opportunity to counterbalance the cross-examination afterward if he or she wishes.

When the witnesses are finished testifying, they should promptly leave the courtroom and not linger, thereby suggesting to the jury that they have undue interest in the outcome of the case. They will care, naturally, but at all times they must give the appearance of being experts — consultants who offer insights and information that the judge and the jury require to make sound decisions. They are not present to win the case.

REFERENCES

Diamond, B. L. (1968). The fallacy of the impartial expert. In R. C. Allen, F. E. Zenoff, & J. G. Rubin (Eds.), *Readings in law and psychiatry* (pp. 145-151). Baltimore: Johns Hopkins Press.

FOR FURTHER READING

Blinder, M. G. (1987). *Psychiatry and the everyday practice of law.* Rochester, NY: Lawyers Cooperative Publisher.

Bluglass, R., & Bowden, P. (1990). *Principles and practice of forensic psychiatry.* London, NY: Churchill Livingston.

Bromberg, W. (1979). *The uses of psychiatry in the law.* Westport, CT: Quorum.

Davidson, H. A. (1965). *Forensic psychiatry, part II: The tactics of testimony* (2nd ed.). New York: The Ronald Press.

Rosner, R. (Ed.) (1994). *Principles and practice of forensic psychiatry.* London, NY: Churchill Livingston.

Sadoff, R. L. (1988). *Forensic psychiatry: A practical guide for lawyers and psychiatrists* (2nd ed.). Springfield, IL: C. C. Thomas.

Simon, R. I. (1992). *Clinical psychiatry and the law* (2nd ed.). Washington, DC: American Psychiatric Press.

Weiner, I. B., & Hess, A. K. (1987). *Handbook of forensic psychology.* New York: John Wiley & Sons.

Ziskin, J. (1970). *Coping with psychiatric and psychological testimony.* Beverly Hills, CA: Law and Psychology Press.

7
Lawsuit Prevention Techniques

Barbara E. Calfee, JD, LSW

Dr. Calfee is President of Barbara Calfee & Associates, Beachwood, OH.

KEY POINTS

- This chapter provides mental health professionals with strategies and preventive measures to avoid cases of professional negligence. By taking action along the lines of risk management, counselors can make major strides to protect their practice and license.

- Professional negligence is a personal injury action that, if proven, may result in a client's receiving financial compensation from the mental health professional or his or her insurer.

- For professional negligence to be proven, the attorney must show that: (a) a client/professional relationship existed, (b) the counselor's behavior fell below the appropriate standard of care for professionals dealing with similar circumstances, (c) the counselor's failure to conform to treatment standards directly caused harm to the client, (d) the harm done to the client was foreseeable, and (e) an actual injury occurred.

- Various types of professional negligence are discussed, including: client abandonment, marked departures from the established therapeutic methods, failure to obtain informed consent, unhealthy transference relationships, practicing beyond the scope of competency, sexual intimacy with a client, misdiagnosis, and failure to control a dangerous client.

AUTHOR'S NOTE

This chapter is designed to provide accurate and authoritative information on lawsuit prevention techniques. Although the author is a health care attorney, this chapter is intended to offer broad guidance and may need to be supplemented by a thorough evaluation of specific state laws, which can be accomplished by seeking the services of a competent professional. In addition, all cases discussed have been presented in national legal reports. The factual descriptions used were taken from court documentation; therefore, the author is limited in discussing the facts from that perspective.

INTRODUCTION

The good news is that lawsuits brought against mental health professionals, chemical dependency specialists, and clergy are few. The bad news is that cases of this nature are on the rise. Therefore, it is appropriate to understand risk management techniques that can reduce the practice of unethical behavior and, therefore, minimize the chance of litigation.

Risk management is a four-step process whereby mental health counselors: (a) identify potential risk areas, (b) evaluate whether the risk area is serious enough to merit further attention, (c) treat any area worth consideration with some method of risk control or prevention, and (d) review treatments periodically to ascertain their effectiveness.

This chapter is the first step in risk identification. Once the eight common types of professional negligence have been reviewed, counselors will become aware of potential risks in their own practice. By examining these areas, counselors can determine which minor adjustments in practice patterns are necessary.

Most of the guidelines discussed are easily incorporated

into practice. Therefore, for a minimal amount of time and effort, a counselor's practice can be further insulated from potential lawsuits. Even the most careful counselor will occasionally run into complaints, letters from attorneys, and lawsuits. However, by following the guidelines in this chapter, counselors hopefully will be better able to avoid such events and manage them effectively if they do arise.

Defining Professional Negligence:

Professional negligence is a personal injury action that, if proven, may result in a client's receiving financial compensation from the mental health professional or his or her insurer. Professional negligence actions are composed of five different elements, each of which must be proven by the client's attorney to demonstrate a successful case of negligence.

1. The attorney must prove that a client/professional relationship existed. In the mental health and addiction fields, these relationships can arise in some of the most peculiar ways: over the telephone, in the emergency room, at a hotline crisis center, in a traditional office visit, at a social gathering, by writing a prescription, by supervising another client's treatment, by offering sample medication, by providing treatment during the evaluation phase of counseling, or by giving advice or opinions to family or friends.

2. The attorney must show that the counselor's behavior fell below the appropriate standard of care for professionals dealing with similar circumstances.

3. A causal link must exist. Therefore, it must be proven that the counselor's failure to conform to

treatment standards directly caused harm to the client.

4. The element known as "proximate cause" must be proven. Proximate cause is akin to foreseeability: the attorney must demonstrate that the harm done to the client was foreseeable.

5. The client must show proof of actual injury.

TYPES OF PROFESSIONAL NEGLIGENCE IN THE COUNSELING SETTING

Client Abandonment:

Client abandonment is alleged when the facts indicate that a counselor unilaterally terminated a client/professional relationship and that this termination resulted in the client's suffering some type of harm. The best way to avoid successful allegations of abandonment is proper documentation. If a counselor wishes to terminate a relationship with a client, he or she certainly may do so unless governmental funding received by the counselor forbids such termination. However, relationship termination must be accomplished carefully, preferably with a written letter sent by certified mail or hand delivered to the client—if appropriate. A client should never be left without proper resources. A referral number or a mental health community service number should always be provided.

Next, records should accurately reflect that a client has been discharged from a counselor's care. If a client has reached an appropriate level of functioning and no longer requires continued treatment, a discharge summary note should be attached to the client's file. This will indicate to the court that the termination of the relationship was rational.

If a client unilaterally decides to terminate the relationship with a counselor, a thorough notation of that discussion should be made in the client's file. If a client says that he or she prefers to discontinue therapy with a counselor, or if he or she begins to cancel appointments, the information should be documented accordingly. The record should always reflect that the client terminated the relationship as opposed to an inference that the counselor abandoned the client while he or she was in need of appropriate follow-up care. In addition, the following actions by a client do not end a professional relationship automatically: the client fails to pay his or her bill, the client fails to abide by his or her treatment plan, the client seeks a second opinion, or the client fails to appear for a scheduled appointment.

If a client still requires treatment, the counselor should avoid terminating care. Rather, a frank discussion with the client about the perceived behavior problems and a need for an improved relationship may be all that is necessary to get the counseling back on track. Courts have determined that the following acts may constitute abandonment: failure to provide a substitute therapist during vacation times, failure to follow a client who has been hospitalized, being extremely difficult to reach between appointments (i.e., ineffective message retrieval), and failure to respond to a request for emergency treatment.

Marked Departures from Established Therapeutic Methods:

Some of the more infamous cases filed against mental health professionals have involved allegations of unorthodox treatment. Cases have been filed alleging client beatings and other severe abusive actions, which therapists later tried to explain as being in the best interest of the client. In court, a counselor's actions will be judged against those commonly used across the country. Therefore, when initiating a new form of therapy or different method of treatment, it is imperative to be able to support the choice with current professional journal articles attesting to its usefulness. Remember, in court, a counselor's attorney will have to find an expert to agree that the therapeutic methods used are acceptable. If it is unlikely that an expert can be found to endorse a certain treatment method, it probably is prudent to discontinue its use.

In *Williams v. The Ohio State Medical Board*, the Board accused a physician of deviating from minimum standards of care by prescribing amphetamines for purposes of weight control. However, the physician presented testimony of two other physicians concurring that there was a majority view and a minority view regarding the use of such prescriptions for that purpose. Therefore, the court ruled that the Board was not justified in determining that the physician had deviated from minimal standards of care. To rule against physicians in such cases, the court must be convinced that the treatment used was below the standard of care, as opposed to being simply the minority view.

In *Glover v. The Board of Medical Quality Assurance*, the court determined that a physician's treatment of a suicidal patient had constituted a substantial deviation from accepted medical standards. The record indicated that the physician had failed to take the patient's history during a 5-year period since his last visit, despite the fact that the patient had a history of violence, depression, and numerous suicide attempts. In addition, the physician failed to secure the patient's signed release for medical records for that period, which would have notified the physician of an attempted suicide by the patient while he was taking antipsychotic medications. Without such knowledge, the physician continued to prescribe large monthly dosages of thioridazine (Mellaril) and amitriptyline (Elavil), even after noticing additional suicide attempts.

Allegations contained within *Roebuck v. Smith* illustrate concrete examples of marked departures from established therapy. In *Roebuck*, the patient complained that his therapist required him to remove his clothes during treatment sessions, exchange his clothing with the therapist's, and subject himself to whippings by the therapist. This kind of abuse obviously is far outside the realm of any legitimate treatment approach.

Failure to Obtain Informed Consent:

Clients occasionally allege that they did not grant consent for a specific type of treatment or the expected outcomes derived from it. Informed consent traditionally has been defined as an oral agreement between a health care worker and a competent client (or appropriate surrogate, such as a guardian or parent) in which the health care worker fully explains the following: the client's condition or diagnosis, the nature and purpose of the recommended treatment, any risks and benefits associated with the treatment, any available alternative treatments, and the client's prognosis with and without the therapeutic intervention.

Entered into voluntarily, this agreement comprises the legal requirement of informed consent. In most jurisdictions, this informed consent discussion does not, by law, need to be put in writing. However, wisdom would suggest otherwise. Some counselors use an actual consent form that a client signs to acknowledge agreement with the proposed therapy. Other therapists prefer to use an introductory letter, which, among other things, explains the type of therapy proposed and the potential outcomes.

Without detailed, written information, it becomes a point of factual issue as to whether a "meeting of the minds" was ever reached between a client and a therapist. A jury would have to determine whether the client actually understood what types of therapy were to be initiated and their potential consequences. For that reason, it is best to have a written document to prove the existence of an informed consent agreement.

Some situations are recognized by law as exceptions to the requirement of informed consent. For example, in an emergency situation, treatment can be rendered without informed consent. (This is often cited as the reason some particularly dangerous clients are medicated against their will.) Also, "therapeutic privilege" may be exercised, which allows treatment to commence without a client's being totally informed of the risk if, and only if, the therapist is convinced that the client's condition would dramatically worsen if he or she were to be told all the facts. Therapeutic privilege does not allow treatment to commence without informed consent if the therapist merely *feels* that the client would not consent if the facts were known. Furthermore, a client may waive the right to informed consent. Some clients implicitly trust their therapists and do not wish to participate in an informed consent discussion. This is also a client's right.

Last, but certainly not least, a counselor must understand how to obtain informed consent when a client is mentally incompetent. It was explained previously that for consent to be truly valid, the client must be competent. Thus, the first responsibility of a counselor is to determine whether the client is incompetent. When doubt exists, judicial intervention may be necessary. If the client is found incompetent by a court, a guardian may be assigned, and, under most conditions, consent can be sought from this person. In the absence of a judicial declaration of incompetence, a counselor takes a risk by obtaining consent from the next of kin.

A minor is considered incompetent by virtue of his or her age. For that reason, a parent or guardian should actively make treatment decisions unless the state law specifically allows minors to seek limited treatment without parental intervention. In the situation of divorce, the parent who was given medical decision-making authority in the divorce decree has authority. Lacking such a decree, it is generally agreed that the custodial parent has the right to make treatment decisions. In the case of joint custody, it is in the counselor's best interest to have both parents agree.

Under all conditions, informed consent discussions should be documented by way of a consent form or a note in the client's record clearly relaying the following information: what was told to the client, the professional opinion of the client's competency, the fact that the client was able to paraphrase what was said (often noted in the record as "the client verbalized understanding"), and the fact that the client willfully agreed to treatment.

Unhealthy Transference Relationships:

In cases pertaining to transference or dual relationship problems between clients and their counselors, some allegations have included inappropriate socialization with clients, burdening clients with personal dilemmas, and putting clients in awkward business situations.

It is best to understand the nature of transference and countertransference and to be particularly mindful of clients who are most susceptible to these issues. If a client cannot be served in a professional manner because of a counselor's personal feelings about that client, the counselor should seek consultation and, perhaps, refer the client to another counselor permanently.

Many questions also arise with regard to dating clients. Dating a current client is never seen as appropriate by any court or accreditation board. More commonly, the question asked is whether or not it is appropriate to date a prior client. Some professionals who believe vigorously that "once a client, always a client" would state that it is never proper to socialize with a prior client. However, a review of ethics codes and professional position papers indicates many professionals believe that a social relationship with a prior client may be appropriate once a 2-year period has elapsed since the last meeting with that person. If at all possible, however, it is best to avoid this type of situation because dating a prior client often results in complications.

An excellent example of many dual relationships is found in *Palmer v. The Board of Regents in Medicine*. In this case, the court found that there was sufficient evidence to support a finding that a psychiatrist had exploited his female patient by using her as a secretary, sexual partner, baby-sitter, and travel companion, all under the guise of therapy.

Although all defendants were exonerated, the case of *Perkins v. Dean* poses extremely interesting problems. In this case, Mr. Perkins began counseling with Mr. Dean, a social worker, regarding the suicide of his daughter. At the time, Mr. Perkins was also drinking heavily and experiencing marital difficulties. Shortly thereafter, Mrs. Perkins also began counseling sessions with Mr. Dean. During one particular counseling session, Mrs. Perkins told Mr. Dean that she wanted to have an affair with him. Mr. Dean allegedly responded, "Check back with me later, and we'll see how it is with my wife and me and you and your husband." Following his resignation from the agency, Mr. Dean continued social contact with the Perkins family. In fact, the Perkins family and the Dean family participated in Alcoholics Anonymous and Alanon meetings together. Mr. and Mrs. Perkins visited the home of Mr. and Mrs. Dean, with some visits culminating in all four spending time together in a jacuzzi. Shortly thereafter, Mrs. Perkins and Mr. Dean began having an affair, which ended some 6 months later. The court determined that Mr. Dean would not be held accountable for his conduct, stating that the professional relationship had terminated and the risks encountered by the couple were purely social. It should be concluded that not all courts would be quite so generous toward the counselor. For a more detailed discussion on dual/multiple relationships, see Chapter 11.

Practicing Beyond the Scope of Competency:

The allegation of practicing beyond the scope of competency is among the more common seen in complaints made against counselors of clients with addictive disorders. Although counselors may like to think they can treat all illnesses or may, quite frankly, desire the extra income, it is extremely dangerous for counselors to take on assignments for which they are not trained. For example, it would be inappropriate for a counselor specializing in chemical dependencies to take on, in an unsupervised capacity, a client with an eating disorder unless he or she had expertise and training in that area.

When in doubt, a counselor always should receive peer input to determine whether or not he or she is practicing outside the scope of his or her competency. If a counselor wishes to broaden his or her skills, it is best to attend continuing education classes or return to college for additional work. Or, a counselor may attempt more challenging cases under the direct supervision of a professional peer who has experience in the management of such cases. Such a supervisor should meet with the counselor often to discuss the case and the method of handling it.

In *Jure v. Raviotta*, an obstetrician was accused of dispensing narcotic drugs and providing psychiatric counseling to a patient when he was not qualified to do so. In *Makris v. the Bureau of Professional and Occupational Affairs*, a massotherapist was accused of offering counseling to clients who came in for massage therapy. Not only did he offer counseling, he also charged for his professional counseling services, for which he was not trained. The Psychology Board of Pennsylvania determined that he had committed violations of the Professional Practice Act.

Sexual Intimacy with a Client:

The following statement cannot be overemphasized: it is *never* appropriate to become sexually or intimately involved with a client! From the cases reviewed, this problem is the most prevalent and most disturbing. Many cases are filed regarding a therapist's sexual involvement with a client and the resulting trauma that occurred. In some states, this is a criminal violation. Studies have shown that this problem is more prevalent than once thought. The damage suffered by clients is often permanent. In addition to severe malpractice consequences (for which there is rarely any insurance coverage), most professional licensure boards will take immediate, harsh action against a counselor's license if this allegation is proven true.

Should a therapist feel any attraction of a sexual nature toward a client, it is imperative to consult a trusted peer and discuss the issue. Also, because of its magnitude, it is suggested that the therapist seek immediate mental health guidance.

Although the majority of such cases reported by the appellate courts are not favorable to counselors, the case of *Sisson v. Seneca Mental Health/Mental Retardation Council* had a different outcome. In this case, an outpatient at a mental health facility claimed that she had a "trust relationship" with a mental health counselor employed at the facility and subsequently had a sexual relationship with him. The basis of her claim was that the trust relationship resulting from counseling services designed to improve her mental and emotional well-being could be easily manipulated by an unscrupulous counselor. However, the court held that since the patient had met the counselor only once in his professional capacity at the hospital, the patient's subsequent association with him had been entirely outside any reasonable semblance of actual therapeutic sessions. Consequently, the sexual relationship had not developed because of a "trust relationship" established during counseling. Undoubtedly, there are some courts that would disagree with the outcome of this case.

Not only may the client involved in the sexual relationship bring a claim, but the client's spouse may initiate a lawsuit as well. For example, in *Figueiredo-Torres v. Nickel*, the husband of a client brought a lawsuit claiming "alienation of affection." Both the husband and wife had sought the counsel of the defendant, a licensed psychologist, for the purpose of preserving and improving their marital relationship. However, during individual sessions, the husband was advised to distance himself from his wife, avoid intimate contact with her, and ultimately separate from her. Meanwhile, the psychologist was engaging in a sexual relationship with the wife. The court determined that the husband had standing to bring legal action. Therefore, a sexual relationship may involve injury to third parties.

Misdiagnosis:

On occasion, a lawsuit may be filed alleging that a misdiagnosis was made by a counselor and inappropriate treatment initiated. As a rule, courts do not like to question a diagnosis because it is not the court's job to practice therapy. However, if it can be shown through a counselor's records that a diagnosis was clearly unfounded and below the standard of care, a case of malpractice might be successful. Once again, an expert witness will be brought in to determine whether he or she can testify on behalf of a counselor's diagnostic capabilities (for more information on counselors as expert witnessess, see Chapter 6). For that reason, it is always wise to require every client, regardless of his or her complaint, to undergo a complete physical examination by a family physician. In so doing, concern for a client's physical health, which might actually have an effect on his or her mental well-being, would be shown. During an initial review, the date of a client's last complete physical examination should always be noted.

The help of a board-certified psychiatrist can be sought if the client's problem might lie beyond the scope of a counselor's competency. This is especially true when dealing with a client with a dual diagnosis (such as the client who has both a chemical dependency and a mental health diagnosis). In such cases, it is especially important for professionals to work hand in hand to ensure that clients receive treatment for both illnesses.

An example of a missed diagnosis is found in *Gandianco v. Sobol*. In this case, a physician's license was revoked for gross negligence and incompetence in the treatment of patients. The record indicated that the physician, who had been employed as a medical specialist to provide emergency medical care at a psychiatric hospital, failed to recognize that a patient was suffering from diabetic ketoacidosis and failed to monitor his fluids, electrolytes, acid-base balance, insulin coverage, and glucose levels. Furthermore, the physician had failed to order an electrocardiogram or blood studies for another patient, who died of myocardial infarction the next morning. The physician also failed to oversee the treatment of a third patient, who had been diagnosed as having rectal cancer. Finally, the physician failed to order a skull x-ray, a computed tomography scan, or a neurologic consultation for a patient who had later been diagnosed as suffering from a right frontal subdural hematoma. Although this physician was working in a psychiatric hospital, his position required him to make medical diagnoses and implement proper care for the hospital's patients.

Failure to Control a Dangerous Client:

A dangerous client presents distinct problems for counselors. First, is there a duty to protect a client from harming himself? Second, is there a duty to protect others from dangerous clients? The answer to both of these questions is *yes*. However, before these dilemmas can be addressed, counselors first must determine which clients are actually dangerous. To do this accurately, it is best to document and compare a client's characteristics with known factors associated with violence. Not only does personality come into play, but counselors must assess a client's socioeconomic background, any situational factors, past violent behavior, and any chemical dependency. If it were determined that a client poses a potential threat of violence to himself or others, it would be best for counselors to take action. The client may require immediate hospitalization or frequent outpatient visits.

In addition, a duty to warn others of potentially violent behavior must be considered. Most states require mental health professionals to warn intended victims of potential harm. Even if a counselor is practicing in a state that does not legally require a warning, it is most likely the proper course of action to take from an ethical perspective.

Sometimes, the duty to warn involves contacting law enforcement authorities. This is especially true when a counselor believes a client is going to drive under the influence of alcohol or drugs. If a counselor is working in a chemical dependency program in which confidentiality is governed by Title 42 of Federal Regulations, he or she might hesitate to alert law enforcement officials about a client. However, the "emergency exception" contained within Title 42 will probably exempt counselors from liability for revealing the identity of a client. For a more in-depth discussion of these issues, see Chapter 8.

In *Reynolds v. National Railroad Passenger Corporation*, a hospital and physician were found to have no special relationship with a patient's fellow employee whom the patient had murdered at his place of employment. The patient had walked away from the hospital during voluntary admission for mental health treatment. The employee was a remote, unidentified third party who had become a victim in the unfortunate incident. The patient had never made a specific threat of violence toward the employee, and there was no special relationship between the defendants and the employee necessary to establish the existence of a legal duty or knowledge that the patient had intended to harm the employee. Furthermore, it was not within the realm of reasonable, foreseeable occurrences that the patient would shoot a co-worker previously unmentioned to staff members during his voluntary admission. In this case, the court emphasized the need for the patient to have specifically mentioned a potential victim for that person to require a warning from the counselor.

A different scenario is presented in *Mikkelsen v. Salama*. In this case, a physician who had prescribed haloperidol (Haldol) negligently failed to warn the patient or her family that she should not drive while taking this medication. Indeed, he informed the patient that she should live a normal life and drive herself to and from her place of employment. However, under the influence of this medication, she had an automobile accident in which a bicyclist also was injured. This case emphasizes the need to be aware not only of violent clients but clients who may be impaired by their illness or medication in normal daily tasks.

CONCLUSION

The material presented in this chapter should help counselors overcome fear of litigation by heightening their awareness of preventive measures. By taking action along the lines of risk management, counselors will have made major strides to protect their practice and license. This guide should be used to answer day-to-day concerns; for specific concerns, the counselor should consult a qualified, personal legal advisor who can discuss these issues in more depth.

REFERENCES

Figueiredo-Torres v. Nickel, 584 A. 2d 69 (MD 1991).

Gandianco v. Sobol, 567 N.Y.S. 2d 909 (NY 1991).

Glover v. the Board of Medical Quality Assurance, 282 Cal. Rptr. 137 (CA 1991).

Jure v. Raviotta, 612 SO.2d 225 (LA 1992).

Makris v. the Bureau of Professional and Occupational Affairs, 599 A. 2d 279 (PA 1991).

Mikkelson v. Salama, 619 SO. 2d 1382 (AL 1993).

Palmer v. the Board of Regents in Medicine, 612 N.E. 2d 635 (MA 1993).

Perkins v. Dean, 570 SO. 2d 1217 (AL 1990).

Reynolds v. National Railroad Passenger Corporation, 576 N.E. 2d 1041 (IL 1991).

Roebuck v. Smith, 418 S.E. 2d 165 (GA 1992).

Sisson v. Seneca Mental Health/Mental Retardation Council, 404 S.E. 2d 425 (WV 1991).

Williams v. the Ohio State Medical Board, 605 N.E. 2d 475 (OH 1992).

FOR FURTHER READING

Barker, R. L. et al. (1993). *Forensic social work*. New York: Haworth Press.

Besharov, D. (1985). *The vulnerable social worker*. Washington, DC: National Association of Social Workers.

Brodsky, S. (1991). *Testifying in court*. Washington, DC: American Psychological Association.

Calfee, B. (1997). *Lawsuit prevention techniques for mental health professionals, chemical dependency specialists, and clergy* (2nd ed.). Huntsburg, OH: ARC Publishing.

Corey, G. et al. (1993). *Issues and ethics in the helping professions*. Pacific Grove, CA: Brooks/Cole.

Group for the Advancement of Psychiatry. (1990). *A casebook in psychiatric ethics*. New York: Brunner/Mazel.

Kagle, J. D. *Social work records* (2nd ed.). Belmont, CA: Wadsworth.

Lakin, M. (1988). *Ethical issues in the psychotherapies*. New York: Oxford University Press.

McIntyre, L. J. (1995). *Families and law*. New York: Haworth Press.

Schroeder, L. O. (1995). *The legal environment of social work*. Maryland: NASW Press.

VandeCreek, L., & Knapp, S. (1993). *Tarasoff and beyond*. Sarasota, FL: Professional Resource Press.

Woody, R. H. (1988). *Fifty ways to avoid malpractice*. Sarasota, FL: Professional Resource Exchange.

8

The "Duty to Protect" Others from Violence

Michael L. Perlin, Esq

Professor Perlin is Professor of Law, New York Law School, New York, NY.

KEY POINTS

- Many therapists and government officials are sued for failing to adequately protect individuals against the commission of tortious acts. Recently, much legal attention has focused on cases in which clients with mental disabilities are "third parties"; that is, cases in which the act of the person with a mental disability precipitated the lawsuit but the defendant is someone else.

- The most significant development in this area has been the establishment of a "duty to protect" others from violence, as articulated in the 1976 case *Tarasoff v. Regents of the University of California*. Subsequent cases have adopted, extended, distinguished, limited, or rejected *Tarasoff*, but, in each case, it has clearly been the benchmark

against which all others have been assessed.

- Under *Tarasoff*, a psychologist can be held liable for the death or injury of a person if, during consultation, the therapist's client threatens to kill or harm that person, and if the therapist fails to notify the proper authorities and/or warn the threatened person or his or her family in the event that the harm is foreseeable and certain.

- The *Tarasoff* decision was immensely controversial from the outset. Confidentiality has been the primary point of contention.

- As of 1995, fourteen jurisdictions outside of California had adopted and applied the *Tarasoff* duty. Some courts have extended it to include persons who are not threatened directly.

INTRODUCTION

In addition to those malpractice and other tort cases brought by or on behalf of individuals with mentally disabilities as plaintiffs,[1] intense attention has recently focused on cases in which persons with mentally disabilities are "third parties." In these instances, either therapists or governmental officials are sued for failing to adequately protect individuals against the commission of tortious acts. In other words, although it is the act of the person who is mentally disabled that precipitated the lawsuit, the defendant is someone else.

By far the most important development in this area has been in the so-called duty to protect, (often inappropriately labeled the "duty to warn") as first articulated in the important case of *Tarasoff v. Regents of the University of California.*[2] Subsequent cases either adopted, extended, distinguished, limited, or rejected *Tarasoff*, but, in each case, *Tarasoff* has clearly been the benchmark against which all other fact patterns have been assessed. This chapter will first examine *Tarasoff* and will then consider its progeny, in an effort to clarify the current state of the law in this most volatile area.[3]

THE *TARASOFF* CASE

Prosenjit Poddar, a graduate student undergoing voluntary outpatient psychotherapy at the University of California hospital, told his therapist (Dr. Moore) that he intended to kill Tatiana Tarasoff,[4] a young woman whom he had known and seen socially for several months a year before, but who did not share his view that the relationship was a serious one.[5] After the therapist (a psychologist) learned that Poddar — whom he viewed as "at times. . . quite rational, at other times. . . quite psychotic"[6] — planned to purchase a gun, he consulted his supervisor (assistant to the director of the department of psychiatry) and the therapist who had originally examined Poddar. He then contacted the campus police (both orally and in writing) to ask for assistance in having Poddar committed.[7]

After the campus police officers took Poddar into custody, they questioned him, extracted a promise that he stay away from Tatiana, and released him without hospitalizing him (when they were satisfied that he was "rational").[8] Subsequently, the director of psychiatry at the university hospital (Dr. Powelson) "asked the police to return Moore's letter, directed that all copies of the letter and notes that Moore had taken as therapist be destroyed, and 'ordered no action to place Prosenjit Poddar in 72-hour treatment and evaluation facility.' "[9]

About 2 months later, Poddar went to Tatiana's home and killed her.[10] Her parents subsequently filed suit against all relevant parties[11] on four separate tort theories, including the failure to warn of a danger (alleging that the defendants negligently permitted Poddar to be released from police custody "without notifying the parents... that their daughter was in grave danger from... Poddar").[12]

After the trial court dismissed the complaint, the plaintiffs appealed.[13] Initially,[14] the California Supreme Court found that a psychotherapist has a duty to warn, when "in the exercise of his professional skill and knowledge, [he or she] determines, or should determine, that a warning is essential to avert danger arising from the medical or psychological condition of his patient."[15] Following a request by the American Psychiatric Association and other professional organizations,[16] however, the Court agreed to rehear the case.

In its second opinion, the Court vacated its earlier decision, holding that a duty existed, but defining the duty more broadly and "with more latitude for professional judgment by the therapist."[17] Writing for a divided court, Justice Tobriner set out the case's holding:

> When a therapist determines, or pursuant to the standards of his profession should determine, that his [client] presents a serious danger of violence to another, he incurs an obligation to use reasonable care to protect the intended victim against such danger. The discharge of this duty may require the therapist to take one or more of various steps, depending upon the

nature of the case. Thus it may call for him to warn the intended victim or others likely to apprise the victim of the danger, to notify the police, or to take whatever other steps are reasonably necessary under the circumstances.[18]

In coming to this conclusion, the Court examined several key factors. First, it asked whether the plaintiff's interests were entitled to legal protection against the defendants' conduct, and concluded that the appropriate test was that if one person was placed in a position with regard to the other so that "if he did not use ordinary care and skill in his own conduct. . . he would cause damage or injury to the person or property of the other, a duty arises to use ordinary care and skill to avoid such danger."[19]

Factors to be balanced in assessing cases under this formula included, most importantly, the foreseeability of harm to the plaintiff,[20] the degree of certainty the plaintiff would suffer injury, the closeness of the connection between defendant's conduct and plaintiff's injury, the moral blameworthiness attached to the defendant's conduct, the burden on the defendant, and the potential consequences to the community.[21]

Second, if avoidance of foreseeable harm requires a defendant to control the behavior of others or to warn, there will only be liability if the defendant bears a "special relationship"[22] to the dangerous person. The therapist-client relationship satisfies this test, the Court found,[23] and a duty may thus be imposed on a therapist to exercise reasonable care to protect others against the dangers that might stem from a client's mental illness. By entering into the therapist-client relationship, the defendant "becomes sufficiently involved to assume some responsibility for the safety, not only of the client himself, but also of any third person whom the [therapist] knows to be threatened by the client."[24]

The Court rejected the defendants' argument that liability should not be allowed, because mental health professionals could not accurately predict dangerousness:

The role of the psychiatrist is like that of the physician who must conform to the standards of the profession, and who must often make diagnoses and predictions based upon such evaluations. Thus, the judgment of the therapist in diagnosing emotional disorders and in predicting whether a [client] presents a serious danger of violence is comparable to the judgment that doctors and professionals must regularly render under accepted rules of responsibility.[25]

Also, in the case before the Court, there was no question as to the failure of defendants accurately to *predict* that Poddar would harm Tarasoff; the negligence alleged was in their failure to *warn* as to the ensuing harm.[26]

The adequacy of the therapist's conduct must be measured, the Court reasoned, "against the traditional negligence standard of the rendition of reasonable care under the circumstances,"[27] stressing that the ultimate question of "resolving the tension between the conflicting interests of [client] and potential victim is one of social policy, not professional expertise."[28] Professional inaccuracy in predicting violence cannot negate the therapist's duty to protect the victim, the Court continued; the risk that unnecessary warnings would be given "is a reasonable price to pay for the lives of possible victims that may be saved."[29]

Rejecting the defendants' argument that the giving of such warnings would be a breach of trust, the Court countered that is was necessary to balance the client's right to privacy with the public's interest in safety from violent assaults.[30] The Court noted a statutory exception to the psychotherapist's privilege in cases where the therapist had "reasonable cause to believe that the [client] is in such mental or emotional condition as to be dangerous to himself or to the person or property of another and that disclosure of the communication is necessary to prevent the threatened danger":[31]

We conclude that the public policy favoring protection of the confidential character of [client]-psychotherapist communications must yield to the extent to which disclosure is essential to avert dangers to others. *The protective privilege ends where the public peril begins.*[32]

However, the police defendants could not be held liable, because they had no "special relationship to either Tarasoff or Poddar sufficient to impose upon such defendants a duty to warn respecting Poddar's violent intentions."[33]

Justice Mosk issued a separate opinion, concurring in part and dissenting in part, stressing that he concurred in the judgment "only because the complaints allege that defendant therapists *in fact* predicted that Poddar would kill and were therefore negligent in failing to warn of that danger."[34] He parted company with the majority, however, regarding that aspect of the Court's holding that allowed for a finding of liability if a therapist failed to predict his or her client's tendency to violence "if other practitioners pursuant to the 'standards of the profession' would have done so."[35] Concluded Justice Mosk:

> I would restructure the rule designed by the majority to elimi-
> nate all reference to conformity to standards of the profession
> in predicting violence. If a [therapist] does in fact predict
> violence, then a duty to warn arises. The majority's expansion
> of that rule will take us from the world of reality into the
> wonderland of clairvoyance.[36]

Justice Clark dissented (for himself and Justice McComb),[37] charging that imposition of the majority's "new duty is certain to result in a net increase in violence."[38] In addition, he read the pertinent statutory provisions[39] to reflect a "clear legislative policy"[40] against disclosure:

> Establishing a duty to warn on the basis of general tort prin-
> ciples imposes a draconian dilemma on therapists — either
> violate the act thereby incurring the attendant statutory penal-
> ties,[41] or ignore the majority's duty to warn thereby incurring
> potential civil liability.[42]

The same result must be reached, he concluded, under a common law tort analysis. Confidentiality must be ensured for three independent policy reasons: (a) without a "substantial assurance" of confidentiality, those requiring treatment will be deterred from seeking assistance[43]; (b) a guarantee of confidentiality is "essential" in eliciting treatment[44]; and (c) without trust in a psychotherapist (in which an assurance of confidentiality is a prerequisite), treatment will be frustrated and most likely will not be successful.[45]

Finally, by imposing a duty to warn, the dissent concluded, "the majority contributes to the danger to society of violence by the mentally ill and greatly increases the risk of civil commitment — the total deprivation of liberty — of those who should not be confined."[46] Because of the "predictive uncertainty"[47] and the concomitant large number of necessary disclosures, treatment will be necessarily impaired: "neither alternative open to the [therapist] seeking to protect himself" or herself — warn or commit — "is in the public interest."[48]

THE CRITICAL RESPONSE TO *TARASOFF*[49]

The *Tarasoff* decision immediately unleashed a "torrent"[50] of "profuse academic comment"[51] and analysis, a significant portion of which was severely critical. Psychiatric commentators[52] attacked the opinion as an unwarranted "judicial intrusion [into] private psychotherapeutic practice"[53] for three major reasons:[54] (a) it was premised on the "false view"[55] that valid professional standards enabling psychotherapists accurately to predict future violence did exist; (b) it compromised confidentiality that was essential to successful psychotherapy[56]; and (c) by raising the therapist's obligation to the public over the obligation to the individual client, it compromised "central professional ethical precepts."[57]

The legal commentators who took issue with the California Supreme Court's decision focused most closely on confidentiality issues, generally predicting that the decision would reduce the success of therapy by: (a) decreasing clients' trust in their therapists, (b) discouraging clients from communicating sensitive information because of fear of subsequent disclosure, and (c) causing clients to terminate treatment when they learn that breaches of confidentiality could have occurred or did occur.[58] At least one student note viewed the decision as, perhaps, a therapeutic Armageddon: *Tarasoff* "may have precipitated the decline of effective psychotherapy in California."[59]

Not all legal commentary was so harsh, however. Professor Merton focused on the law/therapy role conflicts that appeared to be inevitably "exacerbate[d]"[60] by *Tarasoff*, and she noted that the decision "seems to have brought home to many [therapists] the double-bind quality of their professional obligations," and that it may require therapists to act "collectively, to develop a consensus that simply will not permit certain practices,"[61] such as the common (if discredited) long-term prediction of dangerousness at criminal sentencing hearings. And, in a somewhat different context, Professors Shuman and Weiner have suggested that the need for absolute confidentiality in the context of the therapist-client relationship has been "overstated" by its proponents.[62]

TARASOFF'S PROGENY[63]

Subsequent decisions have been far from unanimous in their construction of *Tarasoff*. Some cases have, with slight modifications, adopted its holding; others have extended its reach (as to the identifiability of victim and foreseeability of harm); others have factually distinguished or limited it (on both identifiability and foreseeability issues); several cases have declined to follow it.

Nonetheless, despite the fact that, as of 1995, only fourteen jurisdictions outside of California had explicitly adopted and applied the *Tarasoff* duty in the two decades since the case was decided, *Tarasoff's* symbolic value is so compelling that no one has questioned Dr. James Beck's conclusion that the *Tarasoff* duty to protect "is, in effect, at present a national standard of practice."[64]

Adopting *Tarasoff*:

In the case closest to *Tarasoff* on a factual level, a New Jersey trial court substantially adopted the California court's statement of psychotherapeutic duty to third parties in a wrongful death action brought against a psychiatrist (Milano) after one of his patients (Morgenstein) murdered the plaintiffs' (McIntoshes') daughter (Kimberly).[65]

In denying the defendant's motion for summary judgment at the ensuing civil trial, the Court generally adopted the *Tarasoff* formulation, focusing on the question of predictivity of dangerousness:

It may be true that there cannot be 100% accurate prediction of dangerousness in all cases. However, a therapist does have a basis for giving an opinion and a prognosis based on the history of the [client] and the course of treatment. Where reasonable men might differ and a fact issue exists, the therapist is only held to the standard for a therapist in the particular field in the community. Unless therapists clearly state when called upon to treat [clients] or to testify that they have no ability to predict or even determine whether their treatment will be efficacious or may even be necessary with any degree of certainty, there is no basis for a legal conclusion negating any and all duty with respect to a particular class of professionals. This is not to say that isolated or vague threats will of necessity give rise in all circumstances and cases to a duty. Whether a duty for a therapist to warn or guard against a criminal or tortious event by a [client] to some third party, depends, as with other situations giving rise to a possible legal obligation to exercise due care, ultimately on questions of fairness involving a weighing of the relationship of the parties, the nature of the risk involved, and the public interest in imposing the duty under the circumstances. . . .[66]

The court then summarized its holding:

[A] psychiatrist or therapist may have a duty to take whatever steps are reasonably necessary to protect an intended or potential victim of his [client] when he determines, or should determine, in the appropriate factual setting and in accordance with the standards of his profession established at trial, that the [client] is or may present a probability of danger to that person. The relationship giving rise to that duty may be found either in that existing between the therapist and the [client], as was alluded to in *Tarasoff*. . ., or in the more broadly-based obligation a practitioner may have to protect the welfare of the community, which is analogous to the obligation a physician has to warn third persons of infectious or contagious disease.[67]

Extending *Tarasoff*:

In other cases, courts have extended the *Tarasoff* duty where the victim was a young child of a threatened victim,[68] even where no specific victim has been threatened (on the theories that foreseeable violence may involve a "class of persons at risk,"[69] and therapists have a duty "to take reasonable precautions to protect *anyone* who might forseeably be endangered" by the client in question).[70]

Perhaps most importantly, the Vermont Supreme Court, in *Peck v. Counseling Service of Addison County*,[71] has enlarged the *Tarasoff* duty to include mental health professionals in a case involving property—not personal—injury, holding that a "mental health professional who knows, or, based upon the standards of the mental health profession, should know that his or her [client] poses a serious risk of danger to an identifiable victim has a duty to exercise reasonable care to protect him or her from that danger."[72] Although only property damage was involved, the court noted that arson "is a violent act and represents a lethal threat to human beings who may be in the vicinity of the conflagration."[73]

Peck is significant for several reasons.[74] First, no other post-*Tarasoff* case has extended its holding to property damage questions.[75] Second, the extension of duty to therapists in addition to psychiatrists and individuals with doctorates in clinical psychology (under state law, a mental health professional includes "a person with professional training, experience and demonstrated competence in the treatment of mental illness, who shall be a physician, psychologist, social worker, nurse or other qualified person designated by the commissioner of mental health"[76]) places the duty to warn on a whole range of therapists, including those not specifically enumerated in the statute in question. Third, the decision raises important questions as to what professional standard of care[77] is to be used in the case of a "generic 'mental health practitioner.'"[78] Expert medical testimony was produced at the trial, indicating that the client suffered from temporal lobe epilepsy. Although it might be argued that a nonmedical counselor should not be held to the same standard of care as a physician in the treatment and management of such a client, that question became "irrelevant"[79] when testimony showed that the therapist "was not in possession of [the client's] most recent medical history" because the counseling service had neither a cross-reference system between its therapists and outside physicians nor written policies "concerning formal intrastaff consultation procedures when a [client] presented a serious risk of harm to another."[80]

Concludes Stone in his pessimistic analysis of the *Peck* case:

> The smell of the Vermont-expanded *Tarasoff* decision is in the air. Every mental health professional now faces the *Tarasoff* dilemma: is it in my interest to avoid *potential* liability by warning *potential* victims of the *potential* violence and fire setting of my patient/client?[81]

Distinguishing *Tarasoff*:

Several courts have found that, even though there is a general *Tarasoff* duty, it is inapplicable in specific cases where there was either no identified victim,[82] where the therapist lacked control over the client in question,[83] or where the therapist could have reasonably believed that the client's fantasies did not pose a danger to an identifiable victim.[84]

Declining to Follow *Tarasoff*:

On the other hand, several jurisdictions[85] have declined to follow the California Supreme Court and impose a *Tarasoff* duty to warn, either — or instead — limiting the scope of *Tarasoff*[86] or rejecting it.[87] The latter decision, however, appears to focus on "failure to confine" rather than "duty to warn."[88] There, where the court declined to find liability in a case where a voluntary outpatient killed another outpatient 14 months after his last date of treatment, it ruled that the plaintiff would have to show "more than a mere possibility that the [client] would be very likely to cause harm to himself or to others."[89]

REFERENCES

1. See generally, 3 Michael L. Perlin, MENTAL DISABILITY LAW: CIVIL AND CRIMINAL, Chapter 12 (©Kluwer Law Books 1989).

2. 17 Cal. 3d 425, 131 Cal. Rptr. 14, 551 P. 2d 334 (Sup. Ct. 1976).

3. In addition to the issues raised and discussed here, other important "third party" cases have involved questions of premature release, failure to control petitioners or parolees who are mentally disabled, acts of clients on conditional leave from institutions, and failure to appropriately prosecute involuntary civil commitment applications. These are beyond the scope of this chapter. See generally, 3 Perlin, *supra* note 1, §§13.14 to 13.19.

4. Although Tatiana was not named by Poddar, she was "readily identifiable" by his description. *Tarasoff*, 131 Cal. Rptr. at 21.

5. *People v. Poddar*, 10 Cal. 3d 750, 111 Cal. Rptr. 910, 912, 518 P. 2d 342 (Sup. Ct. 1974).

6. *Tarasoff v. Regents of the University of California*, 33 Cal. App. 3d 275, 108 Cal. Rptr. 129, 529 P. 2d 553 (Sup. Ct. 1974), mod. 17 Cal. 3d 425, 131 Cal. Rptr. 14, 551 P. 2d 334 (Sup. Ct. 1976).

7. *Tarasoff*, 131 Cal. Rptr. at 21.

8. *Id.*

9. *Id.*

10. See generally, *Poddar, supra.*

11. Defendants are listed in *Tarasoff*, 131 Cal. Rptr. at 20 n.2.

12. *Id.* at 21. In addition, plaintiffs also sued on three independent tort theories: (a) the failure to detain a dangerous client, (b) abandonment of dangerous client (seeking punitive damages only from defendant Powelson on this count), and (c) breach of primary duty to a client and the public (stating basically the same allegations as the first count, but characterizing defendants' conduct as a breach of duty "to safeguard their [client] and the public"). *Id.* at 20-21.

13. *Id.* at 20.

14. But see *Tarasoff*, 131 Cal. Rptr. at 22.

15. *Tarasoff*, 118 Cal. Rptr. at 131.

16. See generally, Mills & Beck, *The* Tarasoff *Case*, in Beck, ed., THE POTENTIALLY VIOLENT PATIENT AND THE TARASOFF DECISION IN PSYCHIATRIC PRACTICE 1, 4-5 (1985)(Beck).

17. *Id.* at 5.

18. *Tarasoff*, 131 Cal. Rptr. at 20.

19. *Id.* at 22, quoting *Rowland v. Christian*, 69 Cal. 2d 108, 70 Cal. Rptr. 97, 443 P. 2d 561 (Sup. Ct. 1968), quoting *Heaven v. Pender*, 11 Q.B.D. 503, 509 (1883).

20. A defendant owes a duty of care "to all persons who are forseeably endangered by his conduct, with respect to all risks which make the conduct unreasonably dangerous." *Tarasoff*, 131 Cal. Rptr. at 22, quoting,

inter alia, Rodriquez v. Bethlehem Steel Corp., 12 Cal. 3d 382, 115 Cal. Rptr. 765, 776, 525 P. 2d 669 (Sup. Ct. 1974).

21. *Tarasoff*, 131 Cal. Rptr. at 22.

22. *Id.* at 23; see *Restatement (Second) of Torts* (1965), at §315.

23. *Tarasoff*, 131 Cal. Rptr. at 23-24.

24. *Id.* at 24, quoting Fleming & Maximov, *The Patient or His Victim: The Therapist's Dilemma*, 62 CALIF. L. REV. 1025, 1030 (1974).

25. *Tarasoff*, 131 Cal. Rptr. at 25.

26. *Id.*

27. *Id.*

28. *Id.*, quoting Fleming & Maximov, *supra* note 24, at 1067.

29. *Tarasoff*, 131 Cal. Rptr. at 26.

30. *Tarasoff*, 131 Cal. Rptr. at 26.

31. *Id.* at 27, quoting *Calif. Evid. Code* §1024 (1965).

32. *Tarasoff*, 131 Cal. Rptr. at 27 (emphasis added).

33. *Id.* at 29. Finally, the court rejected defendant therapists' argument that they were statutorily immune, see *Calif. Gov't Code* § 820.2 (1980), declaring that "a public employee is not liable for an injury resulting from his act or omission which was the result of the exercise of the discretion vested in him, whether or not such discretion [was] abuse," construing state law to provide such immunity only in the cases of "basic policy decisions," *Tarasoff*, 131Cal. Rptr. at 29, quoting *Johnson v. State of California*, 69 Cal. 2d 782, 73 Cal. Rptr. 240, 447 P. 2d 352 (Sup. Ct. 1968), and concluding that its scope "should be no greater than is required to give legislative and executive policymakers sufficient breathing space in which to perform their vital policymaking functions," *Tarasoff*, 131 Cal. Rptr. at 30. This, the court concluded, required of publicly employed therapists "only that quantum of care which the common law requires of private therapists." *Id.* at 31. On the other hand, the court found (a) defendant therapists statutorily immune — see *Calif.*

Gov't Code §856 (1980) — from liability for failure to *confine* Poddar (noting the need to protect therapists "who must undertake this delicate and difficult task"), *id.*, citing Fleming & Maximov, *supra* note 24, at 1064, (b) defendant police officers statutorily immune — see *Calif. Welf. & Instn. Code* §514(c) (9186 Supp.) — from liability for *their* failure to confine Poddar (noting that, while campus police were not strictly "peace officers" within the controlling statutory language, they *were* "responsible for [Poddar's] detainment" within the same phrase), *id.* at 33, and (c) no cause of action for punitive damages under state law in a wrongful death action. *Id.*, citing *Pease v. Beech Aircraft Corp.*, 38 Cal. App. 3d 450, 113 Cal. Rptr. 416 (Ct. App. 1974). The case never went to trial on remand, but settled on terms "within the range for wrongful death of a college girl." Merton, *Confidentiality and the 'Dangerous' Patient: Implications of Tarasoff for Psychiatrists and Lawyers*, 31 EMORY L. J. 263, 295 (1982).

34. *Id.* at 33 (Mosk J, concurring and dissenting) (emphasis added): Thus, the issue here is very narrow: we are not concerned with whether the therapists, pursuant to the standards of their professions "should have" predicted potential violence; they allegedly did so in actuality.

35. *Id.* at 34. Asked Justice Mosk rhetorically, "The question is, what standards?" *Id.*, relying on *People v. Burnick*, 14 Cal. 3d 306, 121 Cal. Rptr. 488, 535 P. 2d 352 (Sup. Ct. 1975), to demonstrate that "psychiatric predictions of violence are inherently unreliable." *Tarasoff*, 131 Cal. Rptr. at 34.

36. *Id.*

37. *Id.* at 34 (Clark J, dissenting)

38. *Id.* at 35.

39. See *id.* at 35-38.

40. *Id.*

41. See *Calif. Welf. & Instn. code* §5330(2) (1984), providing for treble damage recovery for unlawful confidential disclosures. See *Tarasoff*, 131 Cal. Rptr. at 35.

42. *Id.* at 38.

43. *Tarasoff*, 131 Cal. Rptr. at 39, citing, *inter alia*, Fisher, "the Psycho-therapeutic Professions and the Law of Privileged Communications," 10 *Wayne L. Rev.* 609 (1974); Rappeport, "Psychiatrist-Patient Privilege," 23 *Md. L. J.* 39 (1963).

44. *Tarasoff*, 131 Cal. Rptr. at 39, citing, *inter alia In re Lifschutz*, 2 Cal. 3d 415, 85 Cal. Rptr. 829, 467 P. 2d 557 (Sup. Ct. 1970).

45. *Tarasoff*, 131 Cal. Rptr. at 39-40, citing, *inter alia*, Dawidoff, "The Malpractice of Psychiatrists," [1966] *Duke L. J.* 696.

46. *Tarasoff*, 131 Cal. Rptr. at 40.

47. *Id.* at 41.

48. *Id.* at 41. Soon after the *Tarasoff* decision, California legislators drafted a series of bills intended to mitigate the decision's impact, culminating in the 1984 introduction to A.B. 2900, which would have granted statutory immunity to psychotherapists for failing to "warn of and protect from" a client's actual or threatened violent behavior except where the client communicated an "actual threat of physical violence against a reasonably identifiable victim or victims." See Comment, *Psychotherapists' Duty to Warn: Ten Years After* Tarasoff, 15 GOLDEN GATE U. L. REV. 271, 292 n.160 (1985) ("Golden Gate Comment"). The bill was supported by mental health professional associations, but was opposed by the Citizens' Commission on Human Rights, which characterized it as "an emotional piece of legislation which open[ed] the door to potential violence by removing current protection afforded the public." *Id.* at 293-295. Although the bill was passed by the legislature, it was vetoed by California's governor who feared that it would increase the likelihood of danger to the public and perhaps "excuse conduct which should be actionable." *Id.* In 1985, the bill was reintroduced with two significant changes. In place of the phrase "an actual threat of physical violence," the new bill substituted "a *serious* threat of physical violence." Also, the duty could be discharged not only by making reasonable efforts to communicate to the victim, but also, in the alternative, "to a law enforce-ment agency." See *Calif. Civil Code* §43.92 (1986 Supp.). With these changes, the bill was signed and became effective January 1, 1986, see *New California Law Limits Therapists' Liability for Violent Acts Committed By Their Patients*, 37 HOSP. & COMMUN. PSYCH. 87 (1986); there has been no subsequent reported litigation as of yet.

49. On the questions of *Tarasoff*'s empirical impact, of suggested thera-

peutic approaches in its wake, and of the concomitant rise of "victimology," see 3 Perlin, *supra* note 1, §§13.10 to 13.13; see generally, Wexler, *Patients, Therapists, and Third Parties: The Victimological Virtues of Tarasoff*, 2 INT'L J. L. & PSYCH. 1 (1979).

50. George *et al.*, *The Therapist's Duty to Protect Third Parties: A Guide for the Perplexed*, 14 RUTGERS L. J. 637 (1983) (George).

51. See Note, *Discovery of Psychotherapist-Patient Communications After Tarasoff*, 15 SAN DIEGO L. REV. 265, 266 (1978), and *id.*, 266-267 n.8 (listing articles).

52. At least one review of the literature has noted that criticism of *Tarasoff* was especially strong by psychiatrists who "advocate psycho-analytic therapy." George, *supra* note 50, at 637.

53. Givelber, Bowers & Blitch, *The* Tarasoff *Controversy: A Summary of Findings From an Empirical Study of Legal, Ethical, and Clinical Issues* (Givelber), in Beck, *supra* note 16, at 35, 37.

54. See, *e.g.*, Stone, *The* Tarasoff *Decision: Suing Psychotherapists to Safeguard Security*, 90 HARV. L. REV. 358 (1976) (Stone 1); Gurevitz, Tarasoff, *Protective Privilege Versus Public Peril*, 134 AM. J. PSYCH. 289 (1976); Roth & Meisel, *Dangerousness, Confidentiality, and the Duty to Warn*, 134 AM. J. PSYCH. 508 (1977).

55. Givelber, *supra* note 53, at 37.

56. See generally, Dubey, *Confidentiality as a Requirement for the Therapist: Technical Necessities for Absolute Privilege in Psychotherapy*, 131 AM. J. PSYCH. 1093 (1974).

57. Givelber, *supra* note 53, at 37.

58. Note, *Where the Public Peril Begins: A Survey of Psychotherapists to Determine the Effects of* Tarasoff, 31 STAND. L. REV. 165, 166 n.9 (1978); See, *e.g.*, sources cited at "Golden Gate Comment," *supra* note 48, at 272 n.7.

59. Note, Tarasoff v. Regents of the University of California: *The Duty to Warn: Common Law & Statutory Problems for California Psychotherapists*, 14 *Cal.* WEST. L. REV. 153 (1978). Concluded the author, "Mental health care and psychotherapy must survive in spite of *Tarasoff*." *Id.* at 181.

60. Merton, *supra* note 33, at 341.

61. *Id.* at 276.

62. Shuman & Weiner, *The Privilege Study: An Empirical Examination of the Psychotherapist-Patient Privilege,* 60 No. CAR. L. REV. 893, 927 (1982).

63. For a helpful discussion of the cases discussed below, see Beck, *The Psychotherapist and the Violent Patient: Recent Case Law* (Beck II), in Beck, *supra* note 16, at 9.

64. Beck II, *supra* note 63, at 33. "[M]ost commentators agree that all psychiatrists should practice as if the *Tarasoff* duty to protect is the law." *Id. Cf.* Roth & Levin, *Dilemma of* Tarasoff: *Must Physicians Protect the Public or Their patients?* 11 L., MED. & HEALTH CARE 104, 110 (1983) (*Tarasoff* doctrine has been adopted "from coast to coast"). *Tarasoff* issues continue to emerge in "new" jurisdictions. See, *e.g.*, Marcus, *Case Underlines Psychiatric Issue: To Keep Confidences or Report Threats,* N.Y. TIMES (May 23, 1986), at A10 (discussing recent Louisiana case).

65. 168 N.J. Super. 466, 403 A. 2d 500 (Law Div. 1979). The *McIntosh* case is discussed extensively in 3 Perlin, *supra* note 1, §13.06.

66. *McIntosh,* 403 A. 2d at 508 (footnotes and citations omitted).

67. *Id.* at 511-512. The *Tarasoff* duty has also been adopted in state and federal cases in Michigan and in the Ninth Circuit. See, *e.g.*, *Davis v. Lhim,* 124 Mich. App. 291, 335 N.W. 2d 481 (Ct. App. 1983); *Chrite v. United States,* 564 F. Supp. 34 1 (E.D. Mich. 1983); *Jablonski v. United States,* 712 F. 2d 391 (9 Cir. 1983). For more recent cases, *see* 3 Perlin, *supra* note 1, §13.09, at 66 n.204.1 (1995 Supp.). *Davis* and *Chrite* are discussed in Givelber, *supra* note 53, at 14-16; *Jablonski* is discussed in Meyers, *The Legal Perils of Psychotherapeutic Practice (Part II): Coping with Hedlund and* Jablonski, 12 J. PSYCH. & L. 39, 40-41 (1984).

68. *Hedlund v. Superior Court of Orange County,* 34 Cal. 3d 695, 194 Cal. Rptr. 805, 669 P. 2d 41 (Sup. Ct. 1983).

69. *Lipari v. Sears, Roebuck & Co.,* 497 F. Supp. 185, 187 (D. Neb. 1980).

70. *Petersen v. Washington,* 100 Wash, 2d 421, 671 P. 2d 230, 237 (Sup. Ct. 1983) (following *Lipari*).

71. *Peck v. Counseling Service of Addison County*, 146 Vt. 61, 499 A. 2d 422 (Sup. Ct. 1985).

72. *Id.* at 427. As Vermont is a comparative negligence case, the trial court had found John's father 50% negligent because he knew his son would be "enraged" if asked to falsify his benefits application. *Id.* This finding was affirmed by the Supreme Court. *Id.*

73. *Id.* at 424 n.3.

74. For a detailed analysis of *Peck*, see Stone, *Vermont Adopts* Tarasoff: *A Real Barn-Burner*, 143 AM. J. PSYCH. 352 (1986) (Stone II).

75. See, *e.g.*, Leong, Tarasoff *and Property Damage*, 143 AM. J. PSYCH. 1488 (1986) (letter to the editor) (*Peck* has "ominous implications for the practice of psychiatry"). *Cf. Bellah v. Greeson*, 73 Cal. App. 3d 911, 141 Cal. Rptr. 92, 94-95 (Ct. App. 1977) (refusing to extend *Tarasoff* to property damage or suicide).

76. *Vt. Stat. Ann.* 18 §7101 (2) (1984 Supp.).

77. See generally, 3 Perlin *supra* note 1, §12.05.

78. Stone II, *supra* note 74, at 354.

79. *Id.*

80. *Peck*, 499 A. 2d at 426.

81. Stone II, *supra* note 74, at 354-355 (emphasis in original).

82. See, *e.g.*, *Thompson v. County of Alameda*, 27 Cal. 3d 741, 167 Cal. Rptr. 70, 614 P. 2d 728 (Sup. Ct. 1980); see also, *Leedy v. Hartnett*, 510 F. Supp. 1125 (M.D. Pa. 1981), aff'd o.b. 676 F. 2d 686 (3 Cir. 1982); *Holmes v. Wampler*, 546 F. Supp. 599 (E.D. Va. 1982); *Furr v. Spring Grove State Hospital*, 53 Md. App. 474, 454 A. 2d 414 (Ct. Spec. App. 1983); *Cairl v. State*, 323 N.W. 2d 20 (Minn. Sup. Ct. 1982).

83. See, *e.g.*, *Hasenei v. United States*, 541 F. Supp. 999 (D. Md. 1982); *Brady v. Hopper*, 570 F. Supp. 1333 (D. Colo. 1983), aff'd 751 F. 2d 329 (10 Cir. 1984).

84. See *White v. United States*, 780 F. 2d 97 (D.C. Cir. 1986).

85. In addition to the cases discussed below, see also, *Hopewell v. Adibempe,* Pitt. L. J. 107, No. G.D. 78-2875 (Pa. Ct. C.P. 181), discussed in Beck II, *supra* note 63, at 30-31, and in Klein & Glover, "Psychiatric Malpractice," 6 *Int'l J. L. & Pysch.* 131, 153 n.59 (1983) (premising its holding on a state confidentiality statute), and *Schneider v. Vine Street Clinic,* No. 15344 (Ill. App. Ct. 1979), discussed in Merton, *supra* note 33, at 328-329. For more recent cases, *see* 3 Perlin, *supra* note 1, §13.17 at 71 n. 330 (1995 Supp).

86. See *Shaw v. Glickman,* 45 Md. App. 718, 415 A. 2d 625 (Ct. Spec. App. 1980), a decision characterized by Professor Merton as "frustratingly opaque." Merton, *supra* note 33, at 326. The *Shaw* case's facts were described floridly by the appelate court:

> This case concerns a new strand to an old yarn, the eternal triangle. It is new in that in addition to the usual cast, *le mari, la femme, et l'amant* (the husband, the wife, and the lover), new characters, the husband's "psychiatric team" have been joined as parties. In fact, the "team" has been sued for injuries inflicted on *l'amant* by *le mari.*

Shaw, supra.

87. See *Case v. United States,* 523 F. Supp. 317 (S.D. Ohio 1981), aff'd o.b. 709 F. 2d 1500 (6 Cir. 1983).

88. *Case v. United States,* 523 F. Supp. 317 (S.D. Ohio 1981) aff'd o.b. 709 F. 2d 1500 (6 cir. 1983).

89. *Id.* at 319. In the course of its opinion, the court simply stated that plaintiff's citation to *Tarasoff* was "not controlling," *id.* at 318, and that that case "stands almost alone in its holding," *id.* n.l.

9

Ethics, Insanity Pleas, and Forensic Psychology

Michael W. Millard, PhD, BCFE

Dr. Millard is in private practice in Hopkins, MN, and specializes in forensic evaluations.

KEY POINTS

- Because the court system itself places relatively few constraints on the power of the expert witness, the only true limit to the power of the psychologist within the forensic environment is a personal system of ethics.

- A forensic evaluation has one of two outcomes: either the individual's freedom will be limited or it will not be limited. The balance between personal freedom and the public safety must be the paramount concern within a competent forensic evaluation.

- "Not guilty by reason of insanity" (NGRI) cases, in which the accused is sane at the time of evaluation but judged to have been insane at the time he or she committed the crime, often place forensic psychologists in an awkward ethical dilemma, especially if freeing the perpetrator would put society at risk.

- *Competency* can be defined in terms of a person's ability to accomplish a particular task; it is contextual, reflecting both the nature of the task and the environment in which it is carried out.

- The M'Naghten standard is applied if the accused person "labors under such a defective reason from disease of mind as to not know the nature and quality of the act(s)" he or she performs.

- If the forensic expert believes the evaluation will lead to dire consequences for society, and that an unbiased and scientific approach is not possible in a particular case, then he or she cannot be deemed competent to carry out this evaluation, and should remove himself or herself from the case.

INTRODUCTION

According to one observer, the practice of forensic psychology often is ". . .spotted with dangerous shoals" (Hess, 1987, p. 659). Hess uses this metaphor to represent difficulties presented by murky ethical dilemmas. As in many areas of life, the shoals encountered by the forensic psychologist have a tendency to present themselves when they are least expected — and very often, when they are least welcome.

The dictionary defines ethics as "the rules of conduct recognized in respect to a particular class of human actions or a particular group. . . ." (*Random House College Dictionary*, 1991). Ethical principles in the practice of psychology apply to forensic specialties as well as to general practice areas. One guideline (American Psychology-Law Society, 1991) states that forensic psychologists must recognize their own personal values and beliefs and be aware that these may interfere with their ability to practice competently.

One way in which personal values can interfere with an evaluator's competency to conduct an evaluation is in the determination of "not guilty by reason of insanity" (NGRI). Finding the perpetrator of a crime to have been insane at the time of the crime, but sane at the time of evaluation, puts the evaluator in a particularly difficult position: Would it put society at risk to allow the perpetrator to be freed on an NGRI defense? The forensic psychologist is thus confronted with an ethical dilemma that may render him or her incompetent to perform an objective, scientific evaluation.

DEFINING "COMPETENCY TO COUNSEL"

Many definitions and conditions have been offered for the determination of competency; most affirm the idea that a person has a set of self-developed constructs that allow him or her to meet particular challenges (Masterpasqua, 1989). This definition of competence needs clarification.

Grisso (1981) defines *competency* in terms of a person's ability to do or not do a particular behavior or task (a legalistic idea of competency). This implies that competence has "fluidity," that it is contextual. The contextuality described in Grisso's model (1986) is reflective of both the nature of the task and the environment in which the task is carried out. For example, most adults can fill out a simplified income tax form; very few, however, can complete an extremely complicated income tax form for a large corporation. Therefore, competency has levels as well as environmental factors.

The standard for competency in psychology is outlined within various sections of codes of ethics. One code (American Psychological Association, 1992, p. 1600) requires that "psychologists provide services. . . only within the boundaries of their competence." Furthermore, "psychologists [must] rely on scientifically and professionally derived knowledge when making scientific and professional judgments." Therefore, in forensic psychology, competency can be said to be a situation in which a relatively neutral study is performed, and scientific principles are contained within each and every area of the assessment and evaluation.

The scientific approach relies on statistical methods and current or past statistical inferences (Sperlich, 1985), the pattern of individuals (Kaplan & Saddock, 1985), and other similar techniques that disallow the formulation of measurement schemes that may be unintentionally biased (Cronbach, 1970).

Although it is clear that the practice of intentional bias is unethical, the concept of unintentional bias presents a definite problem in terms of the "scientificism" (King, 1986) as well as the neutrality of the expert's opinions (Beckham, Annis, & Gustafson, 1989). This is evidenced by the finding that each forensic examiner will exhibit some kind of opinion concerning the relationship between insanity opinions and criminal responsibility. (Beckham et al., 1989). For example, one examiner may be of the opinion that crime is always a direct result of insanity, whereas another believes that each of us is fully responsible for our actions, no matter what the mental state.

This belief, as well as other personal/professional values, can cause a systematic bias within a forensic opinion; this may or may not be able to be teased out during the trial. Forensic psychologists, then, must always be alert to situations in which their personal value system can create unintended ethical dilemmas.

Competency within the forensic area is extremely important, and competency to evaluate someone has many factors. In all cases (forensic or otherwise), it is critical to maintain a neutral stance. In an ordinary therapeutic relationship, the therapist may decide at some point that mental health assistance is not being given to the patient and can refer or disallow the therapy to continue (Gutheil & Appelbaum, 1982). The client who perceives that a particular therapist is not being morally neutral can discontinue therapy. In a forensic evaluation, however, this option is not always open to the client (American Bar Association, 1989), because the client has a limited set of options or no options at all.

Even though a forensic examiner's competence is relative to the situation and environment of each particular case, the court does not (with the exception of cross-examination) place limits on the examiner's testimony. Therefore, in any particular forensic evaluation, such as that of the NGRI plea, the competence of the examiner to render a scientific and professional opinion in a neutral manner must be determined by the examiner himself or herself; no one else can perform such a determination. Therefore, the examiner may be a fairly competent or even extremely competent person for a large majority of cases, but may not be competent to perform an evaluation in a particular case.

CASE STUDY

An examiner was contacted by a well-known attorney with whom he had worked on prior occasions with a good deal of compatibility. In this case, the attorney wished to enter an

NGRI plea for his client. The examiner, having performed such evaluations in the past, saw no particular problem with this plea upon initial consultation.

Crime Details:

The individual (male), with his accomplice (female), had left the home of her parents for a long walk back to his residence. The weather, although not life-threatening, was cold and unpleasant. The couple encountered a private club, broke into it (by their own admission), and proceeded to spend some time there in varied personal activities.

The couple then left, and, still on foot, walked down an intermittently travelled rural road. They came across an unoccupied home. Both of them (by self-report) were in a "manic" mood, and decided to stop there. They broke into the house and fixed themselves some food. Before leaving, they completely stripped the house of portable valuables (i.e., hunting rifles, a coin collection, and a small television). They hid these items across the road in some brush. Then, they reentered the home to prepare food for the balance of their journey.

During this time, the home owners returned. Realizing that the home had been burglarized, the owner attempted to call the police, but found that his telephone had been stolen. He immediately left, contacted the police from a remote location, and agreed to meet them back at the home.

When the police arrived, the perpetrators left through the back door, travelled through the woods approximately one quarter of a mile from where the home was located, and called a friend to pick them up. This friend, knowing nothing about the activities of the night, brought them to their own residence and left.

The next day, the male perpetrator and another friend drove to the cache to pick up the home owners' possessions. However, it was now daylight; the home owner observed them carrying his belongings to a pickup truck and called the police. From the description of the home owner, the police intercepted the individuals at the perpetrator's residence with all of the stolen articles still contained within the second friend's pickup truck.

Defense Strategy:

The case against the subject of the NGRI evaluation is fairly clear: burglary of an inhabited dwelling. The perpetrator was determined to have been at the scene after the break-in occurred and prior to the home owners' return. (He had dropped his wallet in the house.) The possession of everything that was on the list of stolen articles clearly shows that the perpetrator participated in the break-in and was the recipient of the stolen possessions.

But in order to be clearly guilty, the perpetrator must be shown to have a *clear intent to commit the crime* (Thomas & Bishop, 1987), demonstrated by *mens rea* (a guilty mind). The state in which this crime took place uses the M'Naghten standard: The person ". . .labor[ed] under such a defective reason from disease of mind as to not know the nature and quality of the act(s) he was doing. . ." (Shuman, 1986, pp. 275–276). Thus, given the M'Naghten rule, it is quite possible for this person to be simultaneously guilty yet not guilty of a crime — even when he admitted he had committed each act noted above.

The perpetrator in this case had an extensive history of a bipolar disorder. By his own admission, he was not taking his medication during the period of time in which the crime was committed; his relatives verified this. It would be reasonable to formulate the hypothesis that he was in such a mental state at the time of the burglary that he could not be said to have a reasonable idea that what he was doing was wrong. An initial examination confirmed he did not have much of an idea (*mens rea*) of what he was doing at the time of the crime. Therefore, the attorney was quite correct when he began the process of proving that this particular perpetrator was "not criminally responsible if his unlawful act was the product of mental disease or defect" (Shuman, 1986, p. 276).

At this point, there would seem to be no particular ethical dilemma for the examiner. An opinion would have to be written as to whether the perpetrator was or was not suffering from a mental disorder that would destroy his sense of right and wrong at that particular point. Evidence as to the defendant's "irresistible impulse" was gathered from the first friend as well as from the accomplice's parents, who had also been subject to precrime terrorist threats of a manic nature; and the interview with the perpetrator confirmed this state of mind. A trial would have been held, and the jury would have heard all of the prosecution's evidence as well as the NGRI plea of the defendant.

If the jury found him guilty of the crime, the second part of the trial would have involved the determination of insanity. The jury would have found him either to be insane or not insane. If he were found to be sane, he would be processed through the criminal justice system and would pay whatever price it demanded; and the home owner would regain possession of his belongings. In that case, the forensic psychologist would not encounter a major ethical dilemma. However, the case of this particular defendant proved more difficult.

Evaluating Legal Issues:

In reviewing the case, the examiner was given access to the complete criminal file and civil files of the perpetrator. The perpetrator had been involved in a number of "situations" for more than 20 years. Among these situations was a set of assaults as a juvenile in which other persons had been seriously hurt. Indeed, the alleged perpetrator, with the assistance of his family, purchased for others a good many stitches, dental repairs, and auto-body repairs.

For each of these cases, as well as the case at hand, the examiner noticed an emerging pattern. The perpetrator would claim he was in a manic phase of bipolar disorder, he had done the damage, and he was quite willing to make restitution. However, because he had a defect of mind at the time, he should not be required to do any more than stay on probation for a period of time. The courts, for the most part, had agreed with this appeal. Between these periods of escalating violence, the perpetrator would begin to take his medication, which virtually had an immediate effect.

Therefore, although he may very well have been insane at the time of the crime, he could not be considered to have the same mental disorder at the time of the trial. In the state in which these events occurred, if a person is found to be not guilty by reason of insanity, then he or she is released from the criminal system and is at risk for a civil commitment to a psychiatric institution. Thus, if the NGRI plea is successful, the person is examined for a civil commitment at the time of the criminal trial or shortly thereafter.

In this case, however, the perpetrator was on his medication by the time of the examination and was not suffering blatantly from the mental disorder; furthermore, because he had never demonstrated a time of dangerousness while on his medication, he would not be considered to be committable. Therefore, the person would "walk away" from the crime. Essentially, there would be no punishment: He would be free, with neither probation nor any other limits set upon him.

Evaluating Ethical Issues:

The ethical dilemma in this particular case is that the alleged perpetrator posed a dangerous to society, as evidenced by his past behaviors. Because, in the perpetrator's experience, insanity was always a successful plea, this particular crime, like the others, would have no negative consequences. Could the forensic psychologist give an unbiased opinion on this particular insanity plea, when his personal ethics led him to the conclusion that the perpetrator should go to jail?

This person had committed a crime, and had committed many other crimes. This particular crime possessed clear elements of both sanity and insanity. The first aspect of the question is whether the forensic psychologist should perform the evaluation with consideration for the public good. If the insanity plea is successful, a threat to the general society is effected, and the violent behaviors of the perpetrator tend to escalate. Thus, society is at risk. Therefore, the issue is the greatest benefit, or the least amount of harm, for the largest number of people. If this particular NGRI plea were to prevail, society would lose.

The second ethical issue contained within this case is the question of competency of the examiner to formulate an objective opinion. Rodgers (1986, p. 32) states ". . .it is the responsibility of each forensic clinician to decide whether particular insanity evaluations are beyond the scope of his or her expertise." In terms of an expert witness, expertise represents the bringing into court of a scientific opinion based on all the appropriate data available as well as the scientific application of psychological theory and practicalities to the collected data.

If the scientific endeavor is to be completed correctly, the examiner or scientist must be relatively unbiased. The expertise referred to by Rodgers is meant to be judged not only in terms of the mechanics of the evaluation, but should reflect a lack of bias in terms of the examination or results. Therefore, if the forensic expert considers the evaluation to be one that will lead to dire consequences for society, and that an unbiased and scientific approach is not really possible with a particular evaluation, then he or she cannot be said to be competent to carry out this particular evaluation. If the evaluation is biased, and therefore not scientific, it should not be admitted at the expert's level of testimony within the courtroom. More than likely, that psychological evidence should not be admitted at all, because it basically consists of a great deal of heresay evidence from which conclusions are drawn.

The expert in this case was faced with a number of dilemmas. One was concern for society. Another was much more personal: "Am I competent in this case to render an objective, scientific opinion?"

After a great deal of introspection, the examiner resolved his concern about what should be done. First, he consulted with the attorney about the legal ramifications of the case. Then he sent a note to the attorney and the perpetrator categorically resigning from the case, returning any fees on request, and making it known to both sides (the prosecution was aware of the examination) that no report or any testimony would be forthcoming due to the potential of a biased, unscientific, and, therefore, unacceptable report.

DISCUSSION

The central ethical issue illuminated in the case study in this chapter is a question of whether the examiner, regardless of competency to practice forensic psychology in general, has the competency to provide an accurate report in this particular case. The forensic examiner is given a great deal of power. The courts often will wish the examiner to make a decision that is politically or ethically uncomfortable for the judge to pronounce himself or herself (Melton, Petrila, Poythress, & Slobogin, 1987). This is one of the reasons various mental health professionals may be called in on any particular case. A commitment case could have as many as three mental health professionals (one for the prosecution, one for the defense, and one appointed by the judge).

Historically, the courts have not been particularly careful to control the limits of testimony (Smith, 1989). The only area of the trial that could possibly reveal a systematic bias is the cross-examination, which examines questionable areas within an expert's testimony. Although cross-examination may indeed provide some limit to the forensic psychologist's power (Singer & Nievod, 1987), its effectiveness depends on many factors, not the least of which is the skill of the opposing attorney. It may not be possible for even an experienced opposing attorney to uncover an existing systematic bias on the part of the examiner; thus, cross-examination is not necessarily an effective limit to the expert's power. The only true limit to the extraordinary power of the psychologist within the forensic environment is a personal system of ethics. This system should render the psychologist alert to situations in which personal bias may affect the outcome of a case, and, in such situations, should ensure that he or she initiates a withdrawal from the case.

An individual who has no experience with or knowledge of NGRI evaluations cannot be said to be competent to perform one. However, even an experienced and well-trained NGRI psychologist also can be said to have some potential constraints placed on competence. Thus, although there may be many "shoals" within the area of professional ethics, the most fundamental for which the forensic psychologist should be alert during every evaluation is the issue of one's own competency to perform the evaluation in the context of the case at hand.

The competency to conduct a particular evaluation should be questioned at every milepost of the evaluation process. There certainly are many points at which this applies. However, in an NGRI evaluation, the point at which the forensic psychologist typically encounters an ethical dilemma does not occur until late in the procedure, after an evaluation of insanity has been determined. At this point, the evaluator must examine his or her personal ethical system to determine whether personal biases or values may be operative.

A forensic evaluation has one of two outcomes: either the individual's freedom will be limited or the individual's freedom will not be limited. The question that the forensic expert should ask himself or herself is whether he or she would be as comfortable with either of the two outcomes. The balance between personal freedom and the public safety must be the paramount concern within a competent forensic evaluation.

REFERENCES

American Bar Association. (1989). *ABA criminal justice mental health standards.* Washington, DC: Author.

American Psychology – Law Society and Division 41/APA (AP-LS). (1991). Specialty guidelines for forensic psychologists. *Law and Human Behavior, 15,* 655–665.

American Psychological Association. (1992). Ethical principles of psychologists and code of conduct. *American Psychologist, 47,* 1557–1611.

Beckham, G. C., Annis, L. V., & Gustafson, D. J. (1989). Decision making and examiner bias in forensic expert recommendation for not guilty by reason of insanity. *Law and Human Behavior, 13,* 79–87.

Cronbach, L. J. (1970). *Essentials of psychological testing* (3rd ed.). New York: Harper & Row.

Grisso, T. (1981). *Juveniles' waiver of rights.* New York: Plenum Press.

Grisso, T. (1986). *Evaluating competencies.* New York: Plenum Press.

Gutheil, T. G., & Appelbaum, P. S. (1982). *Clinical handbook of psychiatry and the law.* New York: McGraw-Hill.

Hess, A. K. (1987). The ethics of forensic psychology. In I. B. Weiner & A. K. Hess (Eds.), *Handbook of forensic psychology* (pp. 653–680). New York: John Wiley & Sons.

Kaplan, H. I., & Saddock, B. J. (1985). *Comprehensive textbook of psychiatry* (4th ed.). Baltimore: Williams & Wilkins.

King, M. C. (1986). *Psychology in and out of court.* Oxford, UK: Pergamon Press.

Masterpasqua, F. (1989). A competence paradigm for psychological practice. *American Psychologist, 44,* 1366–1371.

Melton, G. B., Petrila, J., Poythress, N. G., & Slobogin, C. (1987). *Psychological evaluations for the courts.* New York: Guilford Press.

Random house college dictionary. (1991). (Rev. ed., p. 459). New York: Random House.

Rodgers, R. C. (1986). *Conducting insanity evaluations.* New York: Van Nostrand Reinhold.

Shuman, D. W. (1986). *Psychiatric and psychological evidence.* Colorado Springs, CO: Sheppards/McGraw-Hill.

Singer, M. T., & Nievod, A. (1987). Consulting and testifying in court. In I. B. Weiner & A. K. Hess (Eds.), *Handbook of forensic psychology* (pp. 529–554). New York: John Wiley & Sons.

Smith, S. R. (1989). Mental health expert witness, of science and crystal balls. *Behavioral Sciences and the Law, 7,* 145–180.

Sperlich, P. W. (1985). The evidence on evidence: science and the law in conflict and cooperation. In S. M. Kassman & L. S. Wrightsman (Eds.), *Psychology of evidence and trial procedure* (pp. 325–361). Beverly Hills, CA: Sage.

Thomas, C. W., & Bishop, D. M. (1987). *Criminal law.* Beverly Hills, CA: Sage.

10

The Multifaceted Ethical Dimension of Treating the Mentally Ill

Mary Ann Carroll, PhD

Dr. Carroll is Professor of Philosophy in the Department of Philosophy and Religion at Appalachian State University, Boone, NC.

KEY POINTS

- Clients generally exhibit varying degrees of helplessness, which automatically places mental health professionals in positions of power and authority. Professionals must guard against conscious or unconscious coercion.

- Professionals in any field encounter ethical dilemmas, but therapists and counselors who treat mentally ill persons are likely to encounter a *wider variety* of such dilemmas than those working in other areas.

- A distinction must be made between clients who are mentally ill and those who are merely eccentric. Mentally ill clients are incapable of fulfilling normal responsibilities of ordinary living and therefore cannot be held fully responsible for neglecting responsibilities; their ability to make free and rational choices, and thus their status as moral agents, is diminished.

- One main goal of treatment should be to foster autonomy by encouraging the client to make his or her own decisions.

- Consent for treatment must be voluntary, informed, and competent. The problem of mental illness compounds the issue of the right to treatment; mentally ill persons may not be competent either to consent to or refuse treatment.

- Issues of confidentiality are discussed regarding children, court-ordered breaches, and the "duty to protect" others from violence.

INTRODUCTION

Suppose you have sore feet and want to buy a specially designed pair of shoes that will alleviate your foot pain. You go to a shoe store that specializes in shoes for people with feet like yours. After trying on a few pairs, you can't decide which pair makes your feet feel better. As you are ponder the various pairs, the shoe seller says, "You *must* buy *one* pair; and if *you* don't decide, *I* will decide for you; your feet will get much worse if you don't buy a pair of shoes *now!*" Not only are you irate at such audacity, you find it very odd — it's your money and your feet. Besides, you are the only person in a position to make a decision about which pair to buy, or whether to buy a pair at all.

Suppose, further, that you finally decide to buy one of the pairs of shoes. A few days later your neighbor asks if your feet feel any better now that you have a new pair of shoes. Surprised by your neighbor's knowledge of your purchase, you ask for the source. "Oh, the shoe seller told me; we're good friends." Though you might think it odd that the seller would tell your neighbor, you do not think it morally outrageous. And although you might think the seller to be a bit eccentric, it is doubtful that you would consider the seller as incompetent.

Now for another scenario. Suppose you have been having anxiety attacks when you are away from home; the attacks make going anywhere stressful and unpleasant. You go to a counselor who specializes in anxiety and who uses a variety of techniques to help clients overcome the problem. The counselor explains these techniques to you and asks which one you would like to try. You say you want to think about it carefully, but the counselor responds, "You *must* decide on one and if you don't, *I* will decide *for* you."

You think to yourself, "This is a professional who knows a lot more than I do; maybe it's true that I'll get worse if I don't make a decision immediately." You feel threatened because you think that if you don't cooperate, the counselor will not accept you as a client; the thought itself is enough to cause you to be anxious. So you say you will go along with whatever the counselor recommends.

Now suppose that a few days later your neighbor asks if you are overcoming your anxiety attacks. Surprised by this question, you ask for the source of the information. "Oh, your counselor told me; we're good friends." For you to say merely that this strikes you as odd would be inappropriate – rather, you should be morally outraged. And, with good reason, you should view this as a matter of the counselor's incompetence – not his or her eccentricity.

Although both scenarios involve professional services and persons who want to purchase something, the dissimilarities between them illustrate the moral dimensions of psychotherapy. Counselors' work, unlike that of sales professionals, involves being in a position of power and of doing something *to* others who are vulnerable. Sales professionals, on the other hand, stand in an equal relationship to those with whom they are voluntarily engaging in an exchange. Although consumers of goods may be pressured into buying, they are not generally coerced. However, because consumers of mental health services are not in an equal relationship with the provider and are, by definition, vulnerable, there is high potential for coercion (conscious or unconscious) on the part of the counselor. Out of this arises certain duties of the provider, which include (for the purposes of this example) obtaining morally valid consent and maintaining confidentiality.

Counselors potentially confront many ethical dilemmas because of the nature of their work. Clients come to them out of a feeling of varying degrees of helplessness, which automatically places the counselor in a position of power and authority. Attempting to fulfill the ethical responsibilities that result from this disparity in power can complicate the task of counseling.

Professionals in any field are likely to encounter ethical dilemmas, but counselors who treat mentally ill persons are more likely to encounter a *wider variety* of such dilemmas than those working in other areas. Unfortunately, it is almost impossible to have either a perfectly defined set of applicability criteria for characteristics such as "competent" or "voluntary," or a neat list of moral rules to resolve the ethical dilemmas in a particular case. The counselor must remember that context is all important. Although the ethical standards set by the profession do indeed provide rigorous guidelines, their accurate application requires a thorough understanding of the details of each situation.

THE MENTALLY ILL CLIENT

People seek help from counselors for a variety of reasons, ranging from problems of low self-esteem to more severe ones such as an inability to function in everyday life. However, not everyone seeking help from a counselor can be labeled mentally ill. A corporate executive may have marital difficulties because she works 70 hours per week. A factory worker may have problems resulting from a lack of self-esteem. An otherwise normally functioning sales representative may be so preoccupied with keeping his house neat that he dusts and mops at every opportunity; thus he is mentally *unhealthy* insofar as his concern with housekeeping occupies most of his free time at the expense of his playing racquetball, a game he enjoys.

Such persons are seeking to improve their lives through the self-understanding gained in the therapeutic process. But their status as moral agents is not diminished. They can still be held responsible for their behavior because they are otherwise capable of choosing freely among options and of understanding their situations, actions, and the consequences of their actions (Wear, 1980).

The persons in the above cases need mental *health* assistance rather than treatment for mental *illness*. To be mentally ill is to be incapacitated to the degree of being unable to fulfill normal responsibilities of ordinary living; this is the crucial distinction between being mentally ill and merely being eccentric. If this delineation is not made, some people will be viewed as mentally ill simply because their lifestyles or behaviors do not conform to a social standard of normalcy.

It is crucial to describe the goal of treatment as enabling the client to make free decisions. Fostering such autonomy involves two main ideas: (a) the client should be encouraged to make his or her own decisions rather than be subject to the will of others; and (b) these decisions ideally should be products of a healthy mind or will rather than being impaired by a debilitating mental condition.

If the goal is described in terms of helping the client become *normal* — if "normal" means typical behavior of the population at large — then there is no way to delineate the merely eccentric from the mentally ill.

A person who is merely eccentric may behave in ways most people would find peculiar (such as taking a duck for walks on a leash, coloring one's hair blue, or choosing to live in a remote area in a house that has no electricity or indoor plumbing). To view such behavior as necessarily indicative of mental illness may result in attempts by family, friends, or social workers to "help" the person, and possibly violate the individual's autonomy in the process.

The characterization of "mentally ill" given above guards against this consequence. Each healthy adult is responsible for details of everyday life that most people fulfill without much effort or thought. Bills must be paid, the laundry done, dishes washed, the garbage disposed of, and so forth. But for those who are mentally ill and experiencing symptoms like hallucinations, paranoia, or major depression, everyday tasks can be difficult — if not impossible — to perform. Granted, many of these responsibilities are relative to one's life situation, and so what counts as "normal responsibilities of ordinary living" cannot be specified in all cases. It follows, then, that what counts as being unable to fulfill them cannot be specified either. If, for example, over a period of time, a respected university professor becomes unable to concentrate enough to read students' papers or to assemble any material for a book already under contract, or if a carpenter begins to make repeated mistakes in measuring for materials, there is *prima facie* evidence of mental illness.

Thus, the characterization of "mentally ill" as "the inability to fulfill ordinary responsibilities of everyday living" can differentiate the mentally ill from the merely eccentric and also indicates that one's status as a moral agent is diminished. Mental illness diminishes one's ability to make free and rational choices among possible alternatives; therefore, the person cannot be held fully accountable for neglecting responsibilities. However, as we shall see later in this chapter, making a precise determination of degree of impairment is problematic.

A word of caution: to diagnose a client as mentally ill does not entail that the client has no responsibility regarding treatment; consequently, this diagnosis does not automatically justify total paternalism on the part of the therapist. Preskorn (1993, pp. 24–25) makes the following point regarding psychiatrists, but it is also applicable to all mental health professionals:

> The physician owes the patient a full explanation of the condition within the confines that current knowledge permits. The patient can then make informed decisions on his or her own behalf and be an active participant in becoming and remaining well. . . . The patient with a psychiatric illness has similar responsibilities [to those of the diabetic], the specifics being dependent upon which illness he or she has. For some, the illness may affect their judgment or comprehension, which in turn may compromise their ability to perform these tasks. Nonetheless, the goal is that they be active participants in their treatment to the fullest extent of their abilities. Such an expectation values the patient and may in itself help to restore some of the self-esteem that he or she may have lost due to the illness. It may also aid with compliance, because the plan of treatment is the result of the patient's choice rather than the physician's dictates.

Although the mentally ill client's status as a moral agent may be diminished, counselors must not assume that the status is thereby erased.

OBTAINING MORALLY VALID CONSENT

One of the fundamental ethical duties of counselors is to obtain morally valid consent of a client before treatment. But ensuring that a client's consent is ethically legitimate when the person suffers from some form of mental illness can be problematic. Anyone who seeks professional help is vulnerable to some extent; the mentally ill client is even more so. This can be seen readily when the general notion of ethically valid consent is analyzed, because much more is involved than merely ensuring that the client agrees to something.

The consent must be: (a) *voluntary,* which excludes any form of coercion on the part of the counselor, no matter how subtle; (b) *informed,* which implies that relevant information has been explained in a manner the client can understand; and (c) *competent,* which means the client is capable of appreciating the information conveyed and can make a decision based on it.

Counselors must not to assume that all children or institutionalized persons are incapable of giving morally valid consent. Though one principle in the *Ethical Principles of Psychologists and Code of Conduct* (American Psychological Association, 1981) actually assumes the opposite (principle 5.d refers to "minors and other persons who are unable to give voluntary, informed consent"), the cognitive abilities of each client— child, adolescent, or adult—must be assessed before determining whether obtaining morally valid consent is possible.

The three conditions of morally valid consent are interconnected. First, clients must know what they are consenting to, and understand the information given to them. Otherwise, the consent can be neither voluntary nor competent. To ensure client comprehension of relevant information, the counselor must explain it in terms the client can understand. Second, and just as important, is communicating "that the individual does not have to consent and has the right to withdraw consent at any time" (Carroll, Schneider, & Wesley, 1985, p. 29). Third, this entire sequence presupposes that the client is competent enough to understand what is being said.

Client Competence:

When questions of competence arise, a blanket statement can be made about lack of competence regarding only the most profoundly mentally handicapped persons. In every other case, counselors must ask, "Competent with respect to what?" A client who may be incompetent with respect to focusing on a project for any length of time may well be competent with respect to understanding and consenting to a particular method of treatment. We must note that determining whether a client is competent enough to understand the information presented is not necessarily related to the legal classification of "mental incompetence" or "mental illness":

> In most states, the label "mental illness" means that the person so labeled is unable to take care of his *personal* affairs (his health, personal safety, etc.), and the label "mental incompetence" means he is unable to take care of his *business* or *legal* affairs (his bank account, taxes, or property). (Ennis & Siegel, 1973, p. 74)

When trying to determine client competence with respect to giving consent to treatment, neither of these legal characterizations will necessarily entail that the client is incompetent. A person who is incompetent with respect to one ability may well be competent in another regard.

A similar point can be made about rationality. Care must be taken to avoid a blanket application of irrationality or incompetence to a client; it must not be assumed that all persons who are diagnosed as mentally ill are incapable of giving ethically valid consent.

Conditions for Obtaining Informed Consent:

Part of the requirement of informed consent is that counselors must convey relevant information in a setting that is as stress free as possible; this allows the client to reflect rationally in making a decision. The *voluntary* consent of a teenage client would be questionable if, for instance, she agreed to cooperate with the counselor in the presence of domineering parents who intimidate her.

Coercion Versus Temptation:

Consent given under duress hardly qualifies as voluntary. But what counts as duress? A distinction must be made between coercion and temptation, because to tempt is not to coerce (Murphy, 1975). "Coercion differs from temptation in that the former involves taking unfair advantage of a person's situation whereas the latter involves using an influence which the person can resist" (Carroll et al., 1985, pp. 30–31). Nevertheless, even though this conceptual distinction can be made, where to draw the line in a particular case is not always clear. Suppose a counselor offers a weekend pass to an institutionalized client if she will attend group therapy, which she abhors; however, she looks forward to weekend passes. Is the client being coerced or merely tempted? Even though the counselor may want her to attend group therapy for her own good, the question still arises as to whether the counselor is taking advantage of the client's situation or merely using an influence she can resist. Answers to such questions can only be given when answers are given to factual questions (e.g., *how* important is a weekend pass to the client?). What constitutes coercion in one case may only be a temptation in another.

CONFIDENTIALITY

A counselor's duty to maintain confidentiality is based on the client's right to privacy. Situations in which this duty can conflict with another duty, such as the duty to protect others, pose some extremely difficult dilemmas that require painstaking deliberation before deciding which takes precedence.

It should be noted, however, that some breaches of confidence are the result of carelessness or unprofessionalism rather than the result of careful moral deliberation. Because these instances easily may be overlooked, it is especially important that counselors are aware of them.

If a counselor has a particularly interesting client, it can be tempting to mention the person in a social situation. Also, client cases provide a good basis for discussion material for counselors who also have teaching responsibilities; thus, care must be taken to avoid any identifying reference to a client if a case is discussed. (See APA [1981] principle 5.b.) Ethical questions of this nature generally do not pose a moral dilemma, because most professionals recognize that discussing specific cases in a social situation is unethical. However, unless the counselor is scrupulously careful, such casual situations can facilitate unintentional breaches of confidentiality (Carroll et al., 1985).

Moral dilemmas typically arise in three types of situations: (a) when the client is a child and the counselor believes that informing a parent of something the child said is crucial to the well-being of the child, (b) when a court order is issued to testify in a case, and (c) when a client threatens harm to another person and the counselor has good reason to believe the client will act on the threat.

Each such situation requires counselors to assess the possible consequences of the confidentiality breach: whom the breach will affect, whether the impact will be positive or negative, and whether the potential benefits outweigh the negative consequences. Because no one can predict a client's future actions with certainty, this determination is no easy task; the practitioner often can confirm that a breach of confidence was warranted only *after* the fact.

When a counselor has good reason(s) for believing that a third party should be informed of something a client has said, in some cases it might be feasible to suggest that the client reveal the information himself or herself. Suppose, for example, a client who is engaged to be married tells his counselor he has tested positive for the human immunodeficiency virus (HIV) but his fiancée does not know this. Perhaps he can be persuaded to reveal this himself. In instances where the client does not understand why a certain third party should be privy to the information, an explanation as to why this particular person should know may persuade the client to convey the information.

In other cases, it may be reasonable to ask the client's permission to divulge information to another party. Thus, it might seem reasonable to assume that the dilemma can be resolved simply by obtaining the client's permission. Unfortunately, this approach can be problematic. In many instances, the client will refuse permission. The counselor then should tell the client—and explain why—the information will have to be revealed to the relevant third party. But even when permission is granted, the counselor must be certain the permission itself is voluntary, competent, and informed. This partly involves discussing the consequences of both divulging and not divulging the information to a relevant third person, as well as taking care to ensure that the client does not feel intimidated in the therapeutic relationship.

Paternalistic Attitudes Toward Children:

That children have a right to privacy in therapeutic situations should be considered a given. However, there may be a temptation to share information more readily with parents simply because the client is a child. It is perhaps easier to justify breaking a confidence here than in cases of adult clients because a paternalistic appeal—to what is in the best interests of the child—is always readily available. All too often it is assumed that children are not competent by adult standards; as a consequence, they are wrongly treated as incompetent. Counselors are in a better position than most to understand that it is indeed possible for children to give voluntary, informed consent, even if not to the extent most adults are able. Counselors must give much more than lip service to a child's right to privacy and so be able to justify any breach of confidentiality as an obvious necessity in promoting the child's mental health.

Court-Ordered Breaches:

Obeying a court order to reveal a confidence in a trial does not necessarily justify doing so, nor is doing so necessarily morally wrong. As is the case whenever complex moral problems arise, deciding what course of action is more morally justifiable requires a close examination of the facts and, often, speculation about future consequences. How crucial is the counselor's testimony? What effect will the testimony have on the client's well-being? If the counselor refuses to reveal a confidence in court and opts for a jail sentence, how long is the duration of the sentence? How will one's other clients fare during this time? What possible good might result?

Sometimes we hear of a mental health professional choosing a jail sentence over revealing in court what a client has said in therapy (or mental health professionals say this is what they would do). This sounds laudable, and it might very well be in many cases. But to assume that it is necessarily morally required is to assume wrongly that such decisions can be made in a vacuum.

Client Threats and Potential Harm to Others:

Ever since the benchmark *Tarasoff v. Regents of the University of California* (1976) case, the "duty to protect" has been cited as justification for breaching confidentiality. This case is discussed in detail in Chapter 8 so only a few of the more salient points will be mentioned.

One obvious difficulty posed by the court's majority opinion is the inability to predict dangerous behavior (Steadman &

Cocozza, 1974; von Hirsch, 1972). Even though Perlin notes in Chapter 8 that the *Tarasoff* decision cited negligence on the part of the therapist because of a failure to *warn* rather than a failure to be able to *predict*, there must be some empirical grounds for predicting—for being justified in believing—a client will in fact harm another.

What constitutes sufficient evidence of posing a real threat to others that would warrant breaking a confidence? Those who would use the duty to protect as justification for overriding the duty to maintain confidentiality should be prepared to suggest some parameters; otherwise, "without strong restrictions on breaking a confidence, confidentiality may become the exception rather than the rule" (Carroll et al., 1985, p. 35). There is reason to take this worry seriously in light of the court's claim that giving even *unnecessary* warnings is justifiable because lives might be saved.

The duty to protect ("often inappropriately labeled the 'duty to warn'" [Perlin, Chapter 8, p. 128]) is not limited to trying to protect the lives of others—it also extends to property. Thus, it is not clear exactly what sorts of threats a client might make in therapy from which therapists have a duty to protect others. What if a client threatens to ruin a colleague financially? To blackmail one's employer? To kidnap a coworker? Before using *Tarasoff* as a model for justification of violating confidentiality, practitioners would be well advised to examine the implications.

INVOLUNTARY COMMITMENT

Psychologists may be asked to participate in a hearing involving involuntary commitment. The legal grounds (not to be confused with moral grounds) for commitment involve the following: "(1) the person in question must be proved, on the basis of convincing scientific evidence given at a fair hearing with appropriate due process, to lack capacities of rational choice and deliberation; and (2) these incapacities must be shown to be highly likely to lead to danger to the person's life and limb or to the life and limb of others" (Richards, 1977, p. 219).

Each is problematic, both in the empirical and in the moral sense. The first condition raises the problems of: (a) whether and to what degree the involuntarily confined person has any autonomy, and (b) what method of treatment is most likely to restore client autonomy without diminishing it in the meantime. The second condition has difficulties because: (a) it requires the ability to predict dangerous behavior, although, as already noted, there is no assurance a prediction will be accurate; and (b) it raises the question of whether interfering with a person's decision to commit suicide is necessarily always justified.

To commit a person involuntarily is to take away the freedom of someone who has committed no crime; such an action stands in dire need of justification. John Stuart Mill (1947, pp. 12-13) argued as follows in his book *On Liberty:*

> The only freedom which deserves the name, is that of pursuing our own good in our own way, so long as we do not attempt to deprive others of theirs, or impede their efforts to obtain it. . . . Mankind are greater gainers by suffering each other to live as seems good to themselves, than by compelling each to live as seems good to the rest.

It is no wonder that one result of the civil rights movement of the 1960s was stricter state laws making involuntary commitment very difficult (Torrey, 1993). Unfortunately, in the concern to protect psychiatric patients, the helplessness of some people — notably the homeless — has been ignored because they legally cannot be treated against their will. Torrey (1993, p. 5) points out that they are "tormented by mental illness yet not aware of the need for help. . ." while "we persist with our legalisms, saying that such individuals must have demonstrated 'dangerousness' to themselves or to others to be treated."

Herein lies the dilemma: on the one hand, our sense of compassion dictates that we should help those suffering from mental illness; on the other hand, we want to respect the right of people to live as they choose. How can we tell, though, whether someone has freely chosen to be what we consider a misfit in society, or whether the person would prefer to have a more "normal" lifestyle? What if, because of mental illness, such a person does not know what another type of lifestyle is like to make this choice?

The homeless mentally ill are typical candidates for involuntary commitment. However, it cannot be assumed that everyone who lives on the streets is mentally ill. Even those who are indeed mentally ill may not be totally dysfunctional or incompetent (Pence, 1991). The main problem is illustrated by the question above and the well-publicized case of Joyce Brown.

In 1987, Mayor Ed Koch of New York City decided that the mentally ill homeless should receive treatment for their illness. Joyce Brown, who called herself by several names, was one of the first homeless persons to be treated. Her appearance and behavior seemed to suggest that she was mentally ill; thus, she was involuntarily admitted to Bellevue Hospital's emergency room, where she was administered antipsychotic and sedative medications. She refused any further treatment, and the American Civil Liberties Union (ACLU) came to her defense. During a 3-day commitment hearing,

> Four psychiatrists testified for the City that Ms. Brown suffered from chronic schizophrenia; they predicted that she would deteriorate if left on the streets. They testified that she was clearly psychotic and should be treated in an institution. Three psychiatrists countered for the ACLU that she was not psychotic, not dangerous, not unreasonable in her answers, and not incapable of caring for herself on the streets. Psychiatrist Robert E. Gould of New York Medical College said she was living on the street by choice (Pence, 1990, pp. 271–272). If we must err, on which side is it better to err?

Erring on the side of a judgment of incompetence endangers personal liberty and creates the potential for abuse; erring on the side of a judgment of autonomy endangers the lives of some and creates an environment in which even the helpless are ignored.

THE RIGHTS TO TREATMENT AND TO REFUSE TREATMENT

If and when involuntary commitment is morally justifiable in particular cases, a moral right to treatment follows. This moral right is also legally protected, thanks to court rulings such as *O'Connor v. Donaldson* (1975). The standard reasoning behind these rulings has been that confining people against their will can be justified only if treatment is provided; depriving a person of liberty requires a better justification than that it makes others feel more comfortable.

However, a right, unlike a duty, does not have to be exercised; thus, the right to treatment also implies the right to refuse treatment. A problem immediately arises in cases where an involuntarily committed person refuses treatment. Just as a mentally ill person may or may not be competent to consent to treatment, so he or she may or may not be competent to refuse treatment. A dilemma similar to the one regarding involuntary commitment arises here as well. Being too eager to do "what is in the client's best interest" can result in violating the person's autonomy; however, being too concerned in the other direction—to let the mentally ill pursue whatever sort of lifestyle they choose—can result in failing to help the client. As Katz (1969, pp. 770–771) pointed out:

> Such a position can be as destructive of human life as its over-readiness to hospitalize. . . . [W]ithout coercion, society will abandon many people to their self-destructive and uncared-for fate. Such an approach is as insensitive as the abuse of

power that leads to indefinite incarceration without treatment or with treatments that are of no value or ineffective or even harmful.

Clearly, the right to refuse treatment can be problematic for practitioners.

CONCLUSION

Competence in counseling involves much more than having the ability to use various therapeutic techniques successfully; it also entails that practitioners appreciate the moral dimensions of their work and be able to identify the sorts of ethical dilemmas they may confront. This in turn requires that they be able to discern the relevant questions to ask when faced with conflicting duties and know how to make a well-reasoned ethical judgment to resolve the dilemma.

Mental health professionals typically will not often find themselves in moral quandaries. Their main ethical concern is confidentiality because their clients' capacity for responsible decision making is assumed.

On the other hand, counselors who primarily treat the mentally ill are much more likely to have to deal with moral dilemmas, most of which stem from questions about obtaining morally valid consent. Because the client's autonomy is impaired to some extent by the illness, it may be difficult to determine whether the client can give consent of the form that is morally required. In ordinary cases, such consent is required to justify doing something to another person; but because competence to consent may be in question when dealing with the mentally ill, so may be the moral permissibility to treat (or not to treat) the person.

Having a well-defined set of moral rules to resolve all ethical dilemmas neatly is simply not possible due to the variables that make each situation unique. Knowing how to incorporate these variables when appealing to more general rules must be an integral part of the criteria for evaluating the competence of psychologists who treat both clients who are basically healthy and those who are mentally ill.

REFERENCES

American Psychological Association. (1981). *Ethical principles of psychologists and code of conduct.* Washington, DC: Author.

Carroll, M. A., Schneider, H., & Wesley, G. (1985). *Ethics in the practice of psychology.* Englewood Cliffs, NJ: Prentice-Hall.

Ennis, B., & Siegel, L. (1973). *The rights of mental patients.* New York: Avon Books.

Katz, J. (1969). The right to treatment—an enchanting legal fiction? *University of Chicago Law Review, 36,* 755–783.

Mill, J. S. (1947). *On liberty.* New York: Crofts Classics.

Murphy, J. (1975). Total institutions and the possibility of consent to organic therapies. *Human Rights, 5,* 25–45.

O'Connor v. Donaldson, 43 U.S.L.W. 4929 (1975).

Pence, G. (1990). *Classic cases in medical ethics.* New York: McGraw-Hill.

Preskorn, S. (1993). The revolution in psychiatry. *National Forum, 73,* 22–25.

Richards, D. (1977). *The moral criticism of law.* Belmont, CA: Dickinson.

Steadman, H. J., & Cocozza, J. (1974). *Careers of the criminally insane.* Lexington, MA: D.C. Heath.

Tarasoff v. Regents of the University of California, 113 Cal., Rptr. 14.551 P.2d 334 (1976).

Torrey, E. F. (1993). Thirty years of shame: The scandalous neglect of the mentally ill homeless. *National Forum, 73,* 4–7, 12.

von Hirsch, A. (1972). Prediction of criminal conduct and preventive confinement of convicted persons. *Buffalo Law Review, 21,* 717–758.

Wear, S. (1980). Mental illness and moral status. *Journal of Medicine and Philosophy, 5,* 292–312

Appendix 10A
ETHICAL CONSIDERATIONS IN TREATING THE MENTALLY ILL:
TWO CASE STUDIES

CASE 1

A 30-year-old woman comes to you seeking help for depression after being unable to go to work for several days in succession. She is a purchasing agent for a corporation and says she has had a good working relationship with the president of the company. However, she has been reluctant to tell him about her depression; she simply told him she has been sick. She appears to be responsible and dedicated to her job. Her primary concern is her job; accordingly, you believe this worry must be alleviated immediately. Because she does not want to explain the real nature of her illness to the president, you ask her if you might talk to him. She agrees.

Is her permission sufficient to justify discussing her illness with her employer?

Some questions to consider:

- Does she appear to be so desperate for help that she might agree to almost anything?

- What is the company president's attitude toward women? Toward mental illness?

- If you decide not to discuss her illness with the employer, will her concern for her job hamper her recovery?

- If you decide to act on her permission, what specific information should you convey?

- Should you make a prediction about when she might be functioning normally?

- What relevant information do you think is missing from the case description?

CASE 2

One of your clients is an 11-year-old boy. He is in counseling because his father, who has custody, tells you the boy has been stealing money from him even though he gives him $10 a week to spend. According to the father, the amounts have been substantial, ranging from $30 to $75; his son had admitted taking some money but claimed it was only a few dollars. The boy tells you he resents his father for rarely being home and that he took the money to punish him. He later confides in you that twice he used some of the money to buy marijuana. You believe you can help him deal with his anger toward his father and that the chances of them establishing a productive relationship are quite good. The pressing problem, you think, is his experimentation with marijuana. Given his present feelings about his father, you wonder if maybe he is doing that as a form of rebellion. Based on some of what this client has told you, you have reason to believe he does not particularly seem to care about consequences of his behavior. Thus, you are concerned that he might begin to experiment with other substances.

Should you inform the father about his son's use of marijuana?

Appendix 10A
ETHICAL CONSIDERATIONS IN TREATING THE MENTALLY ILL:
TWO CASE STUDIES
(CONTINUED)

Some questions to consider:

- Is your concern well grounded?

- What are the chances your client will find out that you relayed the information to his father?

- How will the father react to the information?

- What harmful effects on your client might your breach of confidence have?

- How might your client benefit from a breach of confidence? Does that outweigh respect for his privacy?

- Are there other alternatives to consider?

- What relevant information do you think is missing from the case description?

11

Dual/Multiple Relationships: Toward a Consensus of Thinking

Gerald Corey, EdD, ABPP, NCC, and Barbara Herlihy, PhD, NCC, LPC

Dr. Corey is Professor of Human Services and Counseling at California State University at Fullerton. Dr. Herlihy is Associate Professor of Counseling at Loyola University of New Orleans.

KEY POINTS

- Dual (or multiple) relationships may be sexual or nonsexual in nature. They occur when counselors simultaneously or sequentially assume two or more roles with a client.

- A review of the literature reveals that sexual dual relationships have received the most attention in the media and from professional groups; however, nonsexual dual relationships have become a lively topic of debate.

- Codes of ethics of the professional organizations have standards prohibiting dual relationships that might exploit or cause harm to clients.

- Some problematic aspects in dealing with dual relationships

are that they are pervasive, their beginnings can be difficult to recognize, they are unavoidable at times, and the potential for harm ranges along a continuum from severe to slight.

- The controversy over dual relationships has produced extreme reactions on both sides but is coming closer to a consensus. It is clear that not all dual relationships can be avoided, and it is equally clear that some types of dual relationships (such as sexual ones) should always be avoided.

- Guidelines to minimize the risk of entering into a dual or multiple relationship with a client are provided.

INTRODUCTION

Dual (or multiple) relationships, which may be sexual or nonsexual in nature, occur when counselors simultaneously or sequentially assume two or more roles with a client. Therapists enter into a dual relationship whenever they have another, significantly different relationship with one of their clients (Herlihy & Corey, in press). Some examples of dual relationships include combining the roles of teacher and counselor, or supervisor and therapist; providing therapy to a friend, an employee, or a relative; becoming sexually involved with a client; and going into a business venture with a client. Certain practices in which some professionals engage, that can create dual relationships, include bartering for goods or services, selling a product to a client, attending social events of a client or inviting a client to a social event, and accepting gifts from a client.

Although sexual dual relationships initially received the most attention from both professional groups and the media, nonsexual dual relationships have become a lively topic of debate. Dual relationships affect all counselors, regardless of their work setting or client population. Therefore, professionals must give serious thought to the complexities of dual and multiple relationships. The purpose of this chapter is to share perspectives on dual relationship controversies and to challenge therapists to develop ethical decision-making strategies that effectively address the dilemmas associated with dual or multiple relationships.

PERSPECTIVES ON DUAL RELATIONSHIPS

A review of the literature on dual relationships reveals that the topic is hotly debated among experts. Some writers take a conservative stance, maintaining that codes of ethics are of little value if professionals take great latitude in interpreting them. These writers tend to focus on the problems inherent in dual relationships and to favor a strict interpretation of ethical standards that are aimed at regulating professional boundaries. Pope (1985) and Pope and Vasquez (1991) identify the following problems in dual relationships:

- Dual relationships tend to impair the counselor's judgment

- The potential exists for conflicts of interest

- There is the danger of exploiting the client because the counselor holds a more powerful position than the client

- Boundaries become blurred and distort the professional nature of the therapeutic relationship

According to Pope and Vasquez (1991), counselors who engage in dual relationships are often skillful at rationalizing as a way of evading their professional responsibility to find acceptable alternatives to dual relationships. Bograd (1993, p. 7) summarizes the problematic nature of dual relationships thusly:

The basic argument against dual relationships goes something like this: the hierarchical nature of the therapist-client or teacher-student relationship, which seems a necessary aspect of the professional encounter, undermines the truly equal consent to the nonprofessional connection. Even an ethical practitioner may unconsciously exploit or damage clients or students, who are inherently vulnerable in the relationship. Once the clarity of professional boundaries has been muddied, there is a good chance for confusion, disappointment and disillusionment on both sides.

St. Germaine (1993) points out that although dual relationships are not damaging to clients in every case, counselors must be aware that the potential for harm is always present. She mentions that errors in judgment often occur when the counselor's own interests become part of the equation.

Dual or multiple relationships are a frequent cause of claims against therapists that are made to licensing boards (Neukrug, Healy, & Herlihy, 1992) and ethics committees. As an illustration of the kinds of actual cases brought to an ethics committee, consider the American Association for Marriage and Family Therapy (AAMFT) Ethics Committee Report on Dual Relationships (1992), which outlined the following dual relationship problems among their membership (cited in Goldberg, 1993): sexual intimacy with clients, power differentials, exploitations, role confusions, transference and countertransference issues, diverse goal relationships, triangulation for the client and for the counselor, displacement into both relationships, financial complications, risk of civil suits, and loss of objectivity.

Other writers believe that the standards in ethics codes that address dual relationships are narrow and deceptive. Tomm (1993) believes that the AAMFT's current code implies, in expecting practitioners to maintain their "professional distance," that all dual relationships are wrong. According to Tomm, actively maintaining interpersonal distance focuses on the power differential, promotes an objectification of the therapeutic relationship, and tends to promote a vertical hierarchy in the relationship.

Tomm contends that dual relationships sometimes help counter the vulnerability of clients, who have less power than counselors, and invite greater authenticity and congruence from the therapist. He argues that a counselor's judgment may be improved rather than impaired by dual relationships, which can make it more difficult for counselors to use manipulation and deception or to hide behind the protection of a professional role. Tomm points out that simply avoiding dual relationships does not prevent exploitation. Indeed, counselors may deceive themselves into thinking that they cannot possibly exploit their clients if they avoid dual relationships, when in fact there are many other ways of misusing therapeutic power and influence.

Corey, Corey, and Callanan (1993) remind us that codes of ethics are creations of humans rather than divine decrees of universal truth. Codes of ethics are living documents that evolve over time; each new revision represents a professional group's current philosophy. The roles of professional maturity and judgment, along with flexibility, are crucial. Rather than looking to codes of ethics for absolute answers, it is preferable to use the codes as guidelines in making ethical decisions.

Hedges (1993), writing from a psychoanalytic viewpoint, believes that there is an essential dual relatedness in psychotherapy. He argues that transference, countertransference, resistance, and interpretation *de facto* rest on the existence of a dual relationship. He urges professionals to remember that, when viewed in this light, all beneficial aspects of therapy arise as a consequence of a dual relationship.

The diversity of perspectives that have been presented indicates that the debate over dual relationships has been extensive. A consensus seems to have formed that, because dual relationships are inevitable in some situations, a global prohibition is not realistic. Instead, ethical practitioners must develop their ability to assess each situation. Leslie (1993) notes that there are "gray areas" that deserve careful attention. We contend that ethically self-aware counselors are capable of sorting out the issues involved and dealing appropriately with these gray areas. Tomm (1993) quite correctly points out that it is not duality itself that constitutes the ethical problem; rather, the counselor's tendency to exploit clients is what is central.

There are no simplistic solutions to the complex problems posed by engaging in more than one role with clients. It is neither always possible nor always desirable to play a singular role. We hope to show that, despite some clear clinical and legal risks, some blending of roles is unavoidable and that this is not necessarily unethical or unprofessional. Along with the associated risks, there are also potential benefits to role blending, which are sometimes ignored in the climate of controversy that has surrounded this issue.

CODES OF ETHICS AND DUAL RELATIONSHIPS

What guidance do codes of ethics offer regarding dual relationships? Today, all ethics codes of the major professional associations contain specific standards that prohibit sexual intimacies with clients. Many of the codes and state licensing boards now specify a 2-year "waiting period" after termination as a minimum time before entering into a sexual relationship with a client. Some state licensing boards have gone farther than the professional associations, prohibiting sexual intimacies with former clients regardless of the time elapsed. In at least 12 states, it is a felony for a mental health professional to have sex with a current or former client.

With respect to nonsexual dual relationships, the professional associations now acknowledge that not all dual relationships can be avoided. Both the American Counseling Association (ACA) and AAMFT state in their codes of ethics that members are expected to take professional precautions "when a dual relationship cannot be avoided." The ACA code specifies that these precautions include informed consent, consultation, supervision, and documentation. Similarly, the American Psychological Association's (APA) *Ethical Principles of Psychologists and Code of Conduct* (1992) states that:

> In many communities and situations, it may not be feasible
> or reasonable for psychologists to avoid social or other
> nonprofessional contacts with persons such as patients,
> clients, students, supervisees, or research participants.
> Psychologists must always be sensitive to the potential
> harmful effects of other contacts on their work and on those
> persons with whom they deal. (1.17 a)

Rather than prohibiting all dual relationships, the codes caution professionals against entering into those dual relationships "that could impair objectivity" or that have potential to harm the client. The ACA *Code of Ethics* (1995) states:

> Counselors are aware of their influential positions with respect to clients, and they avoid exploiting the trust and dependency of clients. Counselors make every effort to avoid dual relationships with clients that could impair professional judgment or increase the risk of harm to clients. (Examples of such relationships include, but are not limited to, familial, social, financial, business, or close personal relationships with clients.) (A. 6. a.)

A portion of the APA (1992) code reads:

> A psychologist refrains from entering into or promising another personal, scientific, professional, financial, or other relationship with such persons if it appears likely that such a relationship reasonably might impair the psychologist's objectivity or otherwise interfere with the psychologist's effectively performing his or her functions as a psychologist, or might harm or exploit the other party. (1.17 a)

Similarly, the AAMFT (1991) code states:

> Marriage and family therapists are aware of their influential position with respect to clients, and they avoid exploiting the trust and dependency of such persons. Therapists, therefore, make every effort to avoid dual relationships with clients that could impair professional judgment or increase the risk of exploitation. (1.2)

Leslie (1993) lucidly noted that, as the language of the codes indicates, the likelihood of impaired judgment and exploitation is the determining factor associated with unethical and unprofessional dual relationships. What we consider essential is that safeguards be implemented to minimize the potential dangers that can result from certain forms of dual relating. For example, as counselor educators, we challenge students to consider their personal lives and values, and we invite them to identify and explore a range of feelings and life experiences, especially those that could inhibit the quality of their work with clients if left hidden. Depending on the courses we teach, we sometimes carry out therapeutic functions even though we do not enter into formal therapeutic relationships with our students. Certainly, we are not in favor of a counselor educator establishing an ongoing therapy relationship with a current student, but other types of relationships may also cloud the judgment and reduce the objectivity of the professional. We play many roles, and sometimes it is difficult to separate them neatly.

We believe that students have a right to be informed about potential problems. Furthermore, they have a right to be told about dual relationship concerns as a way of making them active participants in deciding in which relationships they wish to be involved during their training. It is often helpful to discuss with students the procedures we use to minimize the potential negative consequences of any role blending on our parts. These same principles and procedures could be used by practitioners in relating to their clients.

TOWARD A CONSENSUS

The pendulum of controversy over dual relationships, which has produced extreme reactions on both sides, has slowed and now swings in a narrower arc. It is clear that not all dual relationships can be avoided, and it is equally clear that some types of dual relationships (such as sexual intimacies with clients) should always be avoided. In the middle range, it would be fruitful for professionals to continue to work to clarify the distinctions between dual relationships that we should try to avoid and those into which we might enter, with appropriate precautions.

If we adhere to the definition of a dual relationship that we presented at the beginning of this chapter, it seems apparent that what is to be avoided is the simultaneous taking on of the role of *counselor* and another distinctly different role (such as lover, friend, relative, employer, or business partner) with a client, student, or supervisee. Other types of role blending, in which we play more than one *noncounselor* role, do not fit the definition and need not be viewed as problematic. For instance, mentoring a student is often mentioned by counselor educators as one type of "beneficial" dual relationship. However, although serving as a mentor involves playing a multiplicity of roles (perhaps including course instructor, member of the student's thesis or dissertation committee, encourager, co-researcher, and co-author of a professional publication), the mentor does not serve as the student's counselor.

Some roles that mental health professionals play involve an *inherent duality*. One such role is that of supervisor (Borders, 1992). Supervisors often find that countertransference issues can limit the effectiveness of their supervisees. Supervisees typically experience an emergence of earlier psychological wounds as they become involved in working with clients. However, wisdom on the part of the supervisors dictates that they do not abandon their supervisory responsibilities by becoming a counselor to a supervisee. Instead, supervisors can encourage their supervisees to view personal therapy with another professional as a way to become more effective both as counselors and as persons. At the same time, it needs to be recognized that although the supervisor and therapist roles differ, personal issues arise in both relationships. Further study is needed to help supervisors determine when and how these issues should be addressed. For instance, the results of a recent study by Sumerel and Borders (1996) suggest that a supervisor who discusses personal issues in an appropriate manner does not necessarily affect the relationship negatively.

Similarly, in counselor training programs, professors might discover students' personal struggles through the activities involved in various courses. Most programs entail a balance between academic pursuits and the personal development of students. Students of counseling write personal papers, are encouraged to relate personally to course material, and often participate in experiential learning—all of which involve self-disclosure. Thus, even if some role blending is avoidable, some professionals may prefer to proceed with it if they are convinced that the potential for harm to students is minimal and if safeguards ensure that the best interests of students are maintained.

In some situations, by contrast, dual relationships (as opposed to role blending) are *unavoidable*. For instance, in a rural, isolated community the local banker, merchant, or minister might be clients of a particular counselor. In such a setting, counselors may have to perform several professional roles and functions and are likely to find it more difficult to maintain clear boundaries than their counterparts who practice in urban and suburban areas.

GUIDELINES TO MINIMIZE RISK

Some problematic aspects in dealing with dual relationships are that: (a) they are pervasive; (b) their beginnings can be difficult to recognize; (c) they are unavoidable at times; and, (d) as Kitchener and Harding (1990) remind us, the potential for harm ranges along a continuum from severe to slight. The key to learning how to manage dual relationships is to find ways to minimize the risks involved. When a professional functions in more than one role, and a potential for negative consequences exists, it is the professional's responsibility to develop safeguards. Herlihy and Corey (in press) and St. Germaine (1993) identify the following as guidelines to minimize the risks involved in dual relationships:

- Set healthy boundaries from the outset

- Fully inform clients about any potential risks

- Discuss with clients any potentially problematic relationship and clarify areas of concern

- Consult with other professionals periodically if you are engaged in a dual relationship

- Work under supervision in cases where the potential for harm is high

- Document discussions about any dual relationships and relevant steps taken

- If necessary, refer the client to another professional

Counselors will encounter many forms of nonsexual dual relationships in their work. One way of dealing with any potential problem involving dual relationships is to try to avoid them completely. Another alternative is to deal with each dilemma as it arises, making full use of informed consent and, at the same time, seeking consultation and supervision in dealing with the situation. Although this second alternative may be more challenging, we believe that the willingness to grapple with the ethical complexities of day-to-day practice is a hallmark of professionalism.

REFERENCES

American Association for Marriage and Family Therapy. (1992). *AAMFT code of ethics*. Washington, DC: Author.

American Counseling Association. (1995). *Code of ethics and standards of practice*. Alexandria, VA: Author.

American Psychological Association. (1992). *Ethical principles of psychologists and code of conduct*. Washington, DC: Author.

Bograd, M. (1993). The duel over dual relationships. *The California Therapist, Jan/Feb*, pp. 7-16.

Borders, D. L. (1992). Duality within the supervisory relationship. In B. Herlihy & G. Corey, *Dual relationships in counseling* (pp. 124-126). Alexandria, VA: American Association for Counseling and Development.

Corey, G., Corey, M. S., & Callanan, P. (1993). *Issues and ethics in the helping professions* (4th ed.). Pacific Grove, CA: Brooks/Cole.

Goldberg, J. R. (1993, June). Exploring the murky world of dual relationships. *Family Therapy News*, pp. 24-26.

Hedges, L. E. (1993). In praise of dual relationships. Part II: Essential dual relatedness in developmental psychotherapy. *The California Therapist, July/Aug*, pp. 42-46.

Herlihy, B., & Corey, G. (in press). *Boundary issues in counseling: Multiple roles and relationships*. Alexandria, VA: American Counseling Association.

Kitchener, K. S., & Harding, S. S. (1990). Dual-role relationships. In B. Herlihy & L. B. Golden (Eds.), *Ethical standards casebook* (4th ed.) (pp. 146-154). Alexandria, VA: American Association for Counseling and Development.

Leslie, R. (1993). Dual relationships. *The California Therapist, Jan/Feb*, p. 6.

Neukrug, E. S., Healy, M., & Herlihy, B. (1992). Ethical practices of licensed professional counselors: An updated survey of state licensing boards. *Counselor Education and Supervision, 32*, 130-141.

Pope, K. S. (1985). Dual relationships: A violation of ethical, legal, and clinical standards. *California State Psychologist, 20*(3), 3-6.

Pope, K. S., & Vasquez, M. J. T. (1991). *Ethics in psychotherapy and counseling*. San Francisco: Jossey-Bass.

St. Germaine, J. (1993). Dual relationships: What's wrong with them? *American Counselor, 2*(3), 25-30.

Sumerel, M. B., & Borders, L. D. (1996). Addressing personal issues in supervision: Impact of counselors' experience level on various aspects of the supervisory relationship. *Counselor Education and Supervision, 35*, 268-286.

Tomm, K. (1993). The ethics of dual relationships. *The California Therapist, Jan/Feb*, pp. 7-19.

12

Sexual Boundary Violations

Silvia W. Olarte, MD

Dr. Olarte is Clinical Professor of Psychiatry and faculty member of the Psychoanalytic Institute, Department of Psychiatry, New York Medical College, Valhalla, NY.

KEY POINTS

- Sexual relations with clients during the course of treatment is prohibited in most mental health professionals' codes of ethics. Regardless, many sexual boundary violations with clients have been documented.

- Sexual boundary violations negatively affect the client in a number of ways. Harmful effects include distrust of the opposite sex; distrust of therapy and therapists; feelings of guilt, shame, self-blame, anger, rejection, and abandonment; depression, loss of self-esteem, and suicidal ideation; impaired sexual relationships; and reenactment of pathogenic childhood situations. Such violations remain harmful to the client no matter how much time elapses after the termination of therapy.

- Most sexual boundary violations occur between male therapists and female clients because of gender-related socialization patterns. However, no therapist—man or woman—is immune from engaging in an intimate relationship with a client.

- Therapists who commit boundary violations are typically described as being in a "lovesick" state, which often clouds judgment. The most frequent composite of an offending therapist is a middle-aged man who is well trained, orthodox in his methodology, experiencing personal distress, isolated professionally, and overvalues his healing abilities.

- Sexually exploitive therapists can be categorized into clinical clusters according to their characteristics. Common characteristics are examined.

INTRODUCTION

Sexual intimacy with clients during treatment is clearly prohibited in most mental health professionals' codes of ethics. Despite this proscription, sexual boundary violations during therapy have been documented in various groups of health professionals (Bouhoutsos, Holroyd, Lerman, Forer, & Greenberg, 1983; Gartrell, Herman, Olarte, Feldstein, & Localio, 1986; Gartrell, Milliken, Goodson, Theimann, & Lo, 1992; Kardener, Fuller, & Mensh, 1973). Its undoubted deleterious effect on the client includes distrust for the opposite sex; distrust for psychotherapy and psychotherapists, with subsequent difficulty in reinstating counseling; guilt, shame, and self-blame; impaired sexual relationships; depression, loss of self-esteem, and suicidal ideation; and feelings of anger, rejection, abandonment, and reenactment of pathogenic childhood situations, because clients who were sexually abused as children are more vulnerable to being sexually abused by therapists (Apfel & Simon, 1985; Feldman-Summers & Jones, 1984; Schoener, Milgrom, & Gonsiorek, 1990). Sexual intimacy with a former client remains an area of controversy. Some argue that it becomes a consenting act between two mature adults after a specific time has passed following termination (Appelbaum & Jorgenson, 1991). The majority adheres to the belief that such behavior continues to be harmful to the client, no matter how much time has elapsed since termination of treatment (Shopland & VandeCreek, 1991; Vasquez, 1991).

Sexual attraction between a psychotherapist and a client cannot always be described as part of transference or countertransference feelings. Among surveyed counselors, 96% of men and 76% of women acknowledged attraction to one or more of their clients. Of these psychotherapists, only 9.4% of the men and 2.5% of the women reported having had sexual relations with their clients (Pope, Keith-Spiegel, & Tabachnick, 1986). Among surveyed trainees, 86% of men and 52% of women acknowledged sexual attraction to one or more clients (Gartrell, Herman, Olarte, Localio, & Felstein, 1988). Both the psychotherapists and the trainees reported that having been attracted to their clients evoked guilt, confusion, and anxiety. Moreover, they cited their lack of adequate training to contend with their sexual attraction for their clients. The majority reported insufficient training on the recognition and resolution of erotic transference phenomena and minimal discussion during supervision of countertransference feelings pertaining to the development of clients' erotic transference onto therapists.

Most sexual boundary violations occur between male therapists and female clients. Various survey studies found 8%–12% of male therapists and 1.7%–3.0% of female therapists acknowledged sexual contact with their clients (Bouhoutsos et al., 1983; Gartrell et al., 1986, 1992; Kardener et al., 1973).

Phenomena inherent to the psychotherapeutic relationship, such as transference and countertransference, reflect both culturally bound sex role-related factors and intrapsychic factors of the client and the therapist, independent of the gender composition of the dyad. Understanding the role played by such factors fosters appropriate resolution of such inherent therapeutic phenomena and avoidance of the role's misuse. Neither sociocultural nor intrapsychic factors alone can explain such a preponderance of sexual boundary violations among the male therapist-female client dyad. Still, exploration of the possible influence of culturally bound and intrapsychically bound factors on the psychotherapeutic relationship can help therapists understand such a preponderance and focus educational efforts on trying to minimize the occurrence of such boundary violations within the therapeutic relationship.

SEX ROLE-RELATED ISSUES

Kaplan (1984), following Kagan's description of the process of socialization for each sex, describes the therapist's role as a combination of two components, the structural and the functional.

The structural component addresses the therapist's responsibility to define for the client the specific characteristics of the contractual therapeutic relationship. Examples of contractual characteristics are frequency, length, and location of meetings; appropriate subjects of discussion; and type of interactive pattern to be developed. The client can attempt to influence part of this structure, but its definition lies primarily with the therapist. This expected structural role is what confers authority on the therapist. The therapists' personality traits that are most conducive to successful accomplishment of the structural task are independence, assertiveness, and emotional distance—traits most consistent with masculine, rather than feminine, patterns of sex-role socialization. On the other hand, the functional component addresses the therapist's ability to be empathic and intuitive, to be a good listener, and to be capable of showing compassion for others while postponing gratification of personal needs in favor of the client's, traits emphasized in the female socialization process. Men and women therapists need to possess both sets of characteristics to perform both the structural and functional roles.

The presence of such characteristics in both male and female therapists will depend on their socialization patterns, which in turn depend on their intimate interpersonal world and their particular sociocultural context. Therapists of both genders need to be aware of the effect of their sex-related socialization patterns and recognize possible countertransference reactions that stem from such patterns. A male therapist who is not aware of his socially acceptable authority role can be inappropriately accepting of his female clients' tendency to be compliant, to be nonconfrontational, and to idealize his authority by fostering dependency, not growth. Moreover, a male therapist unable to recognize a client's need for an empathic, nurturing stance might deny this client's dependency components on an erotic transference, address only the sexualized aspect of the transference, and mishandle such a phenomenon, facilitating sexual acting out inside or outside of the therapeutic situation (Gabbard, 1990).

A female therapist who may feel that her professional

authority role is not congruent with her sex-role socialization patterns might overvalue her empathic stance, exaggerating the development of a nurturing-symbiotic transference. The client might be inhibited from expressing any transferred erotic longings to the therapist. This might interfere with the client's ability to integrate dependency and erotic longings for the love object.

INTRAPSYCHIC PROCESS

The development of an erotic transference within a psychodynamic therapeutic relationship is considered a universal phenomenon; still, it most frequently develops within a female-client/male-therapist dyad. The child's development of the sense of gender and psychological self will depend on integration of both the different socialization patterns for the boy and girl and the different interpersonal developmental paths followed while relating to the nurturing authority figures of both genders. Pearson (1985) maintains that to understand the difference in the development of the erotic transference in relation to the gender of the client and therapist, the cultural conceptualization of femininity and masculinity, clients' early object relations, and the asymmetric structures of the oedipal complex must be considered.

Women develop their female self-identity in terms of their affiliation to others; the establishment and continuation of relationships is crucial to their self development, and emotional interdependence fosters growth. By contrast, men define their male self-identity through achievement and autonomy (Chodorow, 1988; Gilligan, 1982; Miller, 1984). Both sexes might be equally fearful of psychological engulfment by an image of a powerful, omnipotent, primitive, symbiotic nurturing figure—feelings belonging to an earlier developmental stage—but men and women might react differently to the awakened feelings of dependency longings for the recognized separate love object. That in turn will affect their development and expression of the erotic transference. In a male-client/female-therapist dyad, the client seems to develop a mild, transient — if at all — erotic transference toward his therapist. The client tends to separate his dependency needs on the nurturing figure from his erotic desires, experiencing the therapist as a nurturing maternal ally or as a threatening, intrusive authority. He then projects the transferred erotic wishes *outside* the therapeutic relationship. The female client, on the other hand, is more comfortable with her awareness of her dependency needs and might tend to eroticize her dependency needs *within* the therapeutic relationship (Chodorow, 1988).

THE SEXUALLY ABUSIVE THERAPIST

Prevalence surveys on the existence of sexual boundary violations have been easier to construct and complete than surveys addressing the psychodynamic characteristics of the abusive therapist. Throughout the voluminous literature on the subject, three main methodologies have been used to describe the characteristics of the sexually abusive therapist: composite descriptions, profile descriptions, and descriptions based on voluntary evaluations of offenders.

Composite descriptions are derived from the treatment of a few offenders (Dalberg, 1970; Davidson, 1977). Profile descriptions are based on common characteristics found in anonymous research surveys of responders who acknowledged sexual contact with their clients (Bouhoutsos et al., 1983; Gartrell et al., 1986). An alternative source is review of personnel files and medical records for known cases of staff-client sexual relationships in given institutions (Averill et al., 1989). The third methodology is examination of the description of offenders. It is contingent on voluntary evaluations of such offenders by centers that specialize in treating victims of physical or sexual abuse (Schoener & Gonsiorek, 1990).

Composite Descriptions:

The composite profile that most frequently emerges from the treatment or consultation with offenders is that the therapist is a middle-aged man who is undergoing some type of personal distress, is isolated professionally, and overvalues his healing capacities. His therapeutic methods tend to be unorthodox; he frequently particularizes the therapeutic relationship by disclosing personal information not pertinent to the treatment, which fosters confusion of the therapeutic boundaries. He is generally well trained, having completed at least an approved training program and at times formal psychoanalytic training.

Twemlow and Gabbard (1989) based their observations on their treatment and consultation with offending therapists. They described one who falls in love with clients as the "lovesick therapist." Lovesickness is a reaction separate from any specific underlying pathology because it can be experienced by therapists who, on evaluation, can be considered normal, neurotic, or suffering from assorted personality disorders. Lovesickness is characterized by:

- Emotional dependence

- Intrusive thinking, whereby the thought of the other is almost a constant phenomenon

- Physical sensations like buoyancy or pounding pulse

- A sense of incompleteness, of feeling less than whole, when away from the loved one

- An awareness of the social proscription for such love that seems to intensify the couple's longing for each other

- An altered state of consciousness that fosters impaired judgment on the part of the therapist when in the presence of the loved one

This impaired judgment is not displayed in front of other clients. As a result, the therapist can adequately carry out other clinical functions.

Profile Descriptions:

The most common offender profile extrapolated from anonymous surveys is similar to that derived from treatment of specific offenders: a man who has completed an accredited residency training program and who has undergone some personal psychotherapy or psychoanalysis. A survey by Gartrell and associates (1986) found that among the 6.4% of the mental health professionals who acknowledged sexual relationships with their clients, 89% were men. Of all the therapist-client sexual contacts reported, 88% involved a male therapist and a female client. Of the offenders, 65% reported they had been "in love" with the client. The survey did not clarify this state, but it alerts us to the possible frequency of the above-described lovesick state of the therapist, with its subsequent clouding of judgment and possible fostering of sexual boundary violations. Moreover, 33% of the offenders had been involved with more than one client. All offenders who admitted contact with more than one client were men. Still, 40% of the offenders regretted the contact, and 41% consulted colleagues because of their sexual involvement with clients; female offenders consulted more frequently than men offenders, and repeat offenders were the least likely to seek such consultation.

Sexual exploitation of those admitted to varied mental health institutions is an ongoing problem that is difficult to address. Still, when addressed, two profiles of possible vulnerable staff emerge (Averill et al., 1989). One is a young, exploitative staff member, who acts out his or her exploitative tendencies outside as much as within the hospital setting. This would correspond with the antisocial therapist described by Twemlow and Gabbard (1989) or one of the severely character-disordered abusive therapists described by Schoener and Gonsiorek (1990). The second group (as with the profile from composite sources) encompasses middle-aged, isolated individuals undergoing personal difficulties that trigger longing for nurturing. Men in the second group tend to be disillusioned with the workplace and feel slighted or hurt by the institution. Their sexual acting out might express their anger and disappointment with the organization and might well resonate with similar feelings within the client. Women staff members who abuse clients sexually most often are actualizing rescue fantasies, trying to restore the client's health through love.

Voluntary Evaluation of Offenders:

Schoener and Gonsiorek (1990) have developed a classification of sexually exploitative therapists who have voluntarily agreed to a complete psychological and psychiatric evaluation. They have grouped the offenders into clinical clusters correlated with the offenders' potential for rehabilitation and treatment. These categories have been developed through their extended clinical experience rather than a systematic research approach.

Uninformed or Naïve

These professionals lack knowledge of their expected ethical standards or lack understanding of professional boundaries and confuse personal with professional relationships. If the professional who lacked the appropriate information possesses a mature personality, appropriate supervision and education can correct this lack of knowledge, and the vulnerability to transgress professional boundaries disappears. Such is not the case with those therapists whose lack of information is accompanied by different levels of personal pathology. There, the underlying pathology determines the prognosis for rehabilitation.

Healthy or Mildly Neurotic

These professionals for the most part know their professional standards. Their sexual contact with a client is usually an isolated or limited incident. Frequently at the time of the boundary violation, these therapists are suffering from personal or situational stresses that foster a slow erosion of their professional boundaries. They most often show remorse for their unethical behavior, frequently stop such violations on their own, or seek consultation with peers. With appropriate treatment and supervision, the majority can be rehabilitated.

Severely Neurotic and Socially Isolated

Therapists in this cluster show long-standing and serious emotional problems. They can suffer from depression, low self-esteem, feelings of inadequacy, and social isolation. They frequently confuse personal and professional boundaries and foster inappropriate closeness with their clients in and out of the therapeutic relationship. They share personal information not pertinent to the therapeutic process. When erotic transferences develop, they fail to recognize them because of unresolved countertransference feelings, such as their need for self-gratification (Gabbard, 1990). When they transgress the professional boundaries and their behavior becomes unethical, they tend to deny it or justify such transgression as a therapeutic maneuver to enhance the client's self-esteem, as a restitutive emotional experience, or as a consequence of the client's existing pathology. These therapists can experience guilt or remorse, but seldom do they discontinue their unethical sexual relationship with their client. They frequently are repeat offenders. Because of their more serious personality pathology, rehabilitation through treatment and supervision is difficult; their prognosis is guarded.

Impulsive Character Disorder

These therapists show difficulty with impulse control in

most areas of their lives. Their problem is generally long-standing. Most have received adequate training and are aware of their professional standards, but regulations do not work as a deterrent to their impulsivity in or out of their professional lives. Their judgment is poor. They tend to abuse more than one victim, show minimal remorse for their unethical behavior, and are oblivious to the possible harm inflicted on the client by their impulsive behavior. These therapists are poor candidates for rehabilitation.

Sociopathic or Narcissistic Character Disorder

These therapists also suffer from long-standing serious pathology in most areas of their lives. They tend to be more calculating and deliberate in their abuse of their clients. They successfully manipulate the treatment situation by fostering erotic transference, by blurring the professional boundaries with inappropriate personal disclosure that enhances and idealizes transference, and by manipulating the length or the time of the sessions to facilitate the development of a sexual relationship with the client. They can successfully manipulate the victim or the system to protect themselves from the consequence(s) of their unethical behavior. If caught, they might express remorse and agree to rehabilitation to protect themselves or their professional standard, but they will show minimal or no character change through treatment. Their prognosis is poor.

Psychotic or Borderline Personality

The severity of such professionals' psychopathology will directly interfere with their reality testing or critical judgment. They generally possess the appropriate knowledge of ethical standards and of clinical aspects of professional boundaries; however, their impaired reality testing or poor judgment impedes them in applying such knowledge. Their capacity for rationalization of their unethical behavior—compared with the neurotic individual – is idiosyncratic and simplistic. Reha-bilitation is determined by the seriousness of the underlying pathology, and their prognosis is guarded.

CONCLUSION

Ethical behavior during a professional relationship is always the responsibility of the professional, independent of the client's pathology or the intensity of any given therapeutic processes inherent to the therapeutic relationship. A client's given pa-thology or the intensity of inherent therapeutic phenomena such as the development of an erotic transference can tax the therapeutic relationship, and it may also enhance the therapist's vulnerability or tendency to blur professional boundaries (Gutheil, 1989).

To ensure ethical performance, professional organizations must assume the responsibility of educating their members not only on accepted ethical standards but on all other socio-cultural, personal, and clinical factors that can influence their ethical behavior. For the recognized offenders, professionals are responsible for developing effective evaluatory methods to determine the possibility for treatment and rehabilitation of the offenders to avoid a repeat of their unethical behavior. Only a serious commitment to the education of professionals on ethical matters and a candid, systematic, thorough, nonpunitive evaluation – along with an appropriate treatment and rehabilitative approach for the offenders – can secure professional ethical behavior, protecting the client from the harm such behavior motivates.

REFERENCES

Apfel, R., & Simon, B. (1985). Patient-therapist sexual contact, I: Psychodynamic perspectives on the causes and results. *Psychotherapy and Psychosomatics, 43,* 57–62.

Appelbaum, P. S., & Jorgenson, L. (1991). Psychotherapist-patient sexual contact after termination of treatment: An analysis and a proposal. *American Journal of Psychiatry, 148,* 1466–1473.

Averill, S. C., Beale, D., Benfer, B., et al. (1989). Preventing staff-patient sexual relationships. *Bulletin of the Menninger Clinic, 53,* 384–393.

Bouhoutsos, J., Holroyd, J., Lerman, H., Forer, B. R., Greenberg, M. (1983). Sexual intimacy between psychotherapists and patients. *Professional Psychology Research Practice, 14,* 185–196.

Chodorow, N. J. (1988). *Feminism and psychoanalytic theory.* New Haven, CT: Yale University Press.

Dalberg, C. (1970). Sexual contact between patient and therapist. *Contemporary Psychoanalysis, 6,* 107–124.

Davidson, V. (1977). Psychiatry's problem with no name: Therapist-patient sex. *American Journal of Psychoanalysis, 37,* 43–50.

Feldman-Summers, S., & Jones, G. (1984). Psychological impact of sexual contact between therapists or other health care practitioners and their clients. *Journal of Consulting and Clinical Psychology, 52,* 1054–1061.

Gabbard, G. O. (1990). Therapeutic approaches to erotic transference. *Directions in Psychiatry, 10*(4).

Gartrell, N., Herman, J., Olarte, S., Feldstein, M., & Localio, R. (1986). Psychiatrist-patient sexual contact: Results of a national survey, I: Prevalence. *American Journal of Psychiatry, 143,* 1126–1131.

Gartrell, N., Herman, J., Olarte, S., Localio, R., & Felstein, M. (1988). Psychiatric residents' sexual contact with educators and patients: Results of a national survey. *American Journal of Psychiatry, 145,* 691–694.

Gartrell, N., Milliken, N., Goodson, W. H. III, Theimann, S., & Lo, B. (1992, August). Physician-patient sexual contact—prevalence and problems. *Western Journal of Medicine, 157*, 139-143.

Gilligan, C. (1982). *In a different voice: Psychological theory and women's development.* Cambridge, MA: Harvard University Press.

Gutheil, T. G. (1989). Borderline personality disorder, boundary violations and patient-therapist sex: Medicolegal pitfalls. *American Journal of Psychiatry, 146*, 597-602.

Kaplan, A. G. (1984). Toward an analysis of sex-role related issues in the therapeutic relationship. In P. Perry Reiker & E. H. Carmen (Eds.), *The gender gap in psychotherapy* (pp. 349-360). New York: Plenum Press.

Kardener, S. H., Fuller, M., & Mensh, I. N. (1973). A survey of physicians' attitudes and practices regarding erotic and nonerotic contact with patients. *American Journal of Psychiatry, 130*, 1077-1081.

Miller, J. B. (1984). *The development of women's sense of self* (Work in Progress #12). Wellesley, MA: Stone Center Working Papers.

Pearson, E. S. (1985). The erotic transference in women and in men: Differences and consequences. *Journal of the American Academy of Psychoanalysis, 13*, 159-180.

Pope, K. S., Keith-Spiegel, P., & Tabachnick, B. G. (1986). Sexual attraction to clients. *American Psychologist, 41*, 147-156.

Schoener, G. R., & Gonsiorek, J. C. (1990). Assessment and development of rehabilitation plans for the therapist. In G. R. Schoener, J. H. Milgrom, J. C. Gonsiorek, E. T. Luepker, & R. M. Conroe (Eds.), *Psychotherapists' sexual involvement with clients: Intervention and prevention.* Minneapolis: Walk-In Counseling Center.

Schoener, G. R., Milgrom, J. H., & Gonsiorek, J. C. (1990). Therapeutic responses to clients who have been sexually abused by psychotherapists. In G. R. Schoener, J. H. Milgrom, J. C. Gonsiorek, E. T. Luepker, & R. M. Conroe (Eds.), *Psychotherapists' sexual involvement with clients: Intervention and prevention* (pp. 95-112). Minneapolis: Walk-In Counseling Center.

Shopland, S. N., & VandeCreek, L. (1991). Sex with ex-clients: Theoretical rationales for prohibition. *Ethics and Behavior, 1,* 35–44.

Twemlow, S. W., & Gabbard, G. O. (1989). The love-sick therapist. In G. O. Gabbard (Ed.), *Sexual exploitation in professional relationships* (pp. 71-87). Washington, DC: American Psychiatric Press.

Vasquez, M. J. T. (1991). Sexual intimacies with clients after termination: Should a prohibition be explicit? *Ethics and Behavior, 1,* 45–61.

13

Ethical Standards in Counseling Sexually Active Clients with HIV

Elliot D. Cohen, PhD

Dr. Cohen is Professor in the Department of Social Sciences at Indian River Community College, Fort Pierce, FL, and Editor-in-Chief of the *International Journal of Applied Philosophy*.

KEY POINTS

- Both professional ethics and legal codes uphold two important ethical obligations that may come into conflict in the context of HIV/AIDS. These are (a) maintaining confidentiality with (HIV-positive) clients and (b) warning third parties (who are being exposed to HIV through sexual activity with the client) of "imminent probability of physical harm" by the client.

- This chapter draws on two strands of Western philosophy, utilitarian ethics and Kantian ethics, to develop nine *ethical guidelines* (EGs) for mental health professionals to determine when it is permissible to break confidentiality with sexually active HIV-positive clients. Fourteen *ethical

rules* (ERs) are generated from these guidelines.

- Disclosure is not always mandated. The decision to disclose must also be balanced against any possible contravening harm to the client. Disclosure should not mark the breakdown of mutual respect between the client and professional; the professional should always discuss the potential need to disclose with the client before doing so.

- What the professional determines to be ethical in a certain case may not be legal in some jurisdictions. Therefore, mental health professionals should always consult their state's statutes on the question of legality.

BACKGROUND INFORMATION

Acquired immunodeficiency syndrome (AIDS) is a fatal and contagious disease that is believed to be caused by the human immunodeficiency virus (HIV). Although most reported deaths due to AIDS in the 1980s were among intravenous drug users and homosexual men, the number of reported AIDS cases continues to escalate within the general population (Centers for Disease Control and Prevention [CDC], 1991). This trend augments the likelihood that most mental health professionals eventually will confront ethical problems concerning clients with AIDS or HIV.

The virus invades the T cells (the white blood cells responsible for stimulating production of antibodies to fight infection) of the human immune system. As T cells are destroyed, the body progressively loses its ability to fight infection. Although at the time of this writing there are no vaccines against HIV or cures for the disease, some medications (e.g., azidothymidine [AZT] and the more recent antiviral drugs such as protease inhibitors) can slow the rate of virus reproduction and prolong the life of the patient, especially if the drug regimen is begun in the early stages of infection (Gostin, 1990; Mayer, 1990; Douglas & Pinsky, 1996).

The most common test for HIV is the enzyme immunoassay (EIA) test, which indirectly tests for HIV by detecting HIV antibodies present in the blood (so-called HIV positivity). A person is normally considered to be HIV seropositive only after the administration of a second EIA combined with a more complex and expensive test known as the Western blot (Brant, Cleary, & Gostin, 1990; Douglas & Pinsky, 1996).

Not all HIV-positive persons are classified as having AIDS. The latter diagnosis is made only if the patient also has specific opportunistic diseases, such as Kaposi's sarcoma and *Pneumocystis carinii* (CDC, 1987). HIV can be found in blood, blood products, and other body fluids including semen and cervical-vaginal secretions (Leibowitz, 1989). The primary mode of transmission is sexual intercourse. Although oral-genital sex may transmit the virus, the most probable modes of sexual transmission are vaginal and anal intercourse. Latex condoms are effective in helping prevent the sexual transmission of HIV. The risk of sexual transmission can also be decreased by limiting the number of sexual partners and by selecting partners who do the same (Flaskerud & Nyamathi, 1989).

CONFIDENTIALITY, THIRD-PARTY HARM, AND HIV: A MORAL DILEMMA

An ethical dilemma refers to a situation in which two important ethical interests come into conflict and, thus, cannot both be satisfied completely. For example, counselors who disclose information about their clients' HIV status to endangered third parties may violate client-counselor confidentiality. However, a counselor who preserves this confidentiality may fail to prevent substantial and preventable harm to the third party. In either case, it may be difficult or impossible for a counselor to adhere fully to both professional standards.

This dilemma may appear to be resolvable by referring to legal precedent, state statutes, and professional codes of ethics. For example, in the landmark *Tarasoff v. Regents of the University of California* (1976) decision, it was held that "the right to privacy ends where the public peril begins"; state statutes typically recognize the "clear and immediate probability of physical harm" to others as a legitimate exception to confidentiality (Florida Department of Professional Regulatons, 1993; see also Chapter 8). Moreover, codes of professional ethics typically recognize the prevention of "clear and imminent danger to the client or others" as an overriding professional obligation (American Counseling Association [ACA], 1995).

These sources may seem to suggest that disclosure of confidential information to prevent an unwitting sexual partner from contracting HIV constitutes a legitimate exception to confidentiality. However, such a conclusion requires an inference that the sources in question do not themselves make explicitly.

A closer move toward resolution of the dilemma has been the inclusion by the ACA of a "contagious and fatal diseases" rule in it's recently revised ethics code (ACA, 1995). This rule is a version of "a model rule concerning the limits of confidentiality in cases where clients have a contagious and fatal disease" proposed by Cohen (1990, p. 285). The ACA rule provides that a counselor who has confirming information that a client has an ascertainably fatal and contagious disease is justified in disclosing necessary information to an identifiable third party who is at high risk of contracting the disease from the client (B. 1. d.). However, like most code rules, this rule is general in character and subject to interpretation (Mabe & Rollins, 1986). Direct appeal to this or other similar rules in a cursory manner is thus likely to oversimplify and obscure important ethical considerations and details that undergird a reasonable and informed application of this rule. What is needed, therefore, is a clear understanding of the ethical dimensions of the problem at hand, as well as a set of application criteria consistent with this understanding.

THE ETHICAL GROUNDS OF CONFIDENTIALITY

The dilemma of breaching confidentiality arises because counselors have a professional obligation to hold in confidence what their clients reveal to them in the course of therapy. This obligation can be justified by appealing to classical ethical theories, which are general ethical principles that have enjoyed a central position in the history of Western philosophy. Two such theories are relevant to this chapter: utilitarianism and Kantian ethics.

Utilitarianism:

Utilitarian theories hold that actions, rules, or policies are obligatory when performance or obedience to them can be calculated on the available evidence to maximize "net expected utility" (Brandt, 1959, p. 381). According to classical formulations of this theory, "utility" refers to pleasure and the absence of pain (Bentham, 1989). Net expected utility is calculated by subtracting the amount of expected pain from the amount of expected pleasure (*net* value) multiplied by the *probability* of attaining this value (net *expectable* value). Because probabilities are assessed only in relation to empirical evidence, this theory makes ethical judgments a function of factual ones; that is, before someone can determine the obligatory character of an action, rule, or policy, he or she must first have the (relevant) facts.

There are two types of utilitarianism: act utilitarianism and rule utilitarianism. According to act utilitarianism, an act is ethically obligatory when it can be calculated to maximize net expected utility (Brandt, 1959). A counselor has an obligation to report child abuse only if doing so can be calculated to maximize net expectable utility (e.g., it protects the child). On the other hand, if *not* reporting the abuse can be expected to maximize net expectable value (e.g., it prevents legal custody being transferred to a much more formidable abuser), the counselor would have a *moral* obligation not to report the abuse. (The counselor's moral obligation may then conflict with his or her legal obligation.)

In rule utilitarianism, a rule or policy is obligatory when general obedience to it can be calculated to maximize net expected utility; an act is obligatory when it falls under such an obligatory rule or policy (Brandt, 1959). For example, a rule proscribing sexual intimacy with clients is obligatory because the general obedience to this rule by counselors can be calculated to maximize net expectable value; therefore, a counselor who is sexually intimate with a client would be guilty of an ethical violation.

Similarly, a professional rule or policy requiring counselors to maintain client confidentiality can be justified by appealing to rule utilitarianism. Without such a rule, many clients who would benefit from treatment would probably be deterred from seeking it. Moreover, without the assurance of confidentiality, many clients who seek therapy would probably be deterred from speaking openly to their counselors (*Tarasoff v. Regents of the University of California*, 1976). As a consequence, a rule or policy requiring confidentiality would appear to maximize net expectable utility in the therapeutic context.

Professional rules and policies, however, do permit exceptions. For example, legal rules and professional codes of ethics typically recognize the probability of harm to clients or to third parties as exceptions to confidentiality. From a rule utilitarian perspective, these exceptions can be justified because a rule or policy that recognizes them can be calculated to maximize net expected utility by virtue of preventing substantial harm to clients or to third parties.

Kantian Ethics:

Kantian ethics is the ethical theory developed by Immanuel Kant, an 18th-century German philosopher. Kant referred to his ethical principle as "the categorical imperative," and he presented several formulations of it, two of which are discussed below.

One principle is to "act in such a way that you always treat humanity, whether in your own person or in the person of any other, never simply as a means, but always at the same time as an end" (Kant, 1785/1964, p. 96). That is, persons must never be treated as *mere objects* to be manipulated or used by others. In contrast to objects, persons are rational, autonomous (self-determining) agents. By virtue of their rational, autonomous nature, they possess a right of self-determination. They are "ends in themselves," centers of intrinsic value possessing worth and dignity apart from any use that they might have.

As autonomous agents, persons also have a right to privacy (Parents, 1992). In this context, "privacy" refers to facts about a person that most individuals might share with a few close friends, relatives, or professional associates, but would not usually want others to know. In contemporary America, these facts (which may vary with social trends) include sexual preference, drinking or drug habits, income, marital status, and personal health issues (Parents, 1992).

In therapy, the recognition of a bond of confidentiality between client and counselor constitutes the primary manner in which the right to privacy, so described, may be safeguarded. Within the professional relationship, confidentiality is a primary manner in which the intrinsic worth and dignity of clients as "ends in themselves" may be preserved.

From the Kantian perspective, there can still be disclosures of private facts that do not violate the client's intrinsic dignity. If the disclosure is made with the client's consent, other things being equal, there is no such moral transgression because the client is recognized as a rational, autonomous agent. However, to satisfy Kantian canons of consent, the client must be reasonably informed by the counselor about the nature of the disclosure (what is to be disclosed, to whom the disclosure is to be made, the rationale for disclosure, consequences of disclosure); moreover, the consent must not be exacted through intimidation, threats, or other forms of coercion (explicit or implicit). To omit pertinent information, or to exact consent by coercion, cannot be reconciled with treating clients as "ends in themselves" (Cohen, 1990, p. 283).

Kant emphasizes the need in ethics for *consistency*—the second formulation of the categorical imperative. A rational agent must be willing and able to consistently accept the logical implications of his or her own value judgments. For instance, if it is acceptable for a counselor to disclose a client's confidences without prior consent from the client, then to be consistent with his or her own will, the counselor must be willing to see his or her own confidences disclosed if he or she were in the client's place. Other things being equal, just as the counselor would not want his or her own confidences disclosed without freely given and informed consent, it would be equally wrong for a counselor to subject a nonconsenting client to such treatment.

However, other things may *not* be equal in a given situation and, from a rational perspective, a counselor may be willing to see his or her own confidences disclosed. This suggests that although the bond of confidentiality between counselors and clients is a serious moral obligation that cannot be defeated easily, there are also limits to confidentiality.

ETHICAL THEORY AND VULNERABILITY

Utilitarian and Kantian ethics justify an additional ethical principle that limits confidentiality in professional ethics. This has been dubbed the *principle of vulnerability*, which dictates that "the duty to protect against harm tends to arise most strongly in contexts in which someone is specially dependent on others or in some way specially vulnerable to their choices and actions" (Winston, 1991, p. 175).

Vulnerability implies "risk or susceptibility to harm" (Winston, 1991, p. 175). Furthermore, being specially dependent on others implies the probability of harm unless others intervene. For example, lack of knowledge of impending danger may place one in a situation of dependency on the acts and decisions of another who may be in a position to warn of the impending danger.

This concept of being specially dependent on others also implies a degree of helplessness; that is, the inability to avoid risk of harm on one's own. For example, taking calculated risks or behaving in a reckless fashion does not place one in a relation of special dependency on others insofar as one can, in such cases, foresee or comprehend the risk of harm without the help of others.

In counseling, relations of special dependency may arise between counselors and third parties. By virtue of their confidential relation with clients, counselors may become privy to information concerning the welfare of others. Disclosure of certain confidential information in these cases may be necessary to prevent death or substantial bodily harm to another person. In these cases, the vulnerability of the (potential) victim plus the special dependency of the victim's life or limb on the choices and actions of the therapist firmly establish a duty of disclosure. From a rule utilitarian perspective, this duty arises because net expected utility can be maximized through the therapist's general compliance with a rule requiring disclosure in such cases.

The principle of vulnerability is also justified from a Kantian perspective. First, a counselor who has the power to prevent death or substantial bodily harm to a vulnerable third party through disclosure of relevant, confidential information but who instead knowingly does nothing to prevent it acquiesces in treating the third party as a "mere means" (nonautonomous being) rather than as an "end in itself" (autonomous being). Second, counselors should not knowingly allow vulnerable third parties to be seriously harmed because no rational agent would want to be treated in the same way.

Therefore, from utilitarian and Kantian perspectives, the vulnerability of the potential victim to a counselor's choices and actions firmly establishes the counselor's obligation to disclose confidential information to the extent necessary to prevent the prospective harm, at least when this harm is probable and substantial.

ETHICAL GUIDELINES FOR DISCLOSURE OF CONFIDENTIAL INFORMATION

Ethical guidelines (EGs) derived from the ethical theories discussed above are proposed in Table 13.1 for disclosure of confidential information in the context of counseling.

EGs 1–4 are derived from utilitarian ethics. Together, they serve as guidelines for determining when net expected utility supports disclosure. EGs 5–7 are derived from the two respective formulations of the categorical imperative. EGs 8 and 9 are derived from the principle of vulnerability.

When all EGs have been satisfied in any given situation, the

Table 13.1
ETHICAL GUIDELINES (EGs)

EG 1. There are sufficient factual grounds for considering risk of harm to the third party to be high.

EG 2. The third party in question is at risk of death or substantial bodily harm.

EG 3. Disclosure is likely to prevent or at least significantly reduce the amount of harm to the third party.

EG 4. No contravening harm of equal or greater proportions and probability (than the harm prevented) is likely to result from disclosure.

EG 5. Disclosure can be applied universally.

EG 6. Nondisclosure would permit the client to treat the third party as a mere means (nonautonomous being).

EG 7. Disclosure is made in a manner that promotes the treatment of the client as an end in himself or herself (rational, autonomous agent).

EG 8. The harm to the third party is not likely to be prevented unless the counselor makes the disclosure.

EG 9. The third party cannot reasonably be expected to foresee or comprehend the high risk of harm to self.

case for disclosure of confidential information is strongest. Under these conditions, it is "ethically safe" to say that the counselor has a moral obligation to disclose the information. Because maintaining client confidences in counseling is a serious moral obligation, the case for disclosure must be strong before this obligation can be justly defeated.

APPLYING ETHICAL GUIDELINES

Following are two cases that raise moral dilemmas for counselors (Cohen, 1994). Each case involves a conflict between the obligation to keep client confidences and the possibility of serious harm to third parties. In each case, a client infected with HIV is sexually active with one or more third parties.

Case 1:

> Peter, age 32, is in therapy with Dr. T to work through a depression. His profile includes a history of depression and an attempted suicide. After 3 months of therapy, Peter, who has been very resistant to the therapeutic process, reluctantly reveals to Dr. T that he is HIV-positive (which, he says, was probably the result of having had intercourse with prostitutes). He tells Dr. T that he had attempted suicide after test results of two EIAs were confirmed by the Western blot test.

> Dr. T is aware that Peter is having intercourse regularly with his fiancée without using any means of protection. When Dr. T asks Peter if his fiancée knows about his HIV status, he says he cannot bring himself to tell her because he is sure she would leave him if she knew.

Applying the ethical guidelines to the above case reveals that Dr. T has an obligation to disclose, especially because conclusive medical evidence exists for believing that Peter has HIV. (The EIA and Western blot tests are over 99% accurate; Flaskerud [1989]) Because unprotected vaginal intercourse is a probable mode of HIV transmission, there are sufficient factual grounds for assessing a high risk of harm to the identified third party (EG 1). Moreover, because HIV compromises the body's immune system and is (eventually) fatal, the third party is at risk of death or substantial bodily harm (EG 2).

For purposes of applying EG 1, the mere assessment that Peter himself is at high risk for having HIV would not constitute sufficient factual grounds for considering risk of harm to the third party to be high. Without adequate medical evidence such as EIA and Western blot tests, high risk simply would not be enough to warrant disclosure; otherwise, disclosure might be made, for instance, because a client was homosexual or Haitian. Such a policy would lead to discriminatory disclosure practices, a weakening of the level of trust between counselors and clients within these groups, and the disutility of disclosures made on the basis of incorrect judgments about HIV status.

Regarding Peter's fiancée, either she presently has HIV or she risks getting it in the future as long as the risky sexual behavior continues. If she has HIV, her knowledge of this fact will enable her to begin treatment; although there is no cure for HIV, the earlier treatment is started, the more likely it is that the progress of the virus can be slowed. On the other hand, if she does not have HIV, the knowledge that she is at risk of contracting the disease will enable her to stop the risky sexual activity *before* she contracts it. Therefore, in either situation, disclosure is likely to prevent or at least significantly reduce the amount of harm to the third party (EG 3).

This reduction of harm to Peter's fiancée must also be balanced against the pain or trauma of learning about Peter's HIV status. Although such pain may result in reducing net expected utility, it is not likely to destroy the utilitarian warrant for disclosure (Bok, 1991). Still, the task of maximizing net expected utility would include doing what is feasible to help her cope, such as offering her assistance in the form of counseling or by providing an appropriate referral (Cohen, 1990).

For purposes of applying EG 3, the *amount* of information counselors disclose to third parties at risk is also relevant, because the success or failure of disclosure (in alerting third parties of impending danger) clearly depends on the disclosed information. From a utilitarian perspective, only a general statement (that there is medical evidence indicating that a current sexual partner is HIV positive) should be conveyed. This will suffice to alert Peter's fiancée of the danger and, hopefully, to stop the risky sexual behavior. Given the importance of maintaining confidentiality, saying more would be an unwarranted violation of Peter's right to privacy (Cohen, 1990).

Constructive application of EG 3 must take into account the timeliness of disclosure. If Dr. T continues to delay, the probability of third-party harm and of less effective disclosure in materially reducing this harm increases. Although there is no precise calculus, a disclosure may come so late that it defeats the very purpose for which disclosure has been undertaken (Cohen, 1990).

Given Peter's history of attempted suicide, Dr. T must consider the possibility that disclosure to his fiancée may indirectly lead Peter to attempt suicide if she consequently leaves him. As provided by EG 4, the possibility of such *contravening harm* to Peter must be considered in calculating the net expected utility of disclosure. Nevertheless, this prospect of harm need not override the warrant for disclosure. If Dr. T reasonably believes that Peter is likely to harm himself as a result of disclosure, he must also take reasonable precautions or inform responsible authorities to prevent this possible harm (American Counseling Association, 1988). Under these conditions, the process of disclosure may still proceed, *cautiously.*

In the present case, disclosure also can be universalized (EG 5). As a rational person, Peter could not accept a universal law of *non*-disclosure because it would mean he would also have to be deceived and subjected to the risk of HIV if he were in his fiancée's place.

Because Peter is exposing his fiancée to the risk of contracting HIV without her knowledge or consent, he is treating her as a mere means (a nonautonomous being). If Dr. T chooses not to disclose to Peter's fiancée, he is knowingly permitting the client to treat the third party as a mere means (EG 6).

If disclosure is to be accomplished ethically, it should not mark the breakdown of mutual respect between the counselor and the client. Notwithstanding disclosure, Dr. T must treat Peter as an end in himself; that is, as a rational self-determining agent (EG 7). There are several entailments of this requirement. Before disclosure, Dr. T must adequately inform or educate Peter about HIV and its implications for sexual partners. He must also provide Peter with the "support, understanding, encouragement, and opportunity conducive to the client disclosing the information on his or her own" (Cohen, 1990). From the Kantian perspective, Peter's disclosure to his fiancée must be considered ethically superior to Dr. T's making the disclosure insofar as the former preserves a wider domain of client autonomy than the latter.

To be autonomous, Peter's disclosure must follow from his freely given, as well as informed, consent. This means that Dr. T must not attempt to coerce or threaten Peter into disclosure. If Peter remains steadfast in his refusal to disclose to his fiancée, Dr. T may make the disclosure only after he has apprised Peter of his intention to do so (Cohen, 1990). Otherwise, the client will not have been treated as an end in himself.

If Dr. T is to treat Peter as an end in himself, he must respect Peter's privacy as far as is ethically feasible under the circumstances. For instance, it would be a violation of Peter's right to privacy to disclose over an answering machine, to convey the information to Peter's fiancée through messengers, or to discuss Peter's case where others who have no need to know can hear. Due respect for the client's privacy implies making the disclosure *only* to the one at risk or (in the case of a minor) to his or her parent(s) or legal guardian(s) (Cohen, 1990).

With regard to Peter's fiancée, the conditions of the principle of vulnerability appear to have been fulfilled. Peter intentionally has concealed from her the fact that he is HIV positive; consequently, she is not in a position to foresee or comprehend the high risk of harm to herself (EG 9). Moreover, given that no one is willing and able to inform her of the prospective harm, she is "specially dependent upon" Dr. T for these purposes — the harm is not likely to be prevented unless the counselor makes the disclosure (EG 8).

Case 2:

Jason, age 25, is in therapy with Dr. C due to problems of coping, which stem from the fact that he is in the early stages of AIDS. Among other problems, Jason is experiencing rejection by close relatives and friends, who disassociated themselves from him when they learned of the diagnosis. In the course of therapy, Jason reveals to Dr. C that he is engaging in sexual activities with multiple, anonymous sex partners — routinely "picking up" partners at bars and having unprotected oral, anal, and vaginal sex with many of them. When Dr. C advises Jason to cease his high-risk sexual activities and to wear a condom, Jason agrees to do so. However, 2 months later, he admits that his sexual practices have not changed and that he still does not wear a condom.

Unlike the first case, the third parties in this case are anonymous. Consequently, Dr. C cannot reasonably be expected to contact previous sexual partners for purposes of informing them. However, future sexual encounters might be prevented by contacting the police, who could covertly place Jason under surveillance.

This alternative raises several problems. Police surveillance would be feasible only if it were done covertly, without Jason's knowledge. Therefore, Dr. C could not fully inform Jason of his cooperation with the police. As such, disclosure would not promote the treatment of the client as an end in himself (EG 7 is violated). Instead, Dr. C would acquiesce in the treatment of the client as a means, with manipulation and betrayal replacing candor and trustworthiness in the therapeutic relationship.

In addition, the perception of counselors as "police informants" would undermine the prospects of successful therapy for clients who have already become wary of trusting others. As such, the contravening harm resulting from a policy of disclosure in cases of anonymous sexual partners may be of sufficient magnitude to militate against disclosure (EG 4 may be violated).

This is not to deny the gravity of harm to third parties. As Jason infects others, those whom he infects might in turn infect others, and so on. A consistent policy of disclosing to the police may, however, prove counterproductive in intercepting this cycle of harm. If clients with HIV infection or AIDS are dissuaded from speaking candidly to their counselors about their sex lives or even from seeking therapy at all, a significant opportunity for counselors to encourage clients to cease their dangerous sexual conduct will be lost.

Moreover, disclosing to the police would be useful only if the police were disposed to act on the information imparted. Such a disposition to respond depends on several factors, including whether the police are themselves motivated enough to divert scarce resources away from other concerns to pursue these covert operations, and whether the HIV-positive client's sexual acts are deemed crimes in the legal jurisdiction in which they occur. Without reasonable assurance that the police will respond to the complaint, disclosure could not be expected to reduce the amount of harm to the third parties at risk (EG 3 may be violated). Under such conditions, disclosure would have no redemptive value.

In contrast to the first case, the third parties in this case are engaged in foreseeably high-risk sexual behavior. HIV exists in epidemic proportions within the general population, and its primary means of transmission is sexual intercourse. Thus, it can be reasonably surmised that one places oneself at high risk of contracting HIV when one engages in promiscuous or casual sex without adequate safety precautions. Therefore, these third parties are able to avoid the impending danger through the exercise of their own rational self-determination, but they have chosen not to do so.

Of course, the fact that these third parties have been sexually irresponsible does not mean they deserve to contract HIV for their indiscretion. Nevertheless, third-party responsibility in such cases cannot be dismissed as morally irrelevant to the question of disclosure. From the standpoint of the principle of vulnerability, a counselor's duty of disclosure to third parties who cannot reasonably be expected to foresee the risk of harm is stronger than to third parties who can reasonably be expected to do so. In the first case, the third party needs the counselor's disclosure to comprehend the danger; in the second case, there is already good reason to avoid the high-risk behavior (EG 9 is violated).

Because sexual intercourse is the primary mode of HIV transmission, there are strong utilitarian reasons why helping professionals, including mental health counselors, are obligated to discourage sexual promiscuity. However, it is feasible that service providers can discharge this obligation by providing a therapeutic environment in which clients feel free to discuss intimate details of their sex lives and in which counselors can speak candidly with their clients about the risks of sexual promiscuity. On the other hand, a policy of disclosure under conditions like those described in this case is not likely to discourage sexual promiscuity. In fact, by placing too great a strain on the bond of confidentiality, it may defeat this purpose significantly.

ETHICAL RULES FOR DISCLOSURE OF CONFIDENTIAL INFORMATION

In considering how EGs would apply to the two cases discussed above, more specific ethical directives can be generated in the form of Ethical Rules (ERs), which are presented in Table 13.2.

ERs 1–5 define the conditions or circumstances under which counselors have at least a *prima facie* moral obligation of disclosure; that is, if all five conditions are true and no EGs would be violated, a counselor has a moral obligation to disclose. ERs 6–14, in turn, state how this obligation must be discharged. Therefore, if all of these procedural rules are not executed, the counselor has not satisfied his or her obligation. Because laws governing confidentiality and privileged communication can vary from state to state, it is possible that what

Table 13.2
ETHICAL RULES (ERs)

Conditions of Obligation:

ER 1. Medical evidence based on state-of-the-art testing criteria (e.g., EIA and confirmatory Western blot tests) indicates that the client is HIV positive (EG 1).

ER 2. The third party is engaging in a relationship with the client, such as unprotected sexual intercourse, which, according to current medical standards, places the third party at high risk of contracting HIV from the client (EG 2).

ER 3. The third party can be identified and contacted by the counselor without the intervention of law enforcement (EGs 3, 4, and 7).

ER 4. The client has refused to disclose to the third party and is not likely to do so in the near future, nor is anyone other than the counselor likely to do so (EGs 6 and 8).

ER 5. As far as the clinician is aware, the third party is not engaging in risky sexual behavior, such as promiscuous sex without the use of a condom (EG 9).

Procedural Rules:

ER 6. The counselor makes disclosure in a timely fashion so that the very purpose of such disclosure is not defeated (EG 3).

ER 7. Before disclosure, the counselor makes all reasonable efforts to inform or educate the client adequately about the disease of HIV and its implications for sexual partners (EGs 5 and 7).

ER 8. The counselor provides the client with the encouragement, understanding, and support conducive to the client's making disclosure on his or her own (EGs 5 and 7).

ER 9. The counselor avoids coercion or manipulation in influencing client disclosure, such as by making client disclosure a condition of continued therapy or by engaging in any form of lying or deceit (EGs 5 and 7).

ER 10. Before disclosure, the counselor informs the client of the intention to disclose (EGs 5 and 7).

ER 11. The counselor makes disclosure directly (without messengers or answering machines) to none other than the third party at risk or (in the case of minors) to the parent(s) or legal guardian(s) (EGs 5 and 7).

ER 12. The counselor limits disclosure to general medical information sufficient to inform the third party of the imminent danger (EGs 3 and 7).

ER 13. The counselor takes reasonable measures to safeguard the client from physical harm, such as self-inflicted harm occasioned by disclosure (EG 4).

ER 14. The counselor offers therapy assistance or an appropriate referral to the third party at risk (EG 3).

is ethical according to these rules may not be legal in some jurisdictions. Therefore, counselors must consult their state's statutes on the question of legality.

These rules provide a *primary* level of disclosure criteria in a three-tiered system of theories, guidelines, and rules. ERs comprise the most specific level of disclosure criteria and serve to direct application of the particular EGs from which they were derived. Although ERs should be consulted first, they must be understood and applied in light of their respective EGs. For example, what counts in a given context as "casual sex" for purposes of applying ER 5 may be settled by appealing to EG 9 from which this rule was derived.

Similarly, although ERs 1–5 may be true in a given situation, some further consideration may override the *prima facie* obligation established under these conditions. For example, there may be a contravening harm of equal or greater proportion and probability that is likely to result from disclosure (EG 4). Therefore, it is recommended that counselors review their disclosure decisions with respect to *all* EGs, even when it seems clear to them that the conditions of ERs 1–5 are true. In so doing, counselors can confirm that they have in a given context an actual obligation of disclosure.

In cases in which the import of the EGs is itself dubious, the most general level of ethical theories may be consulted for clarification. For example, Kantian theory may help to clarify whether certain client treatment not explicitly covered under the ERs qualifies as treatment of clients as an ends in themselves. Consideration of ethical theories also may be instrumental to the derivation of additional guidelines (and rules) for resolving ethical problems beyond the scope of the present ethical system.

SUMMARY

Two key traditional ethical theories, Kantian ethics and utilitarianism, have been presented, and it has been shown that the rule of therapist-client confidentiality can be justified by both theories. However, this rule of confidentiality is not absolute. In some cases in which HIV-positive clients are engaging in high-risk sexual activities, the counselor has a moral obligation of disclosure. Nine *ethical guidelines* (EGs) derived from Kantian and utilitarian theories and the principle of vulnerability provide direction for counselors in determining whether disclosure is required in such cases. *Ethical rules* (ERs) are generated by these guidelines. In a three-tiered system of theories, guidelines, and rules, ERs provide mental health professionals with primary disclosure criteria for ethically resolving cases in which HIV-positive clients are sexually active with third parties.

REFERENCES

American Counseling Association. (1995). *Code of ethics and standards of practice*. Alexandria, VA: Author.

Bentham, J. (1989). Morality based on pleasure and pain. In E. D. Cohen (Ed.), *Philosophers at work: An introduction to the issues and practical uses of philosophy* (pp. 27-33). New York: Holt, Rinehart & Winston.

Bok, S. (1991). Lies to the sick and dying. In T. A. Mappes & J. S. Zembaty (Eds.), *Biomedical ethics* (3rd ed.). New York: McGraw-Hill.

Brandt, R. B. (1959). *Ethical theory*. Englewood Cliffs, NJ: Prentice-Hall.

Brant, A. M., Cleary, P. D., & Gostin, L. O. Routine hospital testing for HIV: Health policy considerations. In L. O. Gostin (Ed.), *AIDS and the health care system*. New Haven, CT: Yale University Press.

Centers for Disease Control and Prevention. (1987). Revision of the CDC surveillance case definition for acquired immunodeficiency syndrome. *Morbidity and Mortality Weekly Report, 36*(1S), 1-15.

Centers for Disease Control and Prevention. (1991). The HIV/AIDS epidemic: The first 10 years. *Morbidity and Mortality Weekly Report*, 40(22), 357–369.

Cohen, E. D. (1990). Confidentiality, counseling, and clients who have AIDS: Ethical foundations of a model rule. *Journal of Counseling and Development*, 68, 282–286.

Cohen, E. D. (1994). What would a virtuous counselor do? Ethical problems in counseling clients who have HIV. In E. D. Cohen & M. Davis (Eds.), *AIDS: Crisis in professional ethics* (pp. 149-176). Philadelphia: Temple University Press.

Douglas, P. H., & Pinsky, L. (1996). *The essential AIDS fact book*. New York: Simon & Schuster.

Flaskerud, J. H. (1989). Overview: AIDS/HIV infection and nurses' needs for information. In J. H. Flaskerud (Ed.), *AIDS/HIV infection: A reference guide for nursing professionals* (pp. 1-18). Orlando, FL: Harcourt Brace Jovanovich.

Flaskerud, J. H., & Nyamathi, A. M. (1989). Risk factors and HIV infection. In J. H. Flaskerud (Ed.), *AIDS/HIV infection: A reference guide for nursing professionals* (pp. 169-197). Orlando, FL: Harcourt Brace Jovanovich.

Florida Department of Professional Regulations. (1993). FS 491.0147.

Gostin, L. O. (1990). Hospitals, health care professionals, and persons with AIDS. In L. O. Gostin (Ed.), *AIDS and the health care system* (pp. 3-12). New Haven, CT: Yale University Press.

Kant, I. (1964). *Groundwork of the metaphysics of morals*. New York: Harper & Row. (Original work published 1785)

Leibowitz, R. E. (1989). Sociodemographic distribution of AIDS. In J. H. Flaskerud (Ed.), *AIDS/HIV infection: A reference guide for nursing professionals* (pp. 19-36). Orlando, FL: Harcourt Brace Jovanovich.

Mabe, A. R., & Rollins, S. A. (1986). The role of a code of ethical standards in counseling. *Journal of Counseling and Development*, 64, 294-297.

Mayer, K. H. (1990). The natural history of HIV infection and current therapeutic strategies. In L. O. Gostin (Ed.), *AIDS and the health care system* (pp. 21 -31). New Haven, CT: Yale University Press.

Parents, W. A. (1992). Privacy, morality and the law. In E. D. Cohen (Ed.), *Philosophical issues in journalism* (pp. 92-109). New York: Oxford University Press.

Tarasoff v. Regents of the University of California, 113 Cal., Rptr. 14.551 P.2d 334 (1976).

Winston, M. E. (1991). AIDS, confidentiality, and the right to know. In T. A. Mappes & J. S. Zembaty (Eds.), *Biomedical ethics* (3rd ed., pp. 173-180). New York: McGraw-Hill.

14

Ethics and Multiculturalism: The Challenge of Diversity

Courtland C. Lee, PhD, and Virginia Kurilla, MEd

Dr. Lee is Professor of Counselor Education, University of Virginia, Charlottesville, VA. Ms. Kurilla, a private counseling practitioner, is a graduate student in the Counselor Education Program, University of Virginia.

KEY POINTS

- The great variety of racial, ethnic, and cultural backgrounds in the United States poses an important challenge for mental health and rehabilitation practitioners to become multiculturally literate.

- Clients' cultural backgrounds often predispose them to different world views than those of their counselors.

- To engage in effective, ethical practice across cultures, counselors must be in an ongoing process of professional development; they must upgrade their skills to counsel clients from a variety of cultural backgrounds. The ultimate goal is the emergence of a professional who is culturally responsive and capable of using techniques that are consistent with their clients' life experiences and values.

- Unethical conduct in the counseling or therapy of racial/ethnic minority clients can be the result of lack of multicultural literacy. However, cultural ignorance should be no excuse for unethical conduct.

- The ethical standards of the American Counseling Association provide important guidelines for counseling with clients from diverse backgrounds.

- If a counselor cannot approach a particular client from a different background in an open-minded manner, he or she should consider consultation or referral to another counselor more suited to the client's needs.

INTRODUCTION

Cultural diversity is driving significant change in all sectors of American society. Institutions are being forced to examine the philosophical premises that underlie the principles and standards by which they operate, and this is also true for the counseling profession. Contemporary counseling professionals are confronted with the challenge of addressing the mental health needs of a more culturally and ethnically diverse clientele. The profession must examine counseling theory and practice to ensure that it is culturally responsive, particularly with respect to racial/ethnic minority client groups.

A major part of such introspective examination involves close scrutiny of the ethical standards that guide practice. In recent years, scholars have written extensively on ethical standards as they relate to culturally diverse client populations (Casas, Ponterotto, & Gutierrez, 1986; Casas & Thompson, 1991; Ibrahim & Arredondo, 1986; Pedersen & Marsella, 1982). The literature suggests that ethical standards lack counselor guidance with respect to racial/ethnic minority client groups. It also suggests that those counseling professionals who are not aware of cultural dynamics and their impact on the psychosocial development of racial/ethnic minority clients risk engaging in unethical conduct.

A counselor who is multiculturally literate increases his or her chances of practicing in an ethical fashion with clients from racial/ethnic minority backgrounds. The purpose of this chapter is to explore the multicultural context of ethical standards by emphasizing practice with minority clients. The *Code of Ethics and Standards of Practice* (American Counseling Association [ACA], 1995) is the basis of the exploration.

ETHICS AND MULTICULTURALISM: A PERVASIVE CHALLENGE FOR COUNSELING PROFESSIONALS

The ethical standards of the ACA are designed to guide the

practice of counseling professionals. As Axelson (1993) notes, these standards have ramifications for majority/minority group counselor-client interactions in a multicultural society such as the United States. Pedersen (1988) asserts that counselors have an ethical responsibility to know the cultural experiences of their clients and a responsibility to meet the needs of culturally diverse persons within the context of a multicultural society.

However, the ethical principles and standards of the ACA and those of other professional associations have come under intense fire for not promoting the best interests of clients from ethnic minority backgrounds (Casas et al., 1986; Cayleff, 1986; Ibrahim & Arredondo, 1986; Ivey, 1987; LaFromboise & Foster, 1989). In fact, these standards have been perceived as failing to advance the welfare of minority clients.

In view of the cultural and sociopolitical dynamics that may affect counseling across cultures (Katz, 1985; Lee & Richardson, 1991; Ponterotto, 1988; Sue & Sue, 1990), the issue of client welfare warrants examination with respect to the potential harm that may occur when cultural differences are not considered. From an ethics standpoint, counselors are obligated to protect clients from potential harm and prevent harm whenever possible (beneficence), and they are equally responsible for not inflicting harm on clients (nonmaleficence). There can be little doubt, as Tsiu and Schultz (1988) suggest, that harm can be inflicted when overt and covert cultural biases remain unexplored. Culturally insensitive counselors are certainly less capable of protecting or acting in the best interest of their clients when they are unaware of their own cultural biases. To address the issue of bias and discrimination in the counseling relationship, sections of the ethics code (ACA, 1995) state:

> Counselors do not condone or engage in discrimination based on age, color, culture, disability, ethnic group, gender, race, religion, sexual orientation, marital status, or socioeconomic status. (A.2.a)

Counselors will actively attempt to understand the diverse
cultural backgrounds of the clients with whom they work. This
includes, but is not limited to, learning how the counselor's
own cultural/ethnic/racial identity impacts his/her values
and beliefs about the counseling process. (A.2.b)

Counselors are aware of their own values, attitudes, and behaviors and how these apply in a diverse society, and avoid
imposing their values on clients. (A.5.b)

Counselors do not discriminate against clients, students, or
supervisees in a manner that has a negative impact based on
their age, color, culture, disability, ethnic group, gender, race,
religion, sexual orientation, or socioeconomic status, or for any
other reason. (C.5.a)

Implicit in these statements is the notion that necessary
precautions have been taken by counseling professionals to
ensure that cultural value judgments and biases do not enter
into the counseling relationship and that counselors are consciously aware of any cultural biases and prejudices they may
have. Considering that traditional counseling practice reflects
the values of the dominant European-American culture (Lee &
Richardson, 1991; Ponterotto & Casas, 1991; Wrenn, 1962), the
potential for disregarding or misunderstanding the importance of the values and beliefs of culturally diverse clients is
great. Thus, it is highly probable that the welfare of ethnic/
racial minority clients may be at risk even though counselors'
actions are well intentioned.

CASE STUDY

Mrs. G., a 28-year-old separated Puerto Rican woman, was
referred to a mental health community clinic after being treated
at a hospital emergency department for what she described as
ataques de nervios (attacks of the nerves). According to the
emergency-room report, Mrs. G., escorted by her two children

and a friend, had arrived in a state of panic. Her breathing was labored and she was irrational and incoherent. The report stated that, on arrival, Mrs. G. had to be physically restrained because she was thrashing around uncontrollably. The resident on call examined Mrs. G. for possible seizure activity but found no indication that she was experiencing one. The report further indicated that while being examined, Mrs. G.'s symptoms diminished – at which point the following information was obtained:

Mrs. G. had moved from Puerto Rico a year earlier with her two children, ages 8 and 10, for economic reasons. Mrs. G. and her children speak English, but not fluently. She and her children were living with the friend who had escorted her to the hospital. Except for her children, Mrs. G.'s family members live in Puerto Rico. The report further indicated that Mrs. G., although well educated, had not been able to find employment since arriving in the United States. According to Mrs. G., the attacks had begun several weeks earlier and appeared to be worsening. She reported that when she experienced an attack, she was unable to control her thoughts or behavior. She also expressed feeling terribly afraid, but declined to elaborate further. In addition, the report indicated that Mrs. G. had been spending a great deal of time in her bedroom praying. Her friend stated that Mrs. G. found it very disappointing that church services at the local parish were conducted solely in English. As a result, she had not been attending church as regularly as she had in Puerto Rico.

After examining Mrs. G. more thoroughly and finding no medical reason to admit her, the resident recommended she be evaluated at a neighborhood mental health clinic. The report also noted that Mrs. G. would not commit to following through with the referral because she did not want to embarrass the family.

Despite her reservations, Mrs. G. attended the clinic for her initial screening session. She was interviewed by a non-Hispanic counselor, who used a non-Hispanic bilingual staff member as an interpreter. Mrs. G. was reassured that what she said would be confidential and that the counselor was there to help her and not to pass judgment. With this support and encouragement, Mrs. G. explained she had been feeling very nervous and fearful since the onset of her attacks 2 weeks earlier. When asked to describe her attacks, Mrs. G. explained that her thoughts would become confused and her body would tremble and shake uncontrollably, leaving her petrified with a sense that evil spirits were watching her and telling her that something bad was going to happen. She also indicated that praying made her feel better; but she did not feel religiously strong enough to combat evil. Mrs. G. further pointed out that in Puerto Rico people believe good and evil spirits exist and can be called on to help or can cause torment. When asked who would have called on evil spirits to torment her, Mrs. G. said she suspected that it was the work of her estranged husband's family. When asked specifics about her family structure and relationships, and about the state of her marriage prior to the separation, Mrs. G. said she did not feel it was appropriate to talk about such matters with strangers.

The counselor and his clinical supervisor subsequently concluded that Mrs. G.'s attacks were a manifestation of stress brought on by her marital separation and move from Puerto Rico. They further surmised that her attacks demonstrated a sense of helplessness and that her fears and preoccupation with evil spirits and religion could be a manifestation of unresolved guilt. They felt a thorough psychiatric evaluation was warranted to rule out a thought disorder. To discourage reinforcement of these fears, it was decided that Mrs. G. would be helped best by focusing on the underlying issues and discouraging the topic of spirits. She was instructed to use a relaxation exercise to deal with her attacks. In addition, it was recommended that she attend weekly sessions to address any underlying emotions associated with recent life changes in her life.

Despite initial protest and disappointment, Mrs. G. returned for her next appointment. However, when she began to talk about her fears and religious beliefs, the counselor suggested she direct her energy and attention to feelings that could be hurting her psychologically. Mrs. G. did not return after this session.

Analysis:

The counselor and his clinical supervisor ostensibly followed standard procedure and acted in an ethical manner in Mrs. G.'s case. Following appropriate procedures, they attempted to gather relevant data on the possible precipitants of her anxiety; they focused on her recent immigration experience and marital difficulties to form clinical judgments about stress, helplessness, and unresolved guilt. In doing so, they were supportive and appeared to have Mrs. G.'s welfare in mind.

However, a lack of multicultural literacy on the part of both the counselor and the supervisor highlights the potential for some ethical questions in this case. The major ethical question involves the issue of religion/spirituality. Mrs. G. indicated that, in her view, her nervous problems were the result of evil spirits and that religion was an important therapeutic force for her. Indeed, in many cultures, religion and spirituality are important psychosocial dynamics that contribute significantly to mental health (Lee, 1991a).

Although her friend found her behavior atypical enough that she brought Mrs. G. for medical care rather than to a priest, it is significant in this case that the friend had lived in the contiguous United States for many years; therefore, her level of assimilation into American society was relatively high. In the friend's view, medical care was the most appropriate treatment. Mrs. G., however, was a recent immigrant and still maintained the "world view" of her home culture.

The counselor and his clinical supervisor discounted the issue of spirituality and the potential of religious faith in both the assessment and intervention aspect of this case. It thus appears that they did not understand Mrs. G. on a cultural level. As a consequence, both the counselor and the clinical supervisor arguably violated several standards of the ACA ethical code. The section of the code on professional competence states:

> Counselors practice only within the boundaries of their competence, based on their education, training, supervised experience, state and national professional credentials, and appropriate professional experience. Counselors will demonstrate a commitment to gain knowledge, personal awareness, sensitivity, and skills pertinent to working with a diverse client population. (C.2.a)

It would appear that the counselor and his supervisor had little understanding of or experience with important aspects of Hispanic culture – specifically, the impact of religion/spirituality on the lives of many Hispanic persons (Rogler, 1989). Although not all people of Hispanic origin believe in spirits or the power of religion, spirituality remains a dynamic characteristic of this culture (Rogler, 1989). Within this context, the counselor and supervisor did not consider whether a belief in spirits and the healing power of religion is considered normal in her culture. Instead, they appear to have ignored her belief system and encouraged her to do the same in their intervention strategy. This issue casts doubt on whether these particular counselors' training and experience qualified them to work with Hispanic clients.

The discounting of Mrs. G.'s religious/spiritual belief system is, we believe, a subtle form of discrimination on the part of the counselor and supervisor (see the sections of the ACA ethics code quoted on pages 237-238 of this chapter). Mrs. G. firmly believed that her nervous attacks possessed a spiritual cause and a possible religious cure. Instead of attempting to validate her reality – and perhaps help her find other resources (such as an Hispanic priest) to help her resolve her very real terror – the counselor chose to ignore it and judged it to be a manifestation of emotional difficulties. The counselor encouraged her to concentrate on stress related to her marital problems and her move from Puerto Rico, while discouraging her from dwelling on spirits. Therefore, her cultural beliefs as a person of Puerto Rican origin were compromised.

In addition, the counselor appeared to violate the preamble to the ethical guidelines which states, in part, that ". . .members recognize diversity in our society and embrace a cross-cultural approach in support of the worth, dignity, potential, and uniqueness of each individual." Mrs. G.'s uniqueness as a Hispanic woman with a distinct cultural belief system was not enhanced by the prescribed course of therapeutic action. The ethical code (ACA, 1995) states:

> The primary responsibility of counselors is to respect the dignity and promote the welfare of clients. (A.1.a)

> Counselors encourage client growth and development in ways that foster the clients' interest and welfare; counselors avoid fostering dependent relationships. (A.1.b)

In our opinion, because of their lack of cultural understanding, the counselors in this case neither respected the dignity nor promoted the welfare of their client. Similarly, they failed to foster her interest or welfare. It is therefore not surprising that Mrs. G. did not return after her second session. The counselor's disregard for her cultural realities sabotaged any attempt at effective intervention and can be considered unethical conduct.

MULTICULTURAL LITERACY—THE ANTECEDENT TO ETHICAL PRACTICE

It is obvious from the case of Mrs. G. that unethical or ethically questionable conduct on the part of counseling professionals who offer services to racial/ethnic minority clients can be the result of errors of omission. In other words, questionable or unethical conduct is often due to a lack of multicultural literacy on the part of counselors. However, cultural ignorance should be no excuse for unethical conduct. Korman (1974) supported this perspective and suggested that services to ethnic minority clients by professionals not competent in understanding such groups should be considered unethical.

The multicultural realities of contemporary American society call for counselors who can effectively address the challenges of client diversity. Running an effective ethical multicultural practice is one of the most significant issues facing the counseling profession today. Meeting this challenge requires addressing these issues in the training and continuing education of culturally skilled counselors.

To engage effectively in ethical practice across cultures, counselors must participate in an ongoing professional development process. The focus of this process should concern the development and upgrading of skills to intervene effectively in the lives of clients from a variety of cultural backgrounds. The ultimate training goal is the emergence of a professional who can be identified as a culturally responsive counselor who uses strategies and techniques that are consistent with the life experiences and cultural values of clients.

The concept of comprehensive multicultural counseling training has been addressed extensively in the literature (Casas, 1984; Casas et al., 1986; Copeland, 1983; Lee, 1991a, 1991b; Parker, Valley, & Geary, 1986; Pedersen, 1988; Ponterotto & Casas, 1987; Sue et al., 1982). According to the literature, one must become more aware of one's own heritage, as well as possible biases that may interfere with counseling effectiveness, to become culturally responsive as a counselor. Moreover, one must be knowledgeable about the history and culture of diverse groups of people and develop new skills accordingly.

Such skills include seeking educational, consultive, and training experience to improve understanding and effectiveness in working with culturally diverse clients. It also includes, when appropriate, familiarizing oneself with relevant research findings regarding mental health and mental disorders of various cultural groups and seeking consultation with religious and spiritual leaders and individual mental health practitioners who routinely treat culturally diverse clients.

In conjunction with these notions, Sue, Arredondo, and McDavis (1992) provide an updated conceptual framework through which to consider the facilitation of such competencies. This framework challenges all sectors of the profession to acknowledge the growing influence of cultural diversity on counseling theory and practice. It conceptualizes the development of competencies across three dimensions: beliefs and attitudes, knowledge, and skills. Within this framework, counselors who engage in ethical practice with clients from diverse cultural groups have an awareness of their own cultural assumptions, values, and biases. Also, they have developed an understanding of the culturally different client's world view so that they can develop appropriate intervention strategies and techniques. Such strategies and techniques, for example, would "respect clients' religious and/or spiritual beliefs and values, including attributions and taboos, because they affect world view, psychosocial functioning, and expressions of distress" (Sue et al., 1992, p. 485).

CONCLUSION

Maintaining an ethical counseling practice can be challenging. Competent counselors must be ever-vigilant that their interventions are dedicated to promoting the worth, dignity, and potential of *all* clients. This becomes particularly difficult when clients represent diverse racial, ethnic, or cultural backgrounds. Ethical conduct in a multicultural context is predicated on an awareness of and sensitivity to unique cultural realities and their relationship to optimal psychosocial functioning. Counseling professionals who practice without such awareness and sensitivity risk engaging in unethical conduct. As stated previously, ignorance of cultural dynamics is no excuse for unethical practice.

In all work with clients, it is critical to gain as thorough an understanding of each individual client as possible. The purpose of this chapter is to raise awareness that an individual client's culture or background often predisposes him or her to a different world view than that of the counselor. To treat culturally different clients effectively, it is beneficial — indeed, often crucial — for counselors to educate themselves about the culture in question and to use this knowledge as a possible framework for approaching therapy.

REFERENCES

American Counseling Association. (1995). *Code of ethics and standards of practice.* Alexandria, VA: Author.

Axelson, J. A. (1993). *Counseling and development in a multicultural society.* Pacific Grove, CA: Brooks/Cole.

Casas, J. M. (1984). Policy, training, and research in counseling psychology: The racial/ethnic minority perspective. In S. Brown & R. Lent (Eds.), *Handbook of counseling psychology* (pp. 785-831). New York: John Wiley & Sons.

Casas, J. M., Ponterotto, J. G., & Gutierrez, J. M. (1986). An ethical indictment of counseling research and training: The cross-cultural perspective. *Journal of Counseling and Development, 64,* 347-349.

Casas, J. M., & Thompson, C. (1991). Ethical principles and standards: A racial-ethnic minority research perspective. *Counseling and Values, 35,* 186-195.

Cayleff, S. E. (1986). Ethical issues in counseling gender, race, and culturally distinct groups. *Journal of Counseling and Development, 64,* 345-347.

Copeland, E. J. (1983). Cross-cultural counseling and psychotherapy: An historical perspective, implications for research and training. *Personnel and Guidance Journal, 61,* 10-15.

Ibrahim, F. A., & Arredondo, P. M. (1986). Ethical standards for cross-cultural counseling: Counselor preparation, practice, assessment, and research. *Journal of Counseling and Development, 64,* 349–352.

Ivey, A. E. (1987). The multicultural practice of therapy: Ethics, empathy, and dialectics. *Journal of Social and Clinical Psychology, 5,* 195–204.

Katz, J. H. (1985). The sociopolitical nature of counseling. *The Counseling Psychologist, 13,* 615–624.

Korman, M. (1974). National conference on levels and patterns of professional training in psychology: Major themes. *American Psychologist, 29,* 301–313.

LaFromboise, T. D., & Foster, S. L. (1989). Ethics in multicultural counseling. In P. B. Pedersen, W. J. Lonner, & J. E. Trimble (Eds.), *Counseling across cultures* (3rd ed., pp. 115-136). Honolulu: University of Hawaii Press.

Lee, C. C. (1991a). Cultural dynamics: Their importance in multicultural counseling. In C. C. Lee & B. L. Richardson (Eds.), *Multicultural issues in counseling: New approaches to diversity* (pp. 11-17). Alexandria, VA: American Counseling Association.

Lee, C. C. (1991b). New approaches to diversity: Implications for multicultural counselor training and research. In C. C. Lee & B. L. Richardson (Eds.), *Multicultural issues in counseling: New approaches to diversity* (pp. 209-214). Alexandria, VA: American Counseling Association.

Lee, C. C., & Richardson, B. L. (1991). *Multicultural issues in counseling: New approaches to diversity.* Alexandria, VA: American Association for Counseling and Development.

Parker, W. M., Valley, M. M., & Geary, C. A. (1986). Acquiring cultural knowledge for counselors in training: A multifaceted approach. *Counselor Education and Supervision, 26,* 61–71.

Pedersen, P. (1988). *Handbook for developing multicultural awareness.* Alexandria, VA: American Association for Counseling and Development.

Pedersen, P. B., & Marsella, A. J. (1982). The ethical crisis for cross-cultural counseling and therapy. *Professional Psychology, 13,* 492–500.

Ponterotto, J. G. (1988). Racial consciousness development among white counselor trainees: A stage model. *Journal of Multicultural Counseling and Development, 16,* 146–156.

Ponterotto, J. G., & Casas, J. M. (1987). In search of multicultural competence within counselor education. *Journal of Counseling and Development, 65,* 430–434.

Ponterotto, J. G, & Casas, J. M. (1991). *Handbook of racial/ethnic minority counseling research.* Springfield, IL: Charles C. Thomas.

Rogler, L. H. (1989). *Hispanics and mental health.* Malabar, FL: Krieger.

Sue, D. W., Arredondo, P., & McDavis, R. J. (1992). Multicultural counseling competencies and standards: A call to the profession. *Journal of Counseling and Development, 70,* 477–486.

Sue, D. W., Bernier, J. E., Durran, A., Feinberg, L., Pedersen, P., Smith, E. J. & Vasquez-Nuttall, E. (1982). Position paper: Cross-cultural counseling competencies. *The Counseling Psychologist, 10,* 45–52.

Sue, D. W., & Sue, D. (1990). *Counseling the culturally different client: Theory and practice.* New York: John Wiley & Sons.

Tsiu, P., & Schultz, G. L. (1988). Ethnic factors in group process: Cultural dynamics in multi-ethnic therapy groups. *American Journal of Orthopsychiatry, 58,* 136–142.

Wrenn, C. G. (1962). The culturally encapsulated counselor. *Harvard Educational Review, 32,* 444–449.

Name Index

A

Anderson, S., 76, 95
Annis, L.V., 149, 158
Apfel, R., 196, 207
Appelbaum, P. S., 150, 158, 196, 207
Arkes, H. R., 26, 33
Arredondo, P. M., 236, 237, 245, 247, 248
Austin, K. M., 40, 54, 55
Averill, S. C., 200, 202, 207
Axelson, J. A., 237, 246

B

Backer, T., 59, 70
Barker, R. L., 125
Beale, D., 207
Beckham, G. C., 149, 158
Benfer, B., 207
Benshoff, J. J., 62, 70
Bentham, J., 215, 231
Bergin, A. E., 22, 23, 33
Bernier, J. E., 248
Besharov, D., 125
Beutler, L. F., 18, 22, 33
Bishop, D. M., 152, 159
Blinder, M. G., 108
Bluglass, R., 108
Bograd, M., 185, 193
Bok, S., 222, 231
Borders, D. L., 191, 193
Borders, L. D., 84, 94, 191, 194
Bouhoutsos, J., 196, 197, 200, 207
Bowden, P., 108
Brace, K., 23, 31, 33
Brandt, R. B., 215, 231
Brant, A. M., 212, 231
Brodsky, A., 76, 94
Brodsky, S., 125
Bromberg, W., 108
Buckley, J., 58, 72
Burns, C. I., 79, 94

C

Calfee, B., 125
Callanan, P., 14, 40, 55, 65, 70, 187, 194
Callis, R., 76, 94
Carroll, M. A., 168, 169, 170, 173, 178
Casas, J. M., 236, 237, 238, 244, 246, 248
Cayleff, S. E., 237, 246
Cherry, L., 59, 70
Chodorow, N. L., 199, 200, 207
Claxton, S., 79, 95
Cleary, P. D., 212, 231
Cocozza, J., 173, 178
Cohen, E., 59, 70
Cohen, E. D., 214, 217, 221, 222, 223, 224, 232
Connolly, M., 62, 71
Cook, S. W., 11, 16
Copeland, E. J., 244, 246
Corbet, M., 76, 95
Corey, G., 6, 11, 14, 40, 44, 46, 47, 54, 55, 64, 70, 125, 184, 187, 192, 194
Corey, M. S., 6, 11, 14, 40, 44, 54, 55, 64, 70, 187, 194
Cottone, R., 63, 64, 65, 70, 73
Cronbach, L. J., 149, 158
Culver, C. M., 30, 31, 33

D

Dalberg, C., 200, 207
Davidson, H. A., 108
Davidson, V., 200, 207
Davis, T. E., 54, 55
Dawes, R. M., 26, 33
De Miranda, J., 59, 70
DePauw, M. E., 76, 94
Diamond, B. L., 99, 107
Douglas, P. H., 212, 232
Douglas, R., 62, 71

Doyon, M., 62, 71
Drane, J. F., 19, 20, 33
Durran, A., 248

E

Egan, G., 84, 94
Emener,]. W., 58, 71
Emerson, S., 79, 84, 85, 95
Ennis, B., 168, 178
Erickson, S. H., 9, 14
Everstine, D. S., 4, 15
Everstine, L., 4, 15

F

Feinberg, L., 248
Feldman-Summers, S., 196, 207
Feldstein, M., 196, 207
Fischer, J., 60, 73
Fisher, J., 64, 71
Flaskerud, J. H., 213, 221, 232
Forer, B. R., 196, 207
Forester-Miller, H., 54, 55
Foster, S. L., 237, 247
Frey, D. H., 15
Fuller, M., 196, 208

G

Gabbard, G. O., 198, 201, 203, 204, 207, 209
Garcia, J., 58, 72
Gartrell, N., 196, 197, 200, 202, 207, 208
Gatens-Robinson, E., 64, 71
Geary, C. A., 244, 247
Gert, Bernard, 21, 29, 30, 31, 33
Gibson, G., 76, 95
Gilbride, D., 62, 71
Gilligan, C., 199, 208
Goldberg, J. R., 186, 194
Gonsiorek, J. C., 196, 200, 203, 208
Goodson, W. H. III, 196, 208
Gostin, L. O., 212, 231, 232
Gould, R. E., 175
Greenberg, M., 196, 207
Grisso, T., 149, 158
Gross, D. R., 9, 15
Gustafson, D. J., 149, 158
Guth, L., 80, 94
Gutheil, T. G., 150, 158, 206, 208
Gutierrez, J. M., 236, 246
Guzman, F., 76, 95

H

Handelsman, M. M., 63, 71
Harding, S. S., 192, 194
Hare, R., 19, 33
Harvey, J. H., 26, 33
Haymann, G. M., 15
Healy, M., 186, 194
Hedges, L. E., 187, 194
Heppner, P. P., 11, 16
Herlihy, B., 8, 11, 15, 44, 46, 47, 53, 55, 184, 186, 192, 194
Herman, J., 196, 207
Hess, A. K., 108, 148, 158
Holloway, E. L., 79, 94
Holroyd, J., 196, 207
Howie, J., 64, 71

I

Ibrahim, F. A., 236, 237, 247
Ivey, A. E., 237, 247

J

Johnson, H. G., 15
Jones, G., 196, 207
Jordan, J. S., 26, 33
Jorgenson, L., 196, 207

K

Kagle, J. D., 125
Kant, I., 216, 232
Kaplan, A. G., 197, 208
Kaplan, H. I., 149, 158
Kardener, S. H., 196, 197, 208
Katz, J., 176, 178
Katz, J. H., 237, 247
Keith-Spiegel, P., 4, 11, 15, 33, 80, 95, 196, 208
Kimmerling, G. F., 51, 55
King, M. C., 149, 158
Kitchener, K., 87, 94
Kitchener, K. S., 19, 34, 40, 54, 55, 65, 71, 192, 194
Klein, L., 58, 71
Klein, M., 58, 71
Knapp, S., 125
Koch, Ed, 175
Koocher, G. P., 11, 15, 33
Korman, M., 244, 247
Kottler, J. A., 65, 73

Kurpius, D., 76, 78, 81, 84, 86, 95

L

LaFrombiose, T. D., 237, 247
Lakin, M., 125
Lanning, W., 54, 55
Lavender, L., 58, 71
Leddick, G. R., 84, 94
Lee, C. C., 237, 238, 241, 244, 247
Lee, S., 59, 71
Leibowitz, R. E., 212, 232
Lerman, H., 196, 207
Leslie, R., 187, 189, 194
Lewis, J., 76, 95
Lo, B., 196, 208
Localio, R., 196, 207
Lowe, C. M., 18, 34
Lowery, S., 79, 95
Lowman, R. L., 82, 95
Lucignano, G., 59, 71

M

Mabe, A. R., 214, 232
McDavis, R. J., 245, 248
McDonnell, K., 80, 94
McGinn, F., 64, 71
McIntyre, L. J., 125
Marks, C., 62, 72
Marsella, A. J., 236, 247
Masterpasqua, F., 148, 158
Mayer, K. H., 212, 233
Melton, G. B., 156, 158
Mendoza, D., 80, 94
Mensh, I. N., 196, 208
Milgrom, J. H., 196, 208
Mill, J. S., 174, 178
Millard, R., 58, 59, 64, 65, 66, 72, 73
Miller, J. B., 199, 208
Milliken, N., 196, 208
Moline, M. E., 40, 55
Morgan, L. B., 87, 95
Murphy, J., 169, 178
Murray, E. J., 18, 22, 34
Murrell, P. H., 79, 95

N

Neukrug, E. S., 186, 194
Newman, A. S., 95
Nievod, A., 156, 159
Nyamathi, A. M., 213, 232

O

Olarte, S., 196, 207
Oliver, P., 23, 34
Owen, G., 22, 34

P

Pape, D. A., 58, 71
Paradise, L. V., 54, 56
Parents, W. A., 216, 217, 233
Parker, W. M., 244, 247
Patrick, K. D., 86, 95
Patterson, J. B., 58, 60, 62, 63, 64, 72
Pearson, E. S., 199, 208
Pedersen, P., 236, 237, 244, 247, 248
Pence, G., 175, 178
Perlin, M. L., 173
Petrila, J., 156, 158
Pinsky, L., 212, 232
Ponterotto, J. G., 236, 237, 238, 244, 246, 248
Pope, K. S., 2, 4, 5, 15, 42, 43, 56, 80, 95, 185, 194, 196, 208
Pope, S. K., 94
Poythress, N. G., 156, 158
Preskorn, S., 166, 178
Purtillo, R., 59, 72

R

Rachels, J., 19, 34
Rich, G. L., 2, 15
Richards, D., 174, 178
Richardson, B. L., 237, 238, 247
Roberts, G. T., 79, 95
Robinson, S. E., 9, 15
Rodgers, R. C., 155, 159
Roessler, R., 61, 72
Rogers, S. J., 23, 34
Rogler, L. H., 242, 248
Rollins, C., 63, 64, 65, 71, 72
Rollins, S. A., 214, 232
Romano, M. D., 72
Rosner, R., 108
Rubin, S. E., 58, 59, 60, 61, 63, 64, 65, 66, 71, 72, 73

S

Saddock, B. J., 149, 158
Sadoff, R. L., 108
St. Germaine, J., 185, 192, 194

Sattler, H. A., 6, 15
Schmidt, M. J., 62, 73
Schneider, H., 168, 178
Schoener, G. R., 196, 200, 203, 208
Schroeder, L. O., 125
Schultz, G. L., 237, 248
Schwitzgebel, R. K., 4, 15
Schwitzgebel, R. L., 4, 15
Seiden, R. H., 15
Shaughnessy, P., 11, 16
Sheeley, V. L., 8, 15
Sherry, P., 76, 77, 79, 83, 95
Shopland, S. N., 196, 209
Shuman, D. W., 152, 153, 159
Siegel, L., 168, 178
Siegel, M., 3, 15
Siegelwaks, S., 54, 56
Silverglade, L., 79, 95
Simon, B., 196, 207
Simon, R. I., 108
Singer, M. T., 156, 159
Slobogin, C., 156, 158
Smith, D., 58, 71, 156
Smith, E. J., 248
Smith, S. R., 159
Smull, M., 58, 72
Snider, P. D., 12, 16
Snyder, M., 26, 34
Socrates, 19
Souheaver, H. G., 62, 70
Sperlich, P. W., 149, 159
Stadler, H. A., 54, 56
Steadman, H. J., 172, 178
Stensrud, R., 62, 71
Strong, S. R., 18, 22, 34
Sue, D., 237, 244, 245, 248
Sue, D. W., 237, 248
Sumerel, M. B., 191, 194

T

Tabachnik, B. G., 4, 15, 80, 95, 196, 208
Tarvydas, V., 58, 65, 73
Teschendorf, R., 76, 95
Theimann, S., 196, 208
Thomas, C. W., 152, 159
Thomas, R. E., 79, 95
Thompson, C., 236, 246
Thomsen, C. J., 26, 34
Thoreson, R. W., 11, 16
Tomm, K., 186, 187, 194
Torrey, E. F., 174, 179
Truax, C. B., 18, 22, 34
True, R. H., 15

Tsiu, P., 237, 248
Twemlow, S. W., 201, 203, 209
Tyler, J. M., 80, 94

U

Upchurch, D. W., 76, 81, 83, 85, 95

V

Valley, M. M., 244, 247
Van Hoose, W. H., 65, 73
VandeCreek, L., 31, 33, 125, 196, 209
Vasquez, M. J. T., 5, 15, 42, 43, 56, 185,
    194, 196, 209
Vasquez-Nuttall, E., 248
Vaughn, B., 60, 73
Vetter, V. A., 2, 15
Von Hirsch, A., 173, 179

W

Wear, S., 164, 179
Weary, G., 26, 33
Weiner, I. B., 108
Weinrach, S. G., 87, 95
Welfel, E., 58, 73
Wesley, G., 168, 178
Whiston, S. C., 79, 84, 85, 95
Williams, G. T., 40, 55
Wilson, C., 58, 60, 64, 65, 72, 73
Winston, M. E., 218, 233
Wise, P. S., 79, 95
Wolberg, L. P., 77, 95
Wong, H., 58, 59, 65, 72, 73
Woody, R. H., 125
Wrenn, C. G., 238, 248
Wright, T., 58, 71

Z

Ziskin, J., 108

Subject Index

A

A "Bill of Rights" for Supervisees (*table*), 88
Abandonment, of client, a type of negligence, 112-113
Abuse
  adult, 2
    cause for breach of confidentiality, 4, 7
  child, 2
    cause for breach of confidentiality, 4, 6-7
Academic freedom, 2
Accessibility, 59
Accountability, 78
  professional, 38, 39
Acquired Immunodeficiency Syndrome,
  See AIDS
Acting out, sexual, 198
ADA,
  See Americans with Disabilities Act (ADA)
Addictive disorders, legal complaints against counselors treating, 118
Agencies, cooperation with other, 85
AIDS, 2, 59
  client confidentiality and, 9-10, 213-214
  case studies, 221-227
  counseling sexually active clients with, 211-231
  reporting on, 49
  statistics, 212
Alcoholism, legal trial concerning, 103
American Association of Marriage and Family Therapy (AAMFT)
  code of ethics, 188, 188-189
  guidelines for dual relationships, 186
  provision for guidelines for supervisors, 93
American Civil Liberties Union (ACLU), Joyce Brown case and, 175
American Counseling Association (ACA) Code of Ethics, 40, 44, 46,

49, 188, 189, 213, 236, 242
American Psychological Association
  founding of, 2
  must protect clients from harm, 8
  record keeping guidelines, 12
  requirements concerning breach of confidentiality, 4
Americans with Disabilities Act (ADA), 61-62
Amitriptyline (Elavil), 114
Antiviral drugs, 212
APA,
  See American Psychological Association
Arizona State Psychological Association, 13
Attorneys
  counselors' relationship with, 98
  cross-examination and, 100
Autonomy, 58, 70
  male identity and, 199
  moral principle of, 40-41
Azidothymidine (AZT), 212
AZT (azidothymidine), 212

B

Beneficence, 237
  moral principle of, 40, 41
Bias
  of counselors, 99
  cultural, 237, 238
  intentional, unethical nature of, 149
Bill of Rights, Fourth Amendment to, 3
Brady v. Hopper, 146
Brown, Joyce, homeless person, case of, 175

C

Cairl v. State, 145
California, and laws governing duty to warn, 142

California Supreme Court, *Tarasoff*
decision and, 133
Caring, of counselors, 43
Case v. United States, 146
Child abuse, 2
cause for breach of confidentiality,
4, 6-7
Child custody, trial, 103
Children, confidentiality and, 170, 171-
172
Chrite v. United States, 144
Civil rights movement, spawned laws
against involuntary commitment,
174
Client abandonment, 112-113
Clients
abandonment of, 112-113
competence of, 168
confidentiality and, 4-9
danger to, 7-9
dangerous, failure to control, 122-
123
examination by medical specialist,
26
identification of, 82
mentally ill, ethical dimension of
treating, 161-178, 180-182
mentally incompetent, 116
racially and ethnically diverse,
ethical guidelines, 235-246
records of, 12-14
rules based on respect for, 23-32
self-determination of, 21-22
sexual boundary violations against,
195-206
See also Sexual relationships
threats by,
See Duty to protect
unhealthy transference problems
with, 117-118
vulnerability of, 11
welfare of, 20-21
Code of Ethics (ACA), 40, 44, 46, 49,
188, 189, 213, 236, 242
Code of Professional Ethics for
Rehabilitation Counselors, 64, 65,
66, 67
Codes of ethics,
See Ethics, codes of
Coercion, contrasted with temptation,
169
Commission on Rehabilitation
Counselor Certification, 39
Commitment, involuntary, 173-176
Communication
by expert witnesses to jury, 106

privileged, defined, 3
Competency, 77
case study, 150-156
defined, 149
to counsel, defined, 148
Complaints, counselors and, 111
Computed tomography scan, 101
Confidentiality, 2, 59, 83, 91
clients with HIV and, 213-214
governed by Title 42 of Federal
Regulations, 122
mentally ill clients and, 169-173
when to breach, 4-9, 172, 219-221
Consent
informed, 5, 79, 115-116
conditions for obtaining, 169
morally valid, 167-169
Constitution, interpretation of, 3
Consumer advocacy, 62, 65
Counselors
called on to testify in court, 98
correction of errors in clinical
judgement, 26
credentials, 82-83, 101
credibility, 99, 105
discrimination on part of, case
study, 238-243
duty of disclosure, 225-227, 227-230
duty to protect, 127-138
ethical dimensions of treating
mentally ill by, 161-178
must be sensitive to diversity, 47-
49
power of means more ethical
responsibilities, 18
practicing beyond scope of
competency, 118-119
preventing lawsuits against, 109-
124
rehabilitation
increasing job complexity for,
61-63
preparing to deal with ethical
dilemmas, 57-70
service-based focus, 62
sexual boundary violations and,
195-206
training sites, 86
values of
and clients' self-determination,
22
influence counseling goals, 18
Countertransference, 45, 78-79, 86, 186,
187, 197
Critical-evaluative level, of ethical
consideration, 19

Cross-examination
bias in, 156
counselors task concerning, 100,
102, 105

D

Danger, cause for breach of
confidentiality, 4, 7-9
Dangerousness, question of
predictivity of, 135
Davis v. Lhim, 144
Decision-making, diverse models of,
64-65
Defendants, therapists as, immunity
of, 140-141
Diagnosis, of mental illness, 166
Dilemmas
ethical, 163
case study, 59-60, 221-227
confidentiality types, 170
rehabilitation counselors and,
57-70
seven-step approach to, 54
statistics, 2
Disclosure,
See Confidentiality; Information;
Privacy
Discrimination, 242
in counseling relationship, 237
Diseases
contagious, fatal
reporting on, 49-50, 213-214
See also AIDS
Dissociative identity disorder (DID),
27
Diversity, 78, 80-81
ACA Code of Ethics and, 49
case study, 238-243
cultural, 236
ethics and, 235-246
DSM-IV, diagnosis from part of
information released to insurance
companies, 5
Dual relationships, 2, 78, 79-80
case study, 117-118
Code of Ethics (ACA) and, 50-51
defined, 184, 190
examples of, 184
minimizing the risk, 192-193
toward a consensus in thinking,
183-193
warnings against, 10-12, 185
Duress, consent given under, 169
Duty to protect, 127-138, 172, 173, 218-
219
ethical dilemma of, case studies,
221-227

E

Eccentricity, contrasted with mental
illness, 165
Education
continuing, 38
protection against lawsuits, 119
in ethics, 63-69
EEG,
See Electroencephalogram (EEG)
Elavil (amitriptyline), 114
Electroencephalogram (EEG), 101
End goal development, 19
*Ethical Case Management Practices
Training Program* (Rubin, Millard,
Wong, and Wilson), 65, 66-67
Ethical Considerations in Treating the
Mentally Ill: Two Case Studies
(*appendix*), 180-182
Ethical Guidelines (EGs) (*table*), 220
*Ethical Practices in Rehabilitation
Training Modules* (Rubin, Wilson
et al.), 65, 67, 68-69
Ethical Principles of Psychologists and
Code of Conduct (APA), 2, 76, 82,
167, 188, 189
Ethical reasoning, 58
Ethical rules
defined, 19
for disclosure of confidential
information, 227-230
Ethical Rules (ERs) (*table*), 228-229
Ethical Standards (ACA), 45
pro bono service according to, 51
Ethical Standards Casebook (Callis,
Pope, and DePauw), 76
Ethical theory, defined, 20
Ethics
aspirational, 39, 40, 47
codes of
are living documents, 187
as catalysts for improving
practice, 37-55
excerpts from, 189
limitations, 43-45
living documents, 45-53
making them work, 53-55
defined, 148
insanity pleas and, 147-157
Kantian, 216-219
mandatory, 39, 40

multiculturalism and, 235-246
teaching decision-making in, 63-69
treatment of mentally ill and, 161-
    178, 180-182
utilitarianism, 214-216
Expert witness
  contrasted with standard witness,
      98
  testimony, ethical and legal issues,
      97-107

F

Fidelity, 58
  moral principle of, 40, 42
Figueiredo-Torres v. Nickel, 120, 124
Furr v. Spring Grove State Hospital, 145

G

Gandianco v. Sobol, 121, 124
Glover v. The Board of Medical Quality
    Assurance, 114, 124
Goals
  counseling
    ethical considerations in
        development of, 17-32
    rules in development of, 24-32
  identification of, 82
  incompatibility, 24
"Goodness of fit", 85
Guilt, perpetrator and, 152

H

Hasenei v. United States, 146
Heaven v. Pender, 139
Hispanics, culture, 242
HIV
  confidentiality and, 9, 171, 213-214
  case studies, 221-227
  counseling sexually active clients
      with, 211-231
  reporting on, 49
Holmes v. Wampler, 145
Homelessness, mentally ill clients and,
    175-176
Hopewell v. Adibempe, 146
Human immunodeficiency virus,
    See HIV

I

Identity, self, female, 199

Impartiality, level of, in mental health
    professional, 99
Incapacitated, defined, 7
Information
  confidential, 2-3, 169-173
  ethical guidelines for disclosure
      of, 219-221, 227-230
Informed consent, 79
  conditions for obtaining, 169
  defined, 5, 115
Insanity pleas, ethics and, 147-157
Instrumental goal development, 19
Insurance, liability, no psychologist
    should be without, 9
Intercourse, means of HIV
    transmission, 212
Interpersonal dynamics, 42-43
Intuitive understanding, defined, 19

J

Jablonski v. United States, 144
Jure v. Raviotta, 119, 124
Justice, 58, 70
  moral principle of, 40, 42
  theories of, 87

K

Kantian ethics, 216-219, 230
Kaposi's sarcoma, 212
Koch, Ed, treatment of mentally ill
    homeless and, 175

L

Lawsuits, prevention of, techniques,
    109-124
Learning disabilities, 61
Leedy v. Hartnett, 145
Legal issues, expert witness testimony,
    97-107
Lipari v. Sears, Roebuck & Co., 8, 144
Literacy, multicultural, 241, 243-245
Lovesick therapist, 201
Lovesickness, defined, 201

M

McIntosh v. Milano, 8
Makris v. The Bureau of Professional and
    Occupational Affairs, 119, 124
Malpractice suits, 119, 128
  See also Lawsuits

Mellaril (thioridazine), 114
Men, male self-identity and, 199
Mens rea, a guilty mind, 152
Mental illness
    characterized, 165, 165-166, 168
    defined, 164
    ethical considerations in treating,
        case studies, 180-182
Mikkelsen v. Salama, 123, 124
Minor
    considered incompetent, 116
    defined, 6
    emancipated, defined, 6
Misdiagnosis, lawsuits filed alleging,
    120-122
Moral discomfort, 18
Moral principles
    autonomy, 40-41
    beneficence, 40, 41
    fidelity, 40, 42
    justice, 40, 42
    nonmaleficence, 40, 41
Morality, views of, 21
Morally valid consent,
    See Consent, morally valid
Multiculturalism, ethics and, 235-246

N

National Board for Certified
    Counselors, 39
Negligence
    professional, 110
        defined, 111
    types
        client abandonment, 112-113
        failure to control dangerous
            client, 122-123
        failure to obtain informed
            consent, 115-116
        misdiagnosis, 120-122
        practicing outside scope of
            competency, 118-119
        sexual relationship with clients,
            119-120
        unhealthy transference
            relationships, 117-118
        unorthodox treatments, 113-114
Nondiscrimination, Code of Ethics
    (ACA) and, 47
Nonmaleficence, 58, 237
    moral principle of, 40, 41
Not guilty by reason of insanity
    (NGRI), 148, 150, 157
    case study, 150-156

O

Objectivity, 155
O'Connor v. Donaldson, 176
On Liberty (Mill), 174
Opinions, objective, 155

P

*Palmer v. The Board of Regents in
    Medicine,* 117, 124
Parents, informing, 170
Paternalism
    case study, 30-31
    defined, 30
    therapist's, mentally ill client and,
        166
    toward children, 171-172
Patients, with psychiatric illness,
    responsibilities of, 166
Pease v. Beech Aircraft Corporation, 141
*Peck v. Counseling Service of Addison
    County,* 136, 145
Peer consultation, 60
People v. Burnick, 141
People v. Poddar, 138
Perkins v. Dean, 117, 124
Petersen v. State of Washington, 8, 145
Plagiarism, 2
Pneumocystis carinii, 212
Poddar, Prosenjit
    See People v. Poddar; Tarasoff v.
        Board of Regents of University
        of California (1976)
Power
    of counselors, 18, 42-43
    differential in supervisory
        relationships, 90-91
    of supervisors, 83
Principles, defined, 20
Privacy, 3
    clients' right to, 169
    defined, 216
Privilege, waiving of by client, 6
Pro bono services, 42
    Ethical Standards (ACA) and, 51
Professional disclosure statements, 38
Professional Practice Act, 119
Promises, by counselor, should be
    kept, 27-28, 58
Protease inhibitors, 212
Protect, duty to,
    See Duty to protect
Proximate cause, 112
Psychiatrists

board certified, help of, 121
    expert witness and, 101
Psychologists
    confidentiality and, 4
    should not practice without
        liability insurance, 9
Psychology
    competency in, 149
    current ethical issues in, 1-14
    forensic, 147-157
    slow to address ethics in
        supervision, 94

Q

Quality assurance, 59
Questions, hypothetical, asked during
    trial, 105-106

R

Rationality, 168
Record keeping, 2
    related to confidentiality, 12
Rehabilitation, head trauma, 59
Relationships
    consulting, 81
    counselor-defendant, 101
    dual,
        See Dual relationships
    supervisory, 79-81
Resistance, 187
Respect
    for client's best interest, rules
        based on, 24-29
    for client's ethnic/racial
        differences, 245
    for client's self-determination,
        rules for, 29-32
    for client's welfare, indispensable,
        20, 21
Responsibility, criminal, 149
Reynolds v. National Railroad Passenger
    Corporation, 123, 124
Risk management, four-step process,
    110
Rodriguez v. Bethlehem Steel Corporation,
    140
Roebuck v. Smith, 114, 124
Role
    conflicts, 77-78
    confusions, 186
    examples of inherent duality in,
        191
    sex, dual relationship issues and,

197-199
Rowland v. Christian, 139
Rules
    for guiding goal development in
        psychotherapy, 23-32
    moral, well-defined, not possible in
        counseling, 177

S

Schneider v. Vine Street Clinic, 146
Self-determination, 40
    defined, 21, 22
    rules based on respect for clients',
        29-32
Self-monitoring, by counseling
    professionals, 38
Self-presentation, of credentials, 82-83
Sexual relationships
    between supervisor and supervisee,
        80
    with clients, 11-12, 119-120, 195-
        206
    ethical considerations, 51-53
    prohibiting, 46
    statistics, 196-197, 202
    time limits, 52
    as means of HIV transmission, 212-
        213
Shaw v. Glickman, 146
Sisson v. Seneca Mental Health/Mental
    Retardation Council, 120, 124
Skills, ethical reasoning, need for, 58-
    61
Society, pluralistic, 47
Socrates, moral philosophy and, 19
Spirituality, clients', 241
Standard witness, contrasted with
    expert witness, 98
Standards of Practice (ACA), 46
Students, in counselor training, dual
    relationships of, 191
Subpoena
    duces tecum, 5
    psychological records and, 5
Suicide, prevention of, confidentiality
    and, 10
Supervisees
    feedback provided by, 92
    rights of, 86-93
Supervision
    contrasted with therapy, 90
    defined, 77
    ethics in, 75-94
    parameters of, 89-90

separating from therapy, 84-86
videotaped, 91
Supervisors, countertransference and, 191
Surrogacy, 59

T

T cells, HIV and, 212
Tarasoff v. Board of Regents of University of California (1976), 7, 139-146, 172-173, 213, 216, 233
case described, 128-133
critical response to, 133-134
declining to follow, 138
subsequent decisions, 134-138
Temptation, contrasted with coercion, 169
Testimony, expert witness, ethical and legal issues of, 97-107
Tests
medical
for HIV, 212
as part of legal trial preparation, 101
Therapeutic privilege, 115
Therapeutic relationship
boundaries in, 84
erotic transference can tax, 206
Therapists
gender of, 197-199
sexually abusive
profile of, 200-206
impulsive, 204-205
isolated, 204
naïve, 203
neurotic, 204
psychotic, 205-206
sociopathic, 205
Therapy
contrasted with supervision, 90
separating from supervision, 84-86
Thioridazine (Mellaril), 114
Thompson v. County of Alameda, 145
Title and Content of the Instructional Modules of the Ethical Practices in Rehabilitation Training Modules (*table*), 68-69
Title and Purpose of Each Instructional Unit of the Ethical Case Management Practices Training Program (*table*), 66-67
Transference, 78-79, 86, 186, 187, 197
erotic, 198, 199, 200, 206
nurturing-symbiotic, 199
unhealthy, 117-118

Treatment
abusive, 113
of mentally ill, 161-182
refusal, 176-177
should not harm client, 27
unorthodox, 113-114
Trial
legal
by nature adversarial, 104
criminal, 106
direct examination, 102-105
preparing for, 101-102
Triangulation, 186
Trust, sacred, in counselors, 43

U

Uncertainty, in counseling, principles for reducing, 32
Utilitarianism, theories of, 214-216, 230

V

Values
counselors', 18, 22-23
case study, 23
ethnic clients and, case study, 238-243
personal, 78, 81
Victim, duty to warn, 131
Violence, 2
duty to protect others from, 127-138
Vulnerability
defined, 218
principle of in ethics, 218-219

W

White v. United States, 146
Williams v. The Ohio State Medical Board, 114, 124
Witnesses,
See Expert witness; Standard witnesses
Women, female self-identity and, 199

Contributors

Kerry Brace, PsyD
Psychotherapist, Allegheny East MHMR Center, Pittsburgh, PA.

Barbara E. Calfee, JD, LSW
President, Barbara Calfee & Associates, Beachwood, OH.

Mary Ann Carroll, PhD
Professor of Philosophy, Department of Philosophy and Religion,
Appalachian State University, Boone, NC.

Elliot D. Cohen, PhD
Professor, Department of Social Sciences, Indian River Community
College, Fort Pierce, FL, and Editor-in-Chief of the *International Journal
of Applied Philosophy.*

Gerald Corey, EdD, ABPP, NCC
Professor of Human Services and Counseling, California State University at Fullerton, Fullerton, CA.

Barbara Herlihy, PhD, NCC, LPC
Associate Professor of Counselor Education, Loyola University of New
Orleans, New Orleans, LA.

Virginia Kurilla, MEd
Private counseling practitioner and a graduate student in the Counselor
Education Program, University of Virginia.

Sharon E. Robinson Kurpius, PhD
Professor of Counseling Psychology, Division of Psychology in Education, Arizona State University, Tempe, AZ.

Courtland C. Lee, PhD
Professor of Counselor Education, University of Virginia,
Charlottesville, VA.

Michael W. Millard, PhD, BCFE
In private practice in Hopkins, MN. He specializes in forensic evaluations.

Silvia W. Olarte, MD
Clinical Professor of Psychiatry and faculty member of the Psychoanalytic Institute, Department of Psychiatry, New York Medical College, Valhalla, NY.

Michael L. Perlin, Esq
Professor of Law, New York Law School, New York, NY.

Carolyn Rollins, PhD
Assistant Professor, the Department of Rehabilitation, Social Work, and Addictions, Denton, TX.

Robert L. Sadoff, MD
Clinical Professor of Psychiatry and Director of the Center for Studies in Social-Legal Psychiatry, University of Pennsylvania, Philadelphia, PA.

Catherine L. Tyler, MBA
Former supervisor, State of Indiana, Division of Family and Children.

J. Michael Tyler, PhD
Assistant Professor, Department of Counseling, University of South Florida, Fort Myers, FL.

For information on other books in
The Hatherleigh Guides series, call the
Marketing Department at Hatherleigh
Press, 1-800-367-2550, or write:
Hatherleigh Press
Marketing Department
1114 First Avenue, Suite 500
New York, NY 10021-8325